EXPLORING THE FOURTH DIMENSION

John Dennis Ralphs was born in 1923 in the Potteries district of Staffordshire, England. At school, he developed an interest in physics and mathematics, and in 1943 gained a BSc with Honours in Physics at Birmingham University. Wartime conditions prevented a career in scientific research and directed him into electronics. He was involved in the development of prototype airborne radar systems and, later, instrumentation for nuclear research. After the war, he pursued a career as a designer of scientific and industrial electronic equipment. He later specialised in communications, and for the last twenty years before retirement he was Senior Principal Scientific Officer in the Communications Engineering Department of the Foreign and Commonwealth Office of the British Government. In this capacity, he developed new techniques for communication on extremely weak, noisy or distorted radio signals.

After retirement he took up a long-standing interest in research into the paranormal. His attitude is clear:

'For many years now it has been apparent that far too much time and effort in research into the paranormal has been wasted in trying to produce 'scientific proof' of phenomena, of a standard which will satisfy the ultra-cynical, and so force acceptance by orthodox scientists. This has proved to be a fruitless exercise, since it has been demonstrated on countless occasions that reasons can always be found, or if necessary invented, for rejecting inconvenient evidence. It is time that other approaches were explored.'

EXPLORING THE FOURTH DIMENSION
Secrets of the Paranormal

John D. Ralphs

quantum

LONDON•NEW YORK•TORONTO•SYDNEY

quantum

An imprint of W. Foulsham & Co. Ltd.,
Yeovil Road, Slough, Berkshire SL1 4JH

ISBN 0-572-01624-7

Printed in Great Britain by Cox & Wyman Ltd.,
Reading, Berkshire

CONTENTS

PREFACE

'Before a commander launches an attack, it is essential for him to establish and protect his lines of retreat.'
Colonel Karl von Clausewitz

One of the reasons often advanced by the sceptical to justify their dismissal of the possibility of paranormal events is that there is no satisfactory theory which will explain any one of them. Another reason, possibly even more to the point, is that there is no single coherent theory which attempts to offer a comprehensive explanation of paranormal phenomena in general. I cannot claim that this book will eliminate these objections; one cannot apply the term 'theory' to a network of analogies, illustrations, comparisons, ideas and suppositions, as many readers would not hesitate to point out. However, such a web of miscellaneous items becomes far stronger and more interesting if it is woven from a single thread – in this case the assumption that this universe exists in more than three dimensions, and that the apparent limitation to three lies solely in the limitations of human perception.

This assumption is a Theory in its own right, and has been accepted as such for well over a hundred years. Although it attracted the serious attention of such eminent scientists as James Clark Maxwell and Ernst Mach, it was never popular or well supported. Even in its heyday in the latter half of the 19th century it was derided as ridiculous by the majority of orthodox scientists. For the greater part of this century is has been totally ignored as at best an illogical red herring, and at worst a general-purpose workhorse for cranks.

This prejudice is likely to remain; I have made no attempt to convince the unconvinceable, nor is the book intended to pander to those who are equally dogmatic in their conviction that they have the monopoly of the truth, and who will seize on some suggestion in it as 'proof' of their own beliefs. My approach makes no attempt to be rigid or scientifically analytical; the main conclusions are – inevitably – contentious to a degree, and much of the detailed discussion may be open to accusations of being tendentious or trivial. Such accusations are, in any case, a normal response to unorthodox methods. My attitude could probably best be summed up as: 'I believe nothing; I am prepared to believe anything', (were it not for the fact that, as I explain in the Epilogue, 'belief' should not enter into the discussion).

My justification for flying in the face of precedent in this way is simple. The present situation is intolerable. We have a situation in which many thousands of people – possibly a majority of the world's population – have reason to believe from personal experience or from convincing accounts by others that Hamlet was right, and that 'There are more things in Heaven and earth, Horatio . . .' Yet the public acknowledgement of this almost self-evident fact is blocked by a minority of self-appointed custodians of human knowledge. These people insist that the functions of the human mind, and the whole relationship of man with his surroundings, must only be studied by the same methods that one would use for analysing the action of a steam engine, or predicting a lunar eclipse. By their philosophy, each phenomenon, each report, each idea, must be considered in isolation, and may then be totally rejected and ignored on the basis of some minor weakness or inconsistency, real or invented. What is more, the remnants of the science-worship of the 19th century and the fear of ridicule, ensure that this attitude is outwardly accepted by the general public. This piece-meal approach of scientism is perpetuated, not from scientific logic, but as the only available method which can be relied upon to maintain the status quo.

The situation is not improved by the attitude of a minority – albeit an influential and vocal minority – of scientists, who are quite prepared to speculate on the paranormal, but only in terms of the most advanced and least-understood branch of pure science, namely nuclear or quantum physics. This has the advantage that any such speculation is incomprehensible to all but the specialists, and they seem prepared to accept almost any interpretation of the complex relationships involved, provided that it does not call into question the existing body of scientific knowledge. I discuss what I consider to be the underlying fallacies in extreme scientism in the first two chapters. I give my reasons for suspecting that there may be serious flaws in the very ground-rules of science, so that not even the most fundamental of assumptions are beyond question.

Some effort should be made to investigate totally fresh approaches and this book constitutes a suggestion of one such possibility. Its purpose is to study the literature in a number of widely-separated disciplines, and to apply what Mr De Bono would probably call 'lateral thinking' (I would prefer to think of it as 'imaginative reasoning'), in order to identify 'coincidences' – puzzling factors which would apparently support a common explanation – and then to attempt to trace those explanations to a possible common source in the existence of unknown dimensions.

This is obviously a massive undertaking, requiring for its success a polymathic genius who had spent a lifetime studying all of the subjects involved. My own qualifications do not begin to meet the requirements. Some knowledge of basic physics and a long career in electronics and communication technology will come in useful for a page or so of authoritative discussion, but other than that I am at best no more than an 'informed layman', *but so is any other writer, when dealing with subjects outside his own profession or particular hobby*. There are few theologians with more than a smattering of mathematics; the average astronomer knows little of psychology; and brain surgeons are not particularly knowledgeable on the subject of poltergeists. It is also true that any professional in such a field lays himself wide open to ridicule, and possible damage to his career, if he ventures to show a public interest in the paranormal. I enjoy the considerable advantage that I no longer have a career to hazard, nor professional standing to lose. To that extent, at least, I can start with an open mind.

Inevitably I cannot attempt the thorough analysis the subject deserves, but must limit myself to an outline of possibilities in a broad-brush and imaginative manner, identifying problems and offering tentative suggestions. Such a review, while not pretending great authority or meticulous accuracy, may be of value in that it could arouse interest in the subject, and act as an igniting spark to better qualified minds, who may find it useful as a preliminary sketch-plan, a reference and a reminder.

Despite this approach, it is inevitable that such an exercise will involve some discussions of a technical nature, but to help the reader with little previous scientific or mathematical knowledge I have transferred some of such material to an Appendix. I have also included summaries of the discussion at intervals in the text.

Having carefully disclaimed any specialist knowledge, I must equally thoroughly disclaim any specialist experience. I myself am as psychically sensitive as cold rice pudding. I have never seen a ghost, attended a seance, or even had a picture unaccountably fall off a wall! I am not a member of any organisation remotely associated with psychic research in any form, nor am I acquainted with members of any such organisation. I have certainly heard very interesting accounts from people whose word I trust and who had no motive for lying, but these are no more evidential than a tale overheard in a pub. I must rely entirely on evidence derived from published books and papers, which can in any case be guaranteed to cover all possible shades of opinion and experience.

I emphasise again that I do not seek to convince, and still less to prove, but rather to stimulate interest in, and discussion of, the possibility of a new approach to a very old problem. I hope that I have described this search in an interesting and even entertaining way, which will encourage the open-minded to consider the ideas in more detail. A minority may find, as I have found, a self-consistency and a ubiquity in the concept which is almost startling. To these, and to the even smaller minority who may be able to take the ideas further, and who may eventually find the key that will unlock the mysteries of the other dimensions, I dedicate this book.

John D. Ralphs

ACKNOWLEDGEMENTS

This book relies very heavily indeed on references to, and quotations from, numerous publications, and I have of necessity taken advantage of such latitude as is allowed by Copyright Law and common practice to take short quotations without specific permission, for the purposes of 'fair comment and review'. I have, however, included a comprehensive Bibliography and cross-reference system which should allow most of the substantive quotations to be traced. I would like to express my appreciation to the authors and owners of copyright involved, and indeed to all those whose writings on the subjects discussed have given me such pleasure and mental stimulation over the years.

CHAPTER 1

CLEARING THE DECKS

'The questions which one asks oneself begin, at last, to illuminate the world, and become one's key to the experience of others.'
James Baldwin

I suppose that this book must begin, as do so many others, with a chapter explaining the author's objectives, motives and qualifications. My first problem is to define the subject of the book, which I think is best described as an investigation into some particular aspects of the 'grey areas' between four distinct fields of human thought and experience:

1. The physical world as our senses (of sight, hearing, etc.) know it, and which is investigated by science;
2. The internal world of our mental processes and spiritual experiences;
3. The world of so-called 'paranormal' events (see below); hazy, contradictory and contentious to a degree;
4. The infinite expanse of knowledge and reality which we must presume may exist, but which is so far unknown to us.

Some twenty years or so ago, as a consequence of a habit of omnivorous and undisciplined reading, I began to accumulate one or two ideas, confusing, complex and fascinating. Odd pieces of jig-saw seemed to fit together, and vague patterns began to emerge. They were mostly concerned with various aspects of an elusive, abstract concept, halfway between scientific fact and metaphysical mumbo-jumbo, and often referred to as 'The Fourth Dimension', although cropping up in a variety of disguises. The final incentive to put these ideas on paper and to attempt to make

11

some kind of sense out of them came from reading Arthur Koestler's book *The Act of Creation*,[46] in which he discusses (among other things) the process by which scientific discoveries are made. He points out that in many 'breakthroughs', such as Sir Isaac Newton's exposition of the Laws of Gravity or Einstein's Theories of Relativity, there was no fundamentally new or unknown fact involved in the initial thinking. The genius of the originator consisted in seeing the significance of a relationship between two or more facts, each of which had been recognised for some time *but which had hitherto been considered to be unrelated.*

Newton's work provides an obvious case of what may conveniently be referred to as 'Koestler's Principle', and one which is peculiarly relevant to the present argument. He recognised the common factor between the fall of an apple and the rotation of the moon around the earth. Both phenomena were commonplace enough, and completely accepted. The apple falls because it has weight; the moon goes round the earth because that's the way the world is – and why should there be any connection? Newton's answer, that everything attracts everything else with a universal 'Force of Gravity', not only related the two, but also gave a totally new view of the universe as a whole, and many previously vague and ill-defined ideas clicked into place. And yet Newton's theory involved the concept of 'action at a distance', the idea that one object could affect another through 'empty space', with no rods, strings or fluid between them to carry the force. Most of the scientists of his day had already dismissed this as totally impossible, and Huyghens – another great astronomer – had declared it to be so ridiculous as to be not worth investigating. Liebnitz, a scientist of the same calibre as Newton, wrote: 'That one body should attract another with no intermediary is not so much a miracle as a sheer contradiction, for 'tis to suppose a body can act in a place where it is not:' What is more, *Newton himself agreed*, accepting that the existence of gravitational forces implied that outer space was filled with 'something', and if it was not material – then it must be spiritual!

So I can derive two lessons from the great scientist: not to be afraid of reviewing existing knowledge in search of new discoveries, and to take comfort from his demonstration that the rejection of an idea by the whole of scientific orthodoxy does not automatically guarantee its absurdity. As Sir Karl Popper, Professor of Logic and Scientific Method at the London School of Economics, points out, the more contentious a theory, the greater the progress that is made if it should eventually be proved true.

Objectives

This, then, is my starting point. Taking Koestler's thesis that the essence of discovery is to trace a relationship between apparently unrelated facts, are there any phenomena, or reported phenomena, which are at present unexplained (or badly explained) and which might possibly be related in some way? As the hero of an old Hollywood gangster film would say: 'You can bet your sweet life there are!' For a start, modern science – and particularly nuclear and astronomical physics – deals with such concepts as tachyons, charms, quarks, black holes and so on, all of which imply some degree of contradiction of accepted principles, the assumption of paradoxical characteristics, and (in many cases) doubt as to whether they physically exist at all. Similarly, psychologists find it impossible to explain the normal or abnormal behaviour of a human being without assuming, at least as a working hypothesis, the existence within each of us of a 'subconscious', 'unconscious' or 'subliminal' mind, of which they cannot suggest the location, the origin, the mode of operation or the purpose.

Let me make it quite clear that I am not suggesting that any of these ideas is incorrect, impossible, or ridiculous. I am simply pointing out that each of them calls into question one or more of the fundamental tenets of the materialistic, deterministic, behaviouristic, humanistic, or Logical Positivist views of the universe that have formed the backbone of orthodox science for the last two hundred years. One cannot have one's cake and eat it; and if any set of assumptions or theories fails to explain all observed effects in a completely consistent way, then those theories themselves are open to question. Efforts to protect any of them as sacrosanct are, to say the least, unscientific. The excuse that revision is unthinkable, since it may uncover defects in basic scientific philosophy, and so paralyse current research, is particularly absurd.

Reference to psychology leads to the next huge category of the unexplained, those phenomena generally referred to as supernatural, paranormal, psychic, psi or ESP (and in this book I am not going to waste time in hair-splitting distinctions or definitions – the meaning is plain enough). The common factor in all such events is that they each offend against the materialistic, etc., etc., views of the universe referred to above, but even so, they are not accepted by orthodox science as being in the same category as the black hole, the quark, the subconscious and so on. They are simply dismissed as fundamentally impossible.

A third category of unknown may be summed up as 'religious beliefs'. When one considers the multiplicity of man's attempts to explain his own existence, and his relationship with the universe, it is evident that unless one is prepared to accept without question the complete authority of a single source (such as the Bible, the mythology of a particular community, or the current beliefs of some particular branch of the scientific establishment), all such questions must be considered to be still unanswered. In this book, I hope to suggest (and I emphasise that I use the word 'suggest' quite deliberately and in its literal meaning) that many, if not most, of these large 'unknown quantities' in our knowledge may be related – in some cases almost explicitly – by a single factor, the physical existence of extra dimensions beyond the reach of our normal senses.

Sources and Treatment

The majority of the material I will discuss is derived from books, most of them easily available to the layman. I have tried to avoid the more colourful pot-boilers, with hair-raising accounts of screaming nuns, headless horsemen and ghastly hell-hounds, and also those, ranging from the dreadfully earnest to the delightfully fey, which may be convincing to those already half convinced, but which I find myself viewing with suspicion and cynicism. Although I have not hesitated to use secondary sources such as popular works and reviews which quote from and discuss specialist papers and 'classic' cases, I have nevertheless preferred wherever possible to take actual accounts of paranormal events from the original publication, and particularly those which satisfy the following criteria:

1. The reports should be accounts of phenomena experienced or witnessed by the author himself (or herself), or personally vouched for by him;
2. The accounts should be as clear and factual as the circumstances would allow, and should refer specifically to the reactions and sensations of the experient *at the time*, rather than convey the impression of being biased towards a specific theory;
3. The events described should be relatively recent (allowing – at least in principle – the possibility of some degree of confirmation) and should preferably have been witnessed by, or later investigated by, dispassionate observers;

4. The author should show evidence that he has not prejudged the issue, and is prepared to consider alternative explanations to the one he offers;

5. It is encouraging if the author's accounts are quoted and discussed with respect by other authors in the field (offering a semblance of a 'consensus opinion');

6. The writing itself must convey a strong impression of honesty, convincing the reader that, while the author may be mistaken, misled, confused or subject to other human defects, he is at all times truthful to the limit of his ability.

The last three points (and particularly the final one) are all-important. Although a scientific investigation would reject such subjective criteria, I believe that truthfulness can shine through print, and can be recognised as such without too much risk of gullibility, (although honest self-deception must always remain a possibility).

Having selected my reference on such a basis, I then suspend disbelief and accept it as being honestly written, although still subject to human error. I am not offering a personal opinion on the reality or otherwise of a particular phenomenon. I am simply implying that in my opinion the particular case I quote may be worth studying in the context in which I quote it, as supporting my argument *if the account is true*. In most cases I have a choice of a number of accounts of different events, by different authors, each of which would adequately illustrate the same point, so if the particular example I use were proved totally untrue, the point itself may still be a valid one. In many discussions I have given only a short precis of the original, or quoted extracts in a disjointed form, on the assumption that the interested reader would prefer to consult the original for the background and full details. Similarly, I have often selected examples which I can use to illustrate a number of points at different places in the book. The Bibliography at the end of the book lists most of the sources, and is also a useful cross-reference to names other than authors.

The Exploration

The title of this book is a little ambiguous. It can be read almost literally as a convenient abbreviation for 'A Mental Exploration of the Possibility that a Fourth Dimension May Exist', or meta-phorically, since the slow development of the theme shows many of the characteristics of a rather arduous journey across unknown country, in which there are scientific quagmires, thorny mathematics and mountains of prejudice and preconceptions. Wide and well-beaten paths of belief may end in a solid obstruction. Sometimes I wander in a circle and find myself at a point I passed two chapters before, and I have needed to revise a conclusion I have happily accepted as reasonably well established. Then I have retained both concepts on the grounds that with such contentious material, second thoughts are not always an improvement. On the other hand, an overgrown and indistinct path can on occasion lead to a breath-taking discovery. Like any good explorer, I have occasionally stopped to map my route for the convenience of those who may follow, and to look ahead to anticipate problems, and like all explorations the work remains unfinished. It will need many visits by a host of explorers before a complete description of the new world can be attempted, and indeed it is evident that the full truth about the Fourth Dimension can never be firmly established by such tactics. That must await a determined programme of professional exploration such as I envisage in the final chapter. When that comes (as it undoubtedly will – it is long overdue) I will know how much of my own effort was a waste of time, but whatever the outcome I have no regrets. I have thoroughly enjoyed my exploration, and it would be doubly rewarding to me if others following my tracks enjoyed it as much, and found my account of some help.

The Limitations Of Humanity

Before beginning my exploration, it would be wise to examine the 'equipment' on which I must eventually rely – my own senses. It is commonly accepted that we have five senses: sight, hearing, touch, taste and smell, and that the whole of the knowledge acquired by an individual during a lifetime must be acquired through one or other of those senses. What is true of each individual is true of mankind as a whole; every item of knowledge on every subject must have passed at one time or another through one or other of the sensory organs of a human being. (The situation as regards scientific and technological aids is discussed in Chapter 4.) It follows that the accuracy and completeness of our view of the universe depends entirely on the accuracy and completeness of the information provided by our senses. What evidence have we that our senses may not be telling us the whole truth?

Consider first the opinion of Professor Richard Gregory, Professor of Neuropsychology at Bristol University and an authority on the operation of human perception. He writes:

> Suppose we were to meet something very odd – say a new life form – could we see it properly? The perceptual system is computer programmed by evolutionary experience and by our personal experience of the world. A new kind of object requires the perceptual computer to solve a new problem with an old programme, which may be neither adequate nor appropriate.[25]

This conclusion is confirmed by experiment. It has been shown that if the whiskers of a newly-born rat are trimmed, and maintained short until it matures, it never develops the extremely sophisticated sensory mechanism based on the whiskers, which is the major source of spatial information for a normal rat. Similarly, if a kitten is reared from birth in a large box painted inside with strong vertical stripes of black and white, when it matures it is unable to 'see' horizontal lines. The cat's eyes function perfectly normally, but the process of perception in the animal's brain does not include provision for understanding horizontal lines, *which are therefore invisible to the cat*. This seems perfectly explicit. Sensory information which the process of perception has not been programmed to handle may be distorted or ignored.

Now consider the following quotation from Wollheim's discussion of the work of Sigmund Freud, the 'Father of Psychology':

> First, we must suppose that our ordinary capacity to entertain ideas about some given object involves two components. On the one hand, there is the presentation of the thing, which has been built up of mnemic residues: memory traces of the thing . . . On the other hand there is the presentation of the word, which has similarly been built up of mnemic residues, but this time residues of seeing, and above all, of hearing, the word.
>
> Freud now asserted, first, that thing-presentations cannot become conscious until they have become linked with residues from perception of words, and secondly, that the word-presentations belong to the preconscious, not the unconscious . . .
>
> An unconscious mental state involves a thing-presentation that is without links to the corresponding word-presentation. For the state to become conscious, what is required is that such intermediate links should be laid down.[90]

If I may be allowed to try to express this concept more simply, it seems to mean this: In one area of my brain, words such as C-O-W,

H-O-R-S-E, and so on, are stored as memories of the times that I have read or heard them. Such storage is in my 'preconscious', i.e., normally unconscious but capable of being recalled into consciousness as and when I require them. In a totally separate area of the brain I hold memories of everything I have learned about a cow, a mental 'picture' of an animal with legs, horns and other appendages. However, according to Freud, this knowledge is held in the unconscious mind *and cannot be recalled into the conscious mind until the requisite words are available to discuss it*. The implication is that no subject can be 'thought about' unless the linguistic parts of the brain already contain the required concepts.

A similar conclusion has been reached more recently, and by a totally different route. In his book, *Men of Ideas*, Brian Magee[51] discusses the teachings of Noam Chomsky, Professor of Linguistics and Philosophy at the Massachusetts Institute of Technology, who disagrees with the belief (inherent in behavioural psychology) that all language is learned after birth. Chomsky argues that this is physically impossible, and from study of the structure of language in various cultures he suggests that we are *genetically preprogrammed* to learn to speak and to understand speech, and that all languages have a common structural basis corresponding to this programme. Magee comments:

> This has some important negative implications, too, the chief of which is that anything which cannot be accommodated to this structure . . . is inexpressible and unintelligible within any framework of human language. The general principles common to all languages put inescapable constraints, then, on our capacity to understand the world and communicate with each other.

Chomsky himself argues:

> A Martian scientist looking at us and observing our successes and errors from the standpoint of a higher intelligence might be amazed to discover that whereas in some domains we seem to be able to make substantial scientific progress, in other domains we always seem to be running up against a blank wall, perhaps because our minds are so constructed that we just can't make the intellectual leap required – we can't formulate the concepts, we don't have the categories required to gain insight into that domain.

This is a fascinating idea. It suggests that, just as the physical capabilities to run at speed or jump long distances are limited by the structure of the body, which is genetically controlled, so our capacity for understanding may be similarly limited by genetically-determined constraints on the intellect. Furthermore,

Chomsky's argument implies that what a person cannot express in words or convey in any other conceptual way *may be non-existent as far as his conscious mind is concerned*, so that the limitation applies not only to his ability to understand, but also to his capacity to *imagine*.

I am quite aware that I am extending the significance of the opinions of these authorities beyond the immediate contexts of their work, but even so, it seems that the minimum conclusion, on which all agree, is that our senses (or more correctly, our conscious awareness of sensory information) are limited and finite, and capable of misleading us.

It must be emphasised that this effect is in no way related to the existence of optical illusions and other minor errors of perception. These are largely explainable in psychological or physical terms, as the result of an attempt by the brain to interpret ambiguous, incomplete or contradictory information from the senses. In the effects I am discussing, the senses may report completely and accurately, but the brain distorts or ignores that information simply because it does not comply with certain criteria. It is the difference between a marksman who misses his target because the light is bad, and one who refuses to fire because it is against his principles!

Furthermore, the criteria referred to *are embodied in the programming of the human brain*. It is then an obvious step to suggest that the censor mechanism, which will be referred to frequently in this book, is part of the same programming – and one which is almost certainly genetically controlled, rather than learned. The lesson is clear:

What we observe and experience of the world around us is governed by the processing of sensory information that takes place within the brain. Some of the programming which controls that process is derived from experience, and therefore cannot cater for totally new information. Other parts of the programme are evolutionary, and so have been developed with survival as the objective, or with other purposes which we do not know. There can be no justification for the assumption that the physical world as we experience it, directly through our senses or through man-made aids to those senses, is the total of reality (an assumption which is a foundation-stone of scientific philosophy).

WE CANNOT TRUST OUR SENSES!

The Moral Aspect

I will mention one more aspect which will not be raised again until the closing chapters, (even though this may be equivalent to scrawling 'The Butler Did It' on the first page of a detective novel borrowed from the Public Library). So far, my attempts at complete honesty may have misled the reader into thinking that this is no more than a shallow, rambling collection of stale or ludicrous ideas, put together by the author for his own amusement. It was only after the process of collecting ideas was well under way that I became aware of much deeper implications.

Even the shallowest and most perfunctory thought on world affairs would suggest that the apparent 'progress' of science and technology is (with very few exceptions) a symptom of the total misdirection of man's efforts, and that the awful mess in which humanity finds itself in almost every aspect of existence is directly attributable to the short-sightedness, greed, selfishness, egotism and innate violence of a minority, aided and abetted by the same factors, plus apathy, stupidity and lack of imagination on the part of the majority. It is a cliché to say that man has lost his way, and while the advocacy of such 'cures' as a 'back-to-nature' ecologically-conscious society, or a mass return to some particular religious doctrine, can do no harm, they can only affect a minority and have little real effect. The field is wide open for more drastic suggestions, and fundamental problems call for fundamental suggestions – even if these initially appear to be nonsensical and ludicrous. Thinking in these terms, suppose one starts from the statement I made above, that the principal obstacle to peace, stability and sanity lies in the defects of human nature itself (particularly in bulk – I may manage to love my neighbours as individuals, but when they act as an organised society, the results are invariably horrifying or depressing). Then it is worth considering *what would be required in order to produce a basic change in human nature on a world-wide scale.**

I accept that this sounds crazy, and I am *not* proposing a simple, guaranteed, can't-fail method (such as 'Suppose the whole world took up Zen Buddhism'), but in the last chapter I study the possibility that somewhere buried in this book may be found

---

* If you maintain that this is fundamentally impossible, think what the introduction of Western technology and attitudes has done for the North American Indian, the Eskimo, and the native societies of the Pacific.

clues which, if followed to their conclusion, may lead to discoveries so far-reaching as to produce a major re-think of that nature (and God knows, if anyone does, that even this limited hope is just raving, starry-eyed optimism and, some would claim, blatant egotism). Still, there is nothing lost by trying.

The point to be emphasised *ad nauseam* is that this book tries to present a reasonably coherent sequence of Ideas, to be accepted as such, to be rejected as nonsense if you must, or – preferably – to be thought over carefully. Just how much of reality and true vision is hidden in the mists of conjecture is a matter for each reader to decide for him- or herself and for the future to confirm or correct this judgment. *Good Luck, and Happy Exploring.*

CHAPTER 2

THE CASE AGAINST SCIENTISM

*'The orthodox position is not necessarily vastly superior to all others.
It may even be inferior, especially if its methodological
preoccupations have led it systematically to ignore especially
important but problematic sources of evidence, such as myths,
legends, anecdotes, craft traditions, non-expert testimony of
unreproducible events, and so on.'*[13]
R.G.A. Dolby

I hope I have made it clear that this book can make no pretensions
to being a scientific study. I can *prove* nothing and it would be
inviting ridicule to suggest otherwise. For it to stand a chance of
being taken seriously, it must be transparently honest, emphasis-
ing at all times that it offers one man's thoughts and subjective
opinions, based very firmly on the work of others. This approach,
and indeed the very attempt to discuss in a single volume 'Scientific Facts' such as black holes, 'Absolute Nonsense' such as apparitions and poltergeists, and 'Sacred Beliefs' such as the physical
nature of God, will earn the wrath of many, and I must anticipate
strong and deeply-entrenched antipathy from those who would
defend their own preconceptions by dismissing the whole concept
out of hand. My reply to the theologians among them must wait
until Chapters 14 and 15, but I must deal faithfully with the
scientists here and now.

'Scientism' is defined as '*The methods and mental attitudes of men
of science*', and it is a sad reflection on those men that the word is
often (as here) used in a critical manner to imply a dogmatic belief
in the rightness of the views of orthodox science, and in the
infallibility of the scientific method. Many a scientist may disagree
with those attitudes, but knows that there is little that he can do
without exposing himself to ridicule or worse. In that sense, the
relationship between the individual scientist and 'Science' is

comparable to that between a journalist and 'The Press' or a bishop and 'The Church'; whether he likes it or not he is included in any criticism of his profession. I apologise to the more liberal-minded, but I have little alternative but to use the collective term.

The more extreme supporters of scientism normally advance six basic arguments denying the existence of the paranormal, and decrying attempts to investigate it. It is instructive to take each of these one by one and examine its validity:

1. There is no coherent theoretical basis for any form of paranormal event:

This book itself offers a counter to that criticism, in that it offers a single hypothesis – the existence of a physical Fourth Dimension – and by progression from it advances some kind of an explanation for most paranormal phenomena. The fact that the logic is extremely tenuous, disjointed, full of inconsistencies and gaps, and based more on imagination than experiment, does not justify its dismissal out of hand, since such defects could (in principle at least) be remedied by later and more competent work.

There is another aspect of the problem of theory. A mediaeval scientist could not have advanced a theory to account for radio waves, since he was unaware of their existence, despite his being immersed in (naturally-occurring) radio waves every minute of his life. One cannot formulate a theory until one accepts that there is something to explain, and those scientists who advance this argument against the paranormal are trying to have their cake and eat it – to deny that there is a need for a theory, then to advance the absence of a theory as a reason for not needing one!

A further point has been made by Sir Karl Popper (although as a point of philosophy, and not in this specific context). He argues that if a theory may – in principle – be proved true, this may imply that it is impossible to prove it false – and vice versa. For instance, if I propose that 'It is possible for a green cow to exist', that statement can be proved true simply by the production of a green cow for verification, but it can never be proved false, since a green cow may be born tomorrow in the wilds of Timbuctoo. It seems logical that a Fourth Dimension is in the same category as a green cow. Its existence could be proved by the production of verified observations that could only be explained in those terms, but its non-existence can never be proved because we cannot say what is required of us in order to observe it.

Consider also the principle known as 'Occam's Razor'. William of Occam was a 14th-century philosopher and theologian who proposed that 'entities (or explanations) should not be multiplied unnecessarily', which is usually interpreted as meaning that a simple theory (or one making the *fewest assumptions*) should always be preferred to a more complex one, if they both seek to explain the same facts. Now we are faced with a tremendous range and variety of apparently paranormal phenomena, with countless well-attested examples of each type. To ignore, or to deny the truth of *all* of these one must adopt one of three alternative procedures:

a) Indulge in a massive exercise in head-burying,
b) Be party to the wholesale slander of a multitude of people on no substantive evidence (other than the conviction of one's own infallibility),
c) Undertake a painstaking study of each separate case in search of some excuse, no matter how weak or trivial, for disbelieving it (and no matter how strenuously the people concerned may deny it, this is what much of the 'scientific analysis' reduces to).

The last procedure is doubly dubious, since if there remains a single episode which cannot be explained away, the whole exercise has failed, so that the pressure to distort, select, exaggerate or even invent is enormous: often far greater than the equivalent pressures on those who originated the reports.

In contrast, the theory of a physical fourth dimension is basically simple, being completely expressible in less than a hundred words. It may be difficult to understand in any practical terms, even more difficult to believe, and impossible to prove, but its acceptance, *not* as a statement of proven fact, but as a *working hypothesis* on which to base further investigation and enquiry, enables a tentative explanation of each effect to be offered, with the advantages of a unified and self-consistent approach.

2. Paranormal occurrences do not comply with accepted 'Laws of Nature' or 'Scientific Principles' and therefore they cannot possibly exist:

This is a very popular argument, and yet is easily falsified. It can be expressed in the words of the Scottish philosopher, David Hume, who in a dissertation 'On Miracles' wrote:

A miracle is a violation of the laws of nature; and as a firm and unalterable experience has established these laws, the proof against a miracle, from the very nature of the fact, is as entire as any argument from experience can possibly be imagined . .

Since Hume died in 1776 one may presume that television, heart transplants, aeroplanes and space travel all lay well outside the 'laws of nature' based on the 'firm and unalterable experience' of himself and his contemporaries – which seems to extend considerably the scope of the word 'miracle'. No-one, not even a leading scientist or philosopher, is qualified to pronounce with certainty on what is a miracle and what is not.

In the world of science, major revisions of fundamental attitudes have become almost the norm. As an example, suppose one were to take a number of the text-books of physics used in leading universities a hundred years ago, and compare them with their present-day equivalents. A third or more of the 'scientific facts' in the earlier volumes are now known to be untrue, and the philosophies underlying most of the reasoning would now be regarded as completely incorrect. As Sherwood Taylor pointed out:

> At the turn of the century, Physics seemed to be a science most logically built up on the most unassailable principles . . . To the physicist of 1895 a fundamental change in the bases of the science would have seemed incredible.

That was in the days when each atom was believed to be as solid, indivisible and immutable as a billiard ball, when the observed event and the observer were assumed to be independent entities, and before Relativity and Nuclear Physics had shot the whole of our understanding of the structure of matter and the universe back into the melting pot. There is no logical reason why the scientists of the 1980s should be any more infallible in their pontifical statements of scientific dogmas than their predecessors of the 1880s. It is highly likely that the next hundred years will see equally fundamental revisions of scientific thinking. The whole of the history of science ridicules the suggestion that at any point in time the 'Laws of Nature' are known to such an extent that major changes in the foundations of scientific belief cannot possibly occur.

3. *All anecdotal cases of events not observed under strict laboratory conditions can be attributed to human error, exaggeration, hallucination or fraud:*

A salient feature of the accounts of paranormal experiences is that they are completely genuine and convincing to the experient *at the time*. It is only when the cold light of 'reason' (from disbelieving friends), and the self-examination which results from the continuous defence of the impossible, force a review of what happened, that doubts may creep in. This effect is only to be expected as a consequence of the 'censor mechanism' to be discussed in this book.

It is accepted that fifty or five-hundred anecdotes can prove nothing, but it is farcical to pretend, as scientism pretends, that there can be no alternative to either the complete acceptance of an account, or its total rejection as an absurdity; that each must be tagged 'Possibly True' (i.e., scientifically explainable), or 'False'; that there can be no file labelled 'Not Proven but May be Worth Studying'. One factor which argues strongly for the serious study of anecdotal evidence is that, taken in quantity, it is remarkably consistent between events happening in different societies at different times. A study of world-wide cases of poltergeist hauntings, for instance, has shown that the 'symptoms' may be classified under a relatively small number of headings, and although not all occur in any one case, those that do always happen in the same order. Similarly, Wilson[89] shows that many 'Time of Death' apparitions (as John's on page 98) and 'Near-Death Experiences' (see page 153) show very consistent characteristics.

4. In no case of controlled experiments purporting to demonstrate paranormal events is the evidence repeatable and indisputable, allowing no other possible explanation. This fact alone justifies the rejection of all such evidence:

This objection involves several separate arguments. The first point, that the experiments are not reproducible at will under closely-controlled laboratory conditions, is an extremely weak one, and may be attacked on a number of counts. No reasonable person would refuse to accept a new Olympic record merely because all conditions happened to be favourable at the time, and the athlete could never again hope to achieve that standard of performance. Many claims in medical research, for instance, are made on the basis of investigations into rare diseases and even isolated cases. Such results may be treated with reserve, but they are not dismissed out of hand. Similarly, consider how many of the discoveries in modern science are made in research centres employing highly specialised staff using huge and very expensive equipment, such as large telescopes and 'atom-smashers'. What of the results from space-craft projects, such as the investigation of Halley's Comet or the new 'Eye in Space' telescope? How many such discoveries may be reproduced at will elsewhere?

Then again; how many of the known natural phenomena cannot be reproduced by man at will? Could any of Newton's contemporaries (or Einstein's for that matter) have produced a flash of lightning in the laboratory when he chose? Yet no-one would dream of advancing this fact as proof that lightning cannot exist! Fertilisation of an egg by a sperm has been going on for millions of years, but was only demonstrated in the laboratory a few decades ago.

The second point stems from the first. Scientism claims that such experimental evidence as is available is not 'foolproof'. In fact, under the continuous pressure of scepticism, laboratory techniques in parapsychology have been refined to the state that Collins and Pinch can say:

> All this has been accompanied by an increasing sophistication with statistical analysis and experimental technique such as 'double blind' judging of results and the use of independent observers. It seems likely that the best of modern parapsychology comprises some of the most rigorously controlled and methodologically sophisticated work in the sciences.[11]

This still does not satisfy the sceptic. In the same book, Dolby, in his paper on 'Reflections on Deviant Science' comments:

> Many orthodox scientists are not prepared to trust the claim of parapsychologists to have done the work competently, even though it is admitted that the precautions required are so complex that no one other than a parapsychologist *could* have sufficient expertise.

This aspect has probably caused more heated argument than any other. The (quite open) attitude of scientism is that one may begin from a premise that paranormal events are impossible, and therefore 'scientific analysis' may consist of no more than a search for some excuse, no matter how weak, for rejecting the evidence. Perjury, trickery and fraud on the part of the medium or the experimenters involved are at the top of the list of possibilities. Alan Vaughan discusses:

> . . . the misfortunes that had befallen psychical researchers who had risked their reputation by publishing evidence for ESP that no-one else could verify. Their critics took the view that since ESP is impossible, therefore the researchers must be fraudulent or duped . . . Hardly a researcher in psychology had gone without attacks on his personal integrity and reputation.[79]

This calumny does not stop at those directly involved. One 'explanation' of the positive results of a series of telepathy experiments suggested that a large number of students and staff of the University who were not professionally involved connived at fraud! Professor C.E.M. Hansel, 'scientifically analysing' the evidence for ESP, declares:

If the result could have arisen from a trick, the experiment must be considered unsatisfactory proof of ESP, whether or not it was finally decided that such a trick was in fact used.[29]

Similarly, Mrs Heywood[36] quotes Dr George H. Price of the University of Minnesota, who would only accept the existence of ESP on the evidence of:

. . . one fraud-proof experiment conducted before a committee of twelve prominent men, who were all strongly hostile towards parapsychology and had an adamantine faith that ESP was impossible . . . he admits that there are no other alternatives . . . all concerned in all ESP experiments must have cheated.[36]

One's first reaction is of exasperation. One wonders what would be the views of an archaeologist or astronomer if his work were subject to this kind of destructive criticism, and he himself to this type of character assassination. Imagine the reaction of a doctor who had recently published the results of serious medical research and who was asked to take a lie-detector test! More practically, one could ask Dr Price or Prof. Hansel what proof he would accept that he himself snored in his sleep (assuming that he had already decided that such a thing was impossible).

The final point on this question of experimental weakness is more subtle, but is to me the most telling of all. It is a fact of scientific and technical life that any experiment may fail, or produce unreliable results, until the factors which produce such unreliability are eliminated, and to do this *those factors must first be understood*! This problem can be illustrated graphically by a simple experiment.

Tear off a small piece – about the size of a finger-nail – from the corner of a newspaper and put it on the table. Now take the body of a ball-point pen (or a plastic rule) and rub it briskly for a few seconds in your hair or on dry clothing. Hold it over the paper, which will be attracted to it and cling for several minutes. Now repeat the same process but this time, after rubbing the pen breathe gently on it before holding it over the paper – and there will be no attraction. The explanation is simple. Rubbing the plastic causes it to acquire a high electrical voltage (possibly a thousand volts or more), and when it is brought near to the paper, electrostatic forces pull them together. Since the plastic is a good insulator, this situation may be maintained for a considerable time. Moisture provides a path for the electric charge to leak away, and then the attraction disappears.

The attractive force of an electrostatic field has been known for at least 500 years (probably nearer 2000), but think of the difficulties encountered by an early experimenter, who did not understand what was happening. On a damp, cold morning his efforts may be of no avail, but later that day (after the fire had been burning an hour or so) all his experiments may work perfectly – until someone coughed or sneezed, when results could become very erratic. The more complex experiments used wire or rods which were often supported on a wooden structure. An experimenter who happened to have used well-seasoned wood stored indoors, and who had improved the appearance of his equipment with a coat of French polish (shellac – an excellent insulator, as it happens), could well have produced good and consistent results, while his neighbour (using nominally identical equipment, but not quite so fussy as to its appearance) may have found it impossible to achieve consistency. It would be a salutary lesson in the practical problems of science if one of those shining examples of clear-headed, open-minded and logical scientist quoted above was invited to demonstrate the principles of static electricity in an unventilated cellar in Rangoon in the monsoon season (and if he should complain that he is insufficiently acquainted with the subject to take appropriate precautions, the point would be even more forcibly made).

A more recent example of a similar situation is the discovery and exploitation of radio waves. The characteristics of these waves vary enormously with differing wavelengths; the performance of aerials is an extremely complex subject which took many years to clarify; the development of a reliable detector of minute radio-frequency signals was beset with many difficulties (as anyone old enough to have 'tickled a cat's whisker' will testify); and not only was the existence of the ionosphere (the reflecting layers above the earth's surface which guide a radio wave around the curve of the world) totally unsuspected, but its behaviour is extremely complex and is still far from predictable. It is no wonder that the early years of radio were full of contradictory reports, false clues – *and unrepeatable results*!

The conclusions are perfectly clear, one cannot experiment reliably until one understands the principles behind the experiment. One cannot gain this knowledge without carrying out experiments which must initially, almost by definition, be unreliable and unrepeatable. The attempt by scientism to attack on these grounds the results obtained by research into the paranormal is sheer hypocrisy and obscurantism.

5. The tremendous progress in science and technology over the last two hundred years has all taken place without revealing any evidence for, or

*the need to assume, the existence of the paranormal, therefore it is
logical to assume that there is no such thing:*

The main answer to this argument is that science finds only
what it looks for, and despite its apparently universal range, there
are many areas in which it refuses to look – and so finds nothing.
Colin Wilson writes:

> There is an emotional prejudice behind the choice of 'the facts' the
> scientist is willing to take seriously; a feeling that certain facts are
> 'good taste' and certain others are bad taste. Quite unconsciously,
> he has come to limit his interest to the kind of facts that fit into the
> kind of jigsaw puzzle he is good at solving.[87]

Cosmology and nuclear physics, for instance, are 'In' subjects
because of their esoteric and mathematical nature, and carry
immense professional prestige. Being free of commercial and
military pressures, they are carried out by an introspective and
close-knit international community motivated mainly by incen-
tives of individual ambition and national pride. If a fraction of the
effort applied to these subjects in the last fifty years had been
applied to such problems as the nature of thought and the modes
of operation of the human brain, the questions raised in this book
would probably have been answered many years ago.

There is a second answer. Research into fundamental physics
has produced a number of inconsistent and paradoxical results
which are inexplicable in general terms and so are embarrassing to
scientific orthodoxy. The honest response should be to announce
that 'we cannot explain these results within the limitations of
existing scientific principles, and therefore those principles may
require revision.' Instead, one gets the attitude of the leading
physicist P.A.M. Dirac, who said, 'The only object of the theoretical physicist is to calculate results which can be compared with
experiment and it is quite unnecessary that any satisfying description of the whole course of the phenomenon should be given.' It
seems that we have a triangular 'grey area', bounded on one side
by mathematical expressions, on another by experimental evidence, and on the third by accepted and physically recognisable
fundamental principles. Dirac suggests that if the first two agree
between themselves, the third can go hang. Not only is this a
specific admission of the limitations of man's understanding and
intellect, but it is in direct contradiction to Sir Herbert Dingle's
attitude (see page 256) which rejects as impossible anything which
man cannot imagine! Again the scientific world wants to have its
cake and eat it.

6. Only a professional scientist, trained as he is to exercise dispassionate and objective judgment, and dedicated as he is to the maintenance of the purity of Knowledge, is qualified to pronounce on what is True and what is False.

Despite the efforts of many senior scientists (particularly in the so-called 'pure sciences'), there are notable dissenters to this view. Eysenk writes:

> Many laymen have a kind of stereotyped view of the scientist as an inhuman, completely objective and rational sort of person, who only takes into account facts and is not swayed by emotions or feelings in his judgement. Unfortunately, there is little truth in such a picture. Scientists . . . are just as ordinary, pig-headed and unreasonable as anybody else, and their unusually high intelligence only makes their prejudices all the more dangerous because it enables them to cover these up with an unusually glib and smooth flow of high-sounding talk.

Nor is such an attitude limited to the lower strata of science. It would seem that the higher the status of a scientist, the more likely he is to consider his own beliefs to be unassailable. The great German scientist Von Helmholtz declared (of telepathy):

> Neither the testimony of all the Fellows of the Royal Society, nor even the evidence of my own senses, would lead me to believe in the transmission of thought from one person to another independently of the recognised channels of sense.

William Thompson (Lord Kelvin), a great Victorian physicist, declared that heavier-than-air flying machines were a physical impossibility, and dismissed X-rays as a hoax. The 18th-century meteorologist, Deluc, was similarly adamant. During a long and bitter argument as to whether it was possible for stones to fall from the sky (i.e., meteorites) he declared that if he saw one fall at his feet he would admit that he had seen it, but still say 'I don't believe it.' (One wonders what he would say of the investigations into Halley's Comet. Perhaps he would not believe those results either!)

The hubris of such attitudes is evident and unforgivable. The fact that many sensible people are convinced that paranormal effects have happened to them is brushed aside, on the grounds that science exists to protect the uneducated from their own ignorance and superstition. However, the situation approaches the farcical when the person experiencing the paranormal happens to be just such a scientist. There have been cases, as recounted by Mrs Heywood, in which a speaker at a lecture or symposium has learnedly refuted and derided the possibility of paranormal phenomena, while on the train home that evening, he has discussed with interest his own experiences of them. Furthermore, he has seen nothing illogical in the situation, insisting that while 'as a man' he must accept the evidence of his own senses, 'as a scientist' he cannot possibly support a concept which would require himself, his superiors and his colleagues to revise, and probably scrap completely, their concept of the universe.

This is the nub of the question. It is not possible to consider seriously any phenomenon such as apports, psycho-kinesis, or clairvoyance without calling into question the whole foundation of scientific thought, philosophy and method. To do so would leave almost the whole of 'pure' science at a loose end, unable to proceed because the scientific 'rule book' had been scrapped, but unable to provide a substitute at short notice. Vast numbers of professional scientists would find their life's work – and they themselves – useless; and scientists, despite their image, are as human as the rest of us, with wives and families to keep, and ambitions to fulfil. Such a situation has, understandably enough, been described as 'unthinkable', but the hard fact is that if the only alternative is the kind of hysterical hypocrisy I have described, the unthinkable must be thought, or science itself will ultimately be discredited.

Seen in the light of these arguments, the position of the more extreme devotees of the principle of 'My mind is made up – don't confuse me with facts' is untenable, and is beginning to be recognised as such. The piercing scrutiny of the sociologist has been turned on to the behaviour of the scientists themselves.[81] Their facade of cool and unbiased detachment has been torn down to expose a degree of prejudice and self-interest, and a response to social and market forces, hardly distinguishable from those of any other professional or commercial class. However, there are signs of a major change of heart, particularly among the younger rank and file. Their attitudes are not so public and therefore less influenced by career considerations or possible 'loss of face'. A poll carried out among the readers of *New Scientist* (most of them qualified scientists) in 1973 indicated that some 25 per cent regarded ESP as an established fact and only 3 per cent dismissed it as 'totally impossible'. It is evident that more rational arguments must eventually prevail over the head-in-the-sand attitudes of those ignoble Canutes who are desperately trying to postpone the problems of facing up to the realities of paranormal events by insisting that such phenomena cannot exist.

Going 'Over The Top'

It could be argued that the discussion above may have had some justification in the past, but that modern science is indeed doing its best to adapt to paranormal phenomena. There have been a number of attempts in recent years to introduce 'forbidden' subjects, (such as telepathy, or life after death) into 'legitimate' speculation on such matters as the structure of the nucleus and the origins of the universe. Such unlikely bedfellows can be found particularly in books discussing the latest developments or speculations in nuclear or quantum physics. This tendency was notable from the dawn of the new science; many of the great names in this field, such as Bohr, Dirac, Eddington, Heisenberg and Einstein, saw quasi-mystical possibilities in their discoveries. This is not altogether surprising. The thundering surge of scientific discovery in the 19th century had encouraged an image of Man the Omnipotent, the Master of the Universe, until science collided head-on with the mysteries of the nucleus. These men were the first to contemplate the unseeable, to investigate the unknowable, to grapple with the unimaginable, and it took their breath away. Inevitably, they speculated over their coffee-cups as to what lay at the far borders of the great unknown before them. The fact that some of them were intellectual giants should not lead us to assume that they were infallible, or that their opinions were anything more than temporary musings on half-developed and quarter understood mathematical relationships. For instance Lyall Watson discusses 'Schrödinger's Cat':

> Imagine, suggested Austrian physicist Erwin Schrödinger, a box that contains a radioactive source, a Geiger counter, a bottle of cyanide, and a live cat. Everything is arranged so that in one hour there is a fifty-fifty chance that the counter will detect an atom of radio-active decay, trigger a device that opens the bottle of poison and kill the cat. If there is no decay in that time, nothing happens and the cat lives. There is no way of knowing what has happened to the cat until we open the box at the end of the test period. But, suggested Schrödinger, what if we don't open the box? What then can be said about the cat? According to quantum theory, there is an equal probability that the cat is alive or dead – *and neither is true until we open the lid and it takes on one of these two states*. The cat is both alive and dead in equal proportions, until we impose our conclusions on the equation, and push it, as a photon knocks an electron, one way or the other.[85] [My italics]

The inference seems to be that reality is purely a product of observation – that there is no such thing as an unobserved or unknown fact. One can accept that the process of observation may modify the situation in the area observed; it is not unreasonable that differing experimental techniques may reveal different characteristics of an observed event (and the only unique facet of quantum events is that science has so far failed to explain the wave/particle contradiction – see below); but to deduce from this that the observation creates the reality is to leap out of the indistinct murk of half-understood physics into the inky blackness of speculative mysticism.

Even if the mathematics suggests that this is the case, one would suspect that the mathematics is incorrect, incomplete or ambiguous, rather than accept such an unlikely situation. Opening the lid reveals the state of the cat to an observer in the room, but what of an observer in the next room? Is the cat alive to one man, and alive-and-dead to another? If that is so, can any scientific observation be trusted if it was carried out elsewhere?

The quantum aspect of the problem is itself a red herring. Suppose that the death of the cat is accomplished when a flea jumps off it onto a flea-detector – no radio-activity, no Geiger counter, no quantum physics – would the case be any different?

The proposed situation reduces to the theory of the 17th-century philosopher, Bishop George Berkeley, summarised by M.F. Ashley-Montague:

> A philosopher, one Bishop Berkeley,
> Remarked metaphysically, darkly.
> That what we don't see
> Cannot possibly be
> And the rest is rather unlarkely.

The tradition of such speculation has been maintained to the present day, as in Danah Zohar's book *The Quantum Self*.[91] If I may (somewhat unfairly) summarise her argument:

a) From basic quantum physics, it is known that a photon has a dual existence, behaving simultaneously as a 'particle' and as a 'wave' (see pages 68 and 69). These may be interpreted in terms of an 'object' and an 'influence'.
b) Similarly the human body/mind may be visualised in terms of a duality of object/influence.
c) THEREFORE there is an analogy between the nature of a photon and that of a human being.
d) THEREFORE human consciousness is a quantum phenomenon.

She writes:

> This new conceptual structure for inter-personal relations can be found in the tensions within the wave-particle duality and the ability of an elementary particle to be both a wave and a particle simultaneously.
>
> The tension between particles and waves within the wave/particle duality is a tension between being and becoming. Similarly the tension within ourselves, between the I and the not-I . . . The key to both is quantum wave mechanics.

It is interesting to compare this with the views of Professor Herbert Dingle[12] (page 256), who castigated lesser mortals for 'confusing the symbol with the thing symbolised', whereas Zohar freely uses words such as 'symbol', 'analogy' and 'parallel' as if they represent factual relationships. If a nuclear physicist derives a mathematical expression for his observation of a particle and sees in it characteristics reminiscent (to him) of 'the collapse of a probabilistic wave function', there is no harm in his using the term speculatively when trying to clarify the situation to his peers, but it is pointless – if not downright folly – to use the same term without qualification to describe the execution of an abstract painting, or the death of Schrödinger's poor cat.

Mixed with this line of reasoning is the discovery (so far unexplained) by Professor Fröhlich of Liverpool University, of the existence of 'pumped systems' in the walls of living cells, in which a large number of localised electrical charges vibrate synchronously ('in unison') rather than in the usual random fashion. These two factors, as manipulated by Zohar, form the basis of a magnificent Christmas pudding of speculation, involving quantum physics, Freudian psychoanalysis, neurology of the brain, Marxism, Sartreian existentialism, the mystical aspects of holograms, Eastern mythology, life after death and much, much more. (Note, however, that if God and the human soul are excluded from the term, there is no specific mention of the paranormal.)

Nonetheless, the complete flexibility and malleability of the concepts and the tendentious nature of the discussion, result in a reasonably (if vaguely) understandable and consistent view of reality which finds some echoes in common experience. This luxury is dispensed with by other authors in the field. As an example, may I quote the 'Many Worlds Interpretation of Quantum Mechanics' as described by Gary Zukav.[93] This theory is based directly on Schrödinger's Wave Equation (a mathematical relationship embodying the wave/particle duality referred to above).

If I read Zukav correctly, the situation proposed is this. If I toss a coin, the selection of 'Heads' or 'Tails' is determined by chance at the instant of the toss, and at that instant two distinct and separate 'branches of reality' are created, two distinct universes *both equally real*. In one of these I get Heads, in the other Tails. At the same instant, my own consciousness splits into two versions, (one in each universe), which then continue to exist, each oblivious to the other. Presumably if I spill my coffee (or don't), more universes will be created, and fifty-two if I cut a pack of playing cards!

> When a consciousness happens to be present at such a split, it splits also, one part of it associating with one branch of reality, and the other part(s) of it associating with the other branches of reality. However, each branch of reality is experientially inaccessible [Sic!] to the other(s), and a consciousness in any one branch will consider that branch to be the entirety of reality . . . According to this theory, all of the other states which 'could have' resulted from the same interaction *did happen*, but in other branches of reality. Each of these branches of reality are real. [Zukav's italics]

Apparently, the suggestion of an intangible Fourth Dimension, (which may – as we shall see – imply the existence of one or more 'other' universes), can be dismissed out of hand as ridiculous, but one may discuss with dignity the possibility that almost identical but inaccessible universes are multiplying like midges minute by minute at the whim of chance. Similarly, the idea that mental activity may extend beyond the confines of the skull (as appears to happen in telepathy) is unthinkable, but it is acceptable to theorise there are millions of 'Me' in various universes, all living slightly different lives.

To theorise that physical reality, and the functions of the human brain in particular, are quantum phenomena has been compared to 'trying to study architecture by examining brick-dust under a microscope'. It offends against Common Sense, and if it should be argued that such a factor should not enter into a scientific discussion, then I beg to disagree. I would suggest that, to the Man in the Street, 'Common Sense' consists of his own experiences, plus such received wisdom from parents, teachers, newspapers and other sources *as he is prepared to accept*. He dismisses any unacceptable ideas as 'nonsense'. *Precisely the same definition applies to the so-called 'Laws of Science'*. The whole history of the study of the paranormal demonstrates beyond question that a scientist is always capable of finding (or if necessary inventing) a reason for rejecting data which do not comply with his preconceptions.

Arguing from common sense then, let us list the various physical systems of the universe in order of size, as follows:

a) Atomic nuclei;
b) The atoms of the elements;
c) The small molecules of inorganic compounds;
d) The large molecules of organic compounds found in living organisms;
e) Living organisms themselves, including man;
f) The earth
g) The solar system;
h) The galaxy;
i) The universe.

In general, each step up this progression represents an increase of several orders in size, so that we would expect appreciable interaction to occur only within one category, or between one system and its immediate neighbours. For instance, the chemical characteristics of an inorganic compound can be adequately explained in terms of the arrangements of the electrons in the outer orbits of the atoms in it (c-b), which are related in a simple manner to the gross construction of the nuclei (b-a). The activities of man have played havoc with our own earth (e-f), but we have had no effect on the solar system as a whole. From this line of argument, it seems unreasonable to suggest that phenomena in level (a), occurring only rarely and under very artificial conditions, should constitute a major factor in the physiology, mental functions and social relationships of objects at level (e). It is almost groundless speculation to suggest that major functions of the mind are quantum phenomena.

And yet it must be emphasised that these books are not the products of members of way-out mystical cults. Zukav is describing ideas put to him by research workers in nuclear physics at the University of California at Berkeley and at Birkbeck College, University of London, while Zohar qualified in physics and philosophy at MIT and Harvard, and acknowledges her debt to discussions with academics in Oxford, UK. So what is the fundamental difference between speculation of the Zukav/Zohar variety, which is scientifically acceptable, and the type of thinking in this book, which is not?

The answer lies in the classic vision of scientific philosophy, which accepts a new theory only if it has passed all the tests of rigorous proof and is founded on previous theories which have been accepted on similar terms. The whole structure is like a tower which increases in height safely only if each storey added is soundly built. To erect a structure of speculation on the shaky, new and only partly understood basis of nuclear physics may be frowned upon, but is grudgingly accepted, because it does not seriously affect established work. Speculation as to a fourth dimension (particularly in the blatantly physical and pragmatic terms I will use) is not accepted because it implies that the very foundations of physical science are flawed. If such reasoning is pursued, there is a chance that the whole structure may need to be re-surveyed and be proved unsound – and to a scientist that is unthinkable.

For let there be no prevarication. I will suggest that much of science may be based on false assumptions, my argument proceeding as follows. The proof of a scientific theory rests ultimately on observation – mainly of deliberately prepared experiments. 'Observation' requires that the results of the experiment must be accessible to one or other of man's five senses (usually sight). The use of scientific and technical aids such as telescopes, spectrographs, X-ray machines and so on may have extended very considerably the scope of those senses, but the limitation remains. Any such machine cannot be constructed until its underlying principles are understood – and those principles were only discovered because of effects which were observable. It follows that in all cases the limitations on man's sensory organs and the associated perception processes in the brain form a fundamental limitation to scientific knowledge. And, as explained in the previous chapter, *we cannot trust our senses.*

CHAPTER 3

ONE – TWO – THREE –
? ? ? ?

'The Red Queen shook her head, "You may call it 'nonsense' if you like," she said, "But I've heard nonsense, compared with which that would be sensible as a dictionary."'
Lewis Carroll

The first chapter made it clear that most of the ideas manipulated in this book are second-hand. I do not feel that it is necessary to apologise for this, and indeed the very nature of the subject would make it difficult to advance a totally new argument. As prime examples, Whately Carrington, an eminent Member of the Society for Psychical Research, published in 1920 (under the name of Whately Smith) a book entitled *A Theory of the Mechanism of Survival*, in which he examines the concept of a fourth dimension, and concludes that the dead may continue to exist in a four-dimensional world; a more recent book by Rudy Rucker[73] uses many analogies of the type I quote in this chapter and later to investigate the geometry of four dimensions and the possibilities of travel to other universes through time and four-dimensional space, and so on.

However, a precedent for my approach pre-dates either of these. The proposition that a fourth dimension physically exists was extensively investigated by Johann Zollner,[92] Professor of Physics and Astronomy at Leipzig University, during the second half of the 19th century. As a physicist, he approached the problem in physical and mechanical terms. To him, as to most of his contemporaries, all that was real in the universe was based on mechanical principles. Things pushed, pulled, lifted or accelerated other things by forces applied through solids, liquids or gases; chemical reactions took place when atoms as solid as billiard balls linked with, or broke their links with, other solid atoms. He was not confused by the complexities of the structure of the atomic nucleus, and the cosmology of his day (the study of the origin and structure of the universe) was relatively simple. He therefore saw the fourth dimension as an extension of the existing three, and just as real. However, he laboured under the considerable difficulty that he was trying to prove his theory scientifically to a sceptical and hostile scientific community, who ridiculed his naiveté and gullibility (possibly justifiably) and did not take his 'findings' seriously.

My sights are set lower, and I do not intend anything more ambitious than an armchair investigation of the possibility that the fourth dimension (and others) *may* exist, and the possible consequences if they do. Nonetheless, I share with the Professor the attitude that the primary evidence must be considered in simple physical terms to begin with. If other dimensions exist, then it is reasonable to assume that events in them are as physical as they appear to be in our own, and that the 'Laws of Nature' studied by science are simple extracts from more complex principles. In Chapter 2 I discussed my reasons for being suspicious of the modern urge to extend the findings of nuclear physics into the realm of metaphysics, and for rejecting the current belief that a combination of quantum physics, relativity and the more recent discoveries in cosmology will between them solve all the riddles of the universe. Certainly, the more modern and esoteric sciences must enter into the discussion, but in supporting roles, not in the leading parts.

There is also a philosophical element in my reasoning. I feel strongly that in the present situation 'the proper study of mankind is Man', in that no study of yet another sub-atomic particle or far-distant star is likely to do anything to clarify really fundamental questions such as 'What is Man?', 'Why are we here?', 'How should we behave – and why?'; nor will knowledge of events a few million years ago or in the future help mankind to reduce the imminent possibility of self-destruction from a number of causes.

Basic Dimensions

I begin my investigation, then, with an uneasy feeling that somewhere in the process of the acquisition of knowledge, we have overlooked some vital clue, or ignored some salient fact, and as a consequence have been misled into jumping to false conclusions. In that vein, I will start by considering the oldest branch of mathematics – geometry. The essential concept underlying the ideas I want to discuss is that of Dimension, and since the word is used in slightly different ways by mathematicians, engineers and physicists, I shall clarify my own definitions.

A mathematician would say that a straight line has one dimension – that of Length (see Fig. 1); a rectangular area has two dimensions – Length and Width; while a rectangular volume or block (disregarding technical terms for such shapes), has three dimensions – Length, Width and Height or Thickness. We immediately run into one important factor often overlooked. When a mathematician says 'A straight line has one dimension', he may mean exactly that, but the world of the mathematician differs from the real world of our experience, in that any practical example of a straight line, such as a taut cotton thread or a ruled pencil line, must also have thickness and width, or it is intangible, invisible and non-existent.

I remember this point being made to me many years ago by a workshop foreman, a Cockney with the gift of tongues. I had casually asked him for: '. . . a piece of brass, about three inches by two,' whereupon, after some preliminary discussion of my ances-

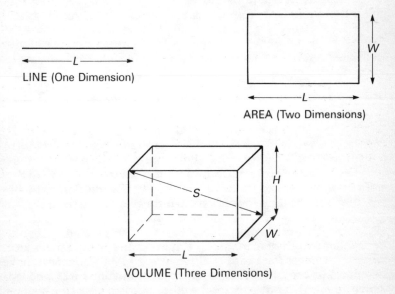

Figure 1. Length, Area and Volume

41

try and personal habits, he requested further information, commenting: 'If a *** fing ain't got no *** fickness, then a'h the *** can you *** well pick it up!' He was quite right, of course. In our real, physical world *everything*, sun, stars, dust or water, must be three-dimensional or it does not exist. What the mathematician implies is that for his purposes two of the dimensions of the line may be ignored as irrelevant to his reasoning. Similarly, we would accept that a football field has two dimensions, simply because no-one is interested in the third. This distinction between abstract theory and practical example is very important in the present context, since we are going to get involved in one- and two-dimensional universes, i.e., worlds in which all objects and movements are apparently limited to that number of dimensions.

One Or Two Is Easy

As a simple case of a two-dimensional world, let us consider the games of chess and draughts (or 'checkers' in America). Either game is played on a flat board marked off in equal-sized squares, the playing area being eight squares wide and eight long. The height of the pieces and the thickness of the board are irrelevant, and a piece removed from the board ceases to exist as far as the game is concerned. Furthermore the position of any piece can be defined by two numbers – counting the squares across the board from the bottom left-hand corner (say), and 'up' the board away from the White player. By all such standards both games are two-dimensional.

Can we extend this concept to help us envisage a one-dimensional world? Consider the children's game of 'Snakes and Ladders'. Again this is played on a flat board, and part of a typical one is shown in Figure 2. Each player has a small counter or token (usually a coloured plastic disc) which he moves along the numbered track according to the throws of a die. If a move ends with the counter on the foot of a ladder, it is immediately transferred to the top, thus advancing it towards the winning square at the end. If a move lands a counter on the head of a snake, it 'slides' down to its tail, thus retarding its progress. At first sight this would appear to be another two-dimensional game, particularly as the snakes and ladders cut across the board at different angles, but in fact it is not. If Square 26 were labelled 'Go to Square 47', and Square 23 labelled 'Go to Square 3' (and so on for the other cases), then all the snakes and ladders could be eliminated without altering the playing of the game in any way (although possibly reducing the fun). The

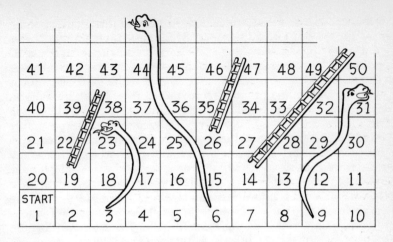

(a)

41	42	43	44	45	46	47	48	49	50
40	39	38	37	36	35	34	33	32	31
21	22	23	24	25	26	27	28	29	30
20	19	18	17	16	15	14	13	12	11
START 1	2	3	4	5	6	7	8	9	10

(b)

| 18 | Go To 38 / 19 | 20 | 21 | 22 | Go To 3 / 23 | 24 | 25 | Go To 47 / 26 | 27 | 28 | 29 | 30 | Go To 9 / 31 |

(c)

| | + 19 | | | − 20 | | + 21 | | | − 22 |

Figure 2.   Snakes and Ladders: (a) Part of a 'Snakes and Ladders' board
(b) Part of the same board laid out in one dimension
(c) As (b) but with relative numbering

game could now be printed on a long strip of card one square wide, with the Start at one end and the Finish at the other. Since the width of the card and the thickness of the board and the counters are irrelevant, and the position of any counter is defined by a single number (that of the square it occupies), we now have a one-dimensional game.

We can use this long thin game to illustrate a few other points. The label on Square 26 saying 'Go to Square 47' could be replaced by one saying 'Go Forward 21 Squares', and that on Square 23 could say 'Go Back 20 Squares', or, expressing the same moves mathematically: 'Move +21' and 'Move −20'. Now all moves (whether determined by the score of the die or by an instruction on a square) are expressed relatively, in that they are counted from the square now occupied, with no reference to the Start or the length of the game. Now there is no need to number the squares themselves, but if we find it convenient to do so we can use any system we choose.

We can now make a significant leap of imagination, from a child's game to a one-dimensional world. Imagine that in the depths of space there is a straight track or thread, stretched across the universe. On it is a single creature like a small bug or beetle; blind, deaf, with very few senses, but with an intelligent mind. He cannot turn round on the track, but can proceed forward or backwards with equal-length steps. He can call one point on the track 'Home', and by counting his steps forward, and subtracting those taken backwards, he always knows how far he is from Home, and in which direction. In effect, his situation is exactly that of a counter on our long board game, in which the squares are numbered − − −, −3, −2, −1, Home, +1, +2, +3, − − − . This is probably as near as we can get to what appears to be a one-dimensional world. We can make several very important assumptions:

a) Our bug knows the meaning of 'forwards' and 'backwards', but since he has never known any other direction, and has nothing to give him any directional reference except his track, the words 'up', 'down' and 'sideways' are completely meaningless to him;

b) Although the track he moves on will have width and thickness, if he has never developed organs capable of sensing these dimensions, he can be totally oblivious of the fact and logically believe that his world is truly (i.e., physically) one-dimensional;

c) Similarly, although he himself will have width and height, if he has never developed the appropriate senses, he will believe himself to be one-dimensional;

d) The track has been described as a straight line, but if it were curved, or wrapped in a spiral, or tied in a loose knot, he would not know it, nor would he know the meaning of such words;

e) (For mathematicians and scientists only). Despite his limitations, if he is a mathematically gifted little bug, there is no reason why he should not develop and use mathematical concepts of 'squares', 'cubes', 'areas' and 'solids', and believe quite logically that he is dealing with mathematical abstractions, incapable of physical realisation.

Think carefully over these points, because if you can grasp what I am driving at, the rest is easy, (or comparatively so!).

Nonetheless, it may be difficult to put ourselves mentally in the position of this poor, primitive, little bug, happily doing his tight-rope act in the elemental dark, and hard to find a practical analogy. (A worm, for instance, can choose to turn up, down or sideways, and has gravity and the earth's surface to give meaning to these words). The whole idea is somewhat macabre, and it may be preferable to return to a two-dimensional world.

There is no need to elaborate on our chess-board analogy; we can proceed directly to describe a creature which lives a 'two-dimensional' life. We need not look far. If you stand by a village pond, a garden pool, or any stagnant water on a summer's day, you are almost bound to see a number of 'pond skaters' or 'water boatmen'; small, slim bugs, which walk, or rather skim, on the surface, (supported – so I am told – by the hairs on their feet resting on the surface tension of the water). I am not interested in the entomological details of these creatures; I am simply using them as an illustration, endowing them for my purposes with largely imaginary characteristics. I shall assume that they spend all their lives on the surface, being incapable of diving, flying or walking on land. I am also going to assume that they have never developed any organs capable of sensing the third dimension in any way. This means that the words 'up' and 'down' are completely mean-ingless to them; they cannot comprehend the existence of a fish, a bird or a man since all these exist outside their universe, which is limited to the surface of the pond. In dry weather their universe shrinks; after rainfall it expands; any waves may be sensed as sideways movements, but vertical movements are not detected.

Such a bug would be aware that he himself had length and width, but not that he had height, but despite these limitations, he may be quite intelligent and completely capable of learning all about his two-dimensional world. If he can measure distances and can get one directional reference (let us say that he is sensitive to magnetism and so can identify magnetic North), he can 'draw a map' of his universe (as far as the shores of the pond) and on this map any stick or stone which breaks the surface of the pond is a 'no-go' area, as shown in Figure 3. He can call any particular spot 'Home', and by measuring his distance North of Home (South being reckoned as negative – as for a one-dimensional world) and

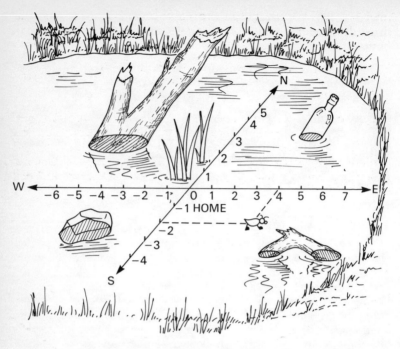

Figure 3. The 'World' of a Two-Dimensional Bug. The shaded areas are those marked on the Bug's 'Map'. He is at '−2 South, +4 East' of Home

East of Home (West being negative) he can identify any point in his world by two measurements. A mathematician would say he has set up two 'axes' (plural of 'axis') crossing at an 'origin'. The principle is obviously similar to the method of identifying a point on the earth's surface by measurements of latitude and longitude with reference to the axes of the equator and the Greenwich meridian.

Three Is Familiar

The next step up our dimensional scale is a three-dimensional creature in a three-dimensional world, and the obvious example is man himself. We are quite capable of describing our world in three-dimensional terms. On a small scale, if I take my axes as being:

'Along the room towards the door',
'Across the room towards the window' and
'Up – Down';

and my origin as the corner of my desk, then the centre of the light bulb is about 2 m, −1.5 m, and 1 m (see Fig. 4), and by the same procedure I can describe the position of any point of the room or its contents. By extensions of the same principle an architect can describe a block of flats, a geologist can make a scale model of a

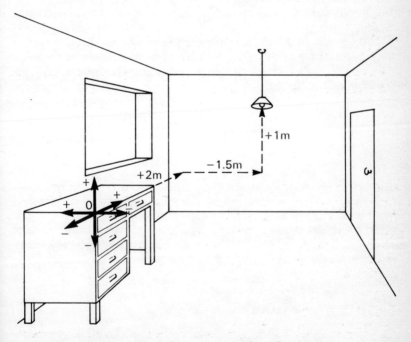

Figure 4. Describing a room in three dimensions

mountain, and an astronomer can define the position of a star. There are other systems of measurement than the 'rectangular orthogonal Cartesian coordinates' that I have described, but in each case *three* (and in any optimum system no more than three) measurements are needed for each point, so similar reasoning applies.

If a creature living in a 3-D world is only able to sense two of them, this can lead to misunderstandings. For instance, imagine that you cut out a square of thin card, and float it on the surface of a pond that is the 'world' of one of our two-dimensional bugs. He will explore round it and will conclude that it is a square 'no-go' area. Since it is occupying his own two dimensions, his view of it will be reasonably accurate. Now hold the card on edge, so that it is partly submerged (see Fig. 5). The bug is unaware of areas of the card above and below the surface, and he will conclude that it is simply a thin line. This line consists of all the points on the card which are also in the two dimensions of the pond. Note that if you rotate the card, or move it up and down, the length of this line will vary – to the extent that it may disappear altogether, (although if the pond and the card are large enough, there is always such a line).

This leads to a related observation. Suppose I, as a three-dimensional creature, wish to convey to my friend the 'two-dimensional' bug the true shape of something that I can see

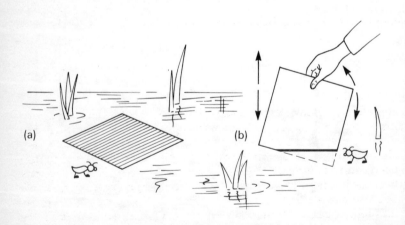

Figure 5. 'No-Go Areas' produced by a square card:
(a) Flat on the surface (b) Held vertically

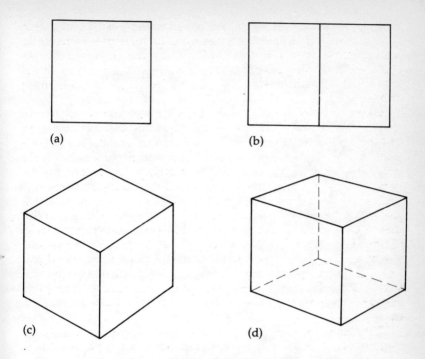

Figure 6. Four two-dimensional views of a cube: (a) Face on (b) Edge on (c) Corner on (d) Skewed and transparent

completely – say a cube of sugar – and try to do so by drawing it on his two-dimensional world. According to the angle at which you view it, any one of the sketches in Figure 6 is as valid as any other, although none of them is correct. Sketch (d) is most frequently used, and is immediately recognisable by us as a cube, partly because it follows the artistic conventions of perspective, and also because the illusion of depth is greatly assisted by drawing the 'unseen' edges as if the cube were transparent. Nonetheless, we still have unequal edge lengths and incorrect angles, so that the best of such sketches will be misleading to a two-dimensional creature.

49

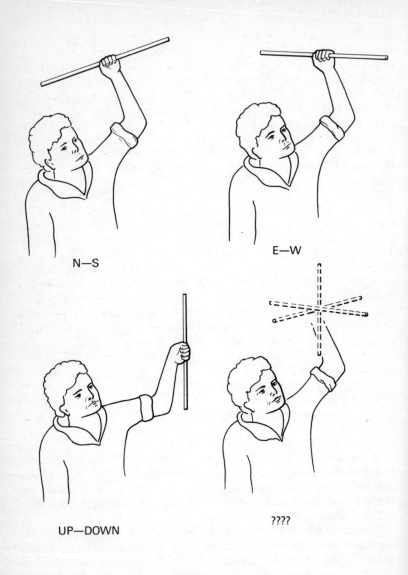

N—S

E—W

UP—DOWN

????

Figure 7.   Where is the fourth dimension?

The Difficult Step

These conclusions regarding the interaction between two-dimensional and three-dimensional worlds and creatures are of importance because we can use them in the next stage of the discussion, in which I try to imagine the different ways in which a 3-D creature like man, living in a 4-D world, could become aware of the fact. But first there is a major problem to be faced, that of conceiving how a four-dimensional world can exist at all! This is the nub of the whole discussion. We cannot imagine a four-dimensional world in physical terms; we have no means of expressing or measuring distances in a fourth dimension, and we apparently have no organs or senses capable of responding in any way to more than three dimensions. Try this simple experiment. Take a straight rod, such as a measuring rule or garden cane, and hold it by its centre above your head so that it points North-South (see Fig. 7). Now rotate it horizontally so that it points East-West, then vertically so that it points Up-Down. Now try to rotate it once more through 90° so that it points in a new direction – a fourth axis. You cannot. Any such move returns you to one of the others. Three axes at right angles to each other through an origin are sufficient to describe all the known universe. There seems no way in which a fourth axis or dimension can even be contemplated. And this is most surprising since there is not (to my knowledge) any logical or mathematical proof that a fourth dimension cannot exist, in fact, quite the contrary.

Referring to Figure 1 (see page 41), I can say of a straight line, 'It is two metres long' – its only dimension. I can say, 'This room is 5 metres long and 4 metres wide, therefore it has a floor area of 20 square metres [5 × 4]'; and similarly, 'This room is 5 metres by 4 metres and is 3 metres high, so its volume is 60 cubic metres [5 × 4 × 3].' But what happens if I try to include another dimension? What physical shape can be represented by 8 × 4 × 6 × 2, where each of those measurements is a length? The answer is that we cannot conceive of such an object, and we have no name for such a measurement.

This does not prevent mathematicians from dealing in 'multi-dimensional mathematics', discussing such 'bodies' as if they were physically real. For instance, a 'hypercube' is the four-dimensional 'equivalent' of a cube, and its geometry can be studied in detail and all its characteristics calculated.[73] We know that, just as a cube can be assembled from six squares of card, a hypercube is formed from an assembly of eight identical cubes; it

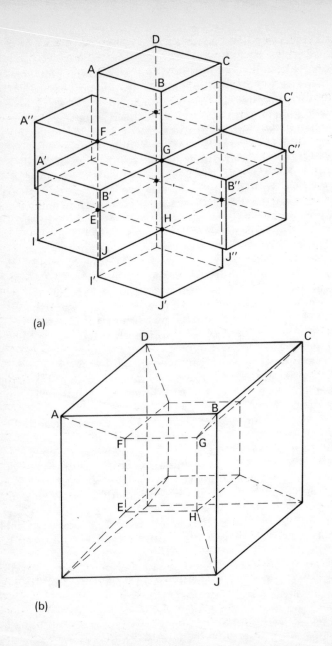

(a)

(b)

Figure 8. Models of a Hypercube: (a) First attempt (b) Second attempt

has 24 faces or sides, each of which is common to two of the cubes, and 32 edges, each of which is common to three of the cubes, and so on. Although we cannot visualise such a body, or make a model of it, we can get somewhere near to it, but we need to approach carefully, recognising that, just as the bug's view of a solid object will be incomplete and misleading, so must be our view of a four-dimensional object.

A model of a hypercube can best be approached in two stages. Consider first the simple model shown in Figure 8(a), which consists of seven identical cubes, six of which are stuck to the faces of the centre cube. Now imagine the cubes to be made of very flexible rubber, and that the three points B, B', and B'' are pulled together, so that the line AB coincides with A'B', BC coincides with B''C'', and so on. Now repeat this procedure all around the model. We now have the arrangement shown in Figure 8(b), which is considerably nearer to our hypercube, in that we have now formed the eighth cube by the outside faces. Furthermore, we have satisfied two other requirements, in that each face is now common to two 'cubes', and each edge is common to three of them. Unfortunately, in the process we have sadly distorted six of our cubes, so that they are no longer cubic, and even the two true cubes we have are not the same size as each other. It is manifestly impossible to arrange eight identical cubes in the same general configuration – we have got as near as we can get to a hypercube in the absence of a fourth dimension.

It is evident that the deficiencies of our model of a hypercube are very reminiscent of those of our drawings of a cube – distorted shapes, wrong angles and wrong edge lengths. Nevertheless, when combined with the purely mathematical approach, it is sufficiently accurate to allow the calculation of all the geometrical characteristics of a body which cannot exist or even be imagined! (Just as our water-bug may be perfectly capable of calculating for himself all the characteristics of a cube.)

But what would be the point of such abstract mathematical exercises? As an attempt to answer that question, imagine a colony of our two-dimensional bugs living, not on a flat pond, but on the surface of an enormous bubble, as shown in Figure 9(a). To them with their limited senses, it is obviously a flat surface which could extend to infinity, until the day when the intrepid explorer Columbus Bug sets out on a journey to discover the edge of the universe, determined to skate in a straight line until something stops him. A long time later, to their – and his – amazement, he rejoins his companions, skating towards them from the opposite direction to that in which he set out. This causes consternation among Scientist Bugs, most of whom insist that he must have cheated, skating in a large circle. But among the more advanced Mathematician Bugs who have studied the esoteric science of 'Solid Geometry', and have invented the idea of abstract bodies called 'cubes', there are mutterings of completely impossible ideas like surfaces curved in three dimensions, and weird things called 'spheres' which are apparently shaped something like discs, but bent in a totally impossible way. They may start to do experiments to support their ideas. On the surface of their 'flat' world, they draw an equilateral triangle (i.e., one with three equal sides), and find, as Euclid did before them, that the three angles each measure 60° giving a total of 180°. But then they increase the size of the triangle, and they find that, when it reaches huge proportions, the angles increase to give a total greater than 180° until eventually they draw an equilateral triangle with three right angles! To demonstrate that this is possible, imagine standing at the North pole of the earth, and start to travel down the line of 0° Longitude. Continue until you reach the equator, then turn due East through 90°. Continue along the equator to longitude 90°, then turn due north (through 90° again). Return to the pole, and you will return on a line which is at 90° to that on which you set out. Your route will have consisted of an equilateral triangle with three right angles. (see Figure 9(c).)

This leaves our bugs in a quandary. Their world is obviously two dimensional, in that it satisfies the requirements corresponding to those discussed on page 42, but the geometrical 'laws' they have discovered can only be true on a surface which is curved. The conclusion that they must reach, if they are to be logical, is that their world is two-dimensional, but it must be the surface of a body which is curved in a third dimension, so *they must exist in a three-dimensional universe*. One or two of them may even start asking ridiculous questions like, 'Is there something "Under" us?' and 'Where is "Up"?'. The point is that although the bugs are asking questions that they are not equipped to answer, this does not in any way prove that there is no answer, nor that the answers are not expressible in a completely physical form – provided one had the mental equipment.

Einstein and All That

Our own scientists have carried out mathematical computations, well supported by experimental observations, which are far more

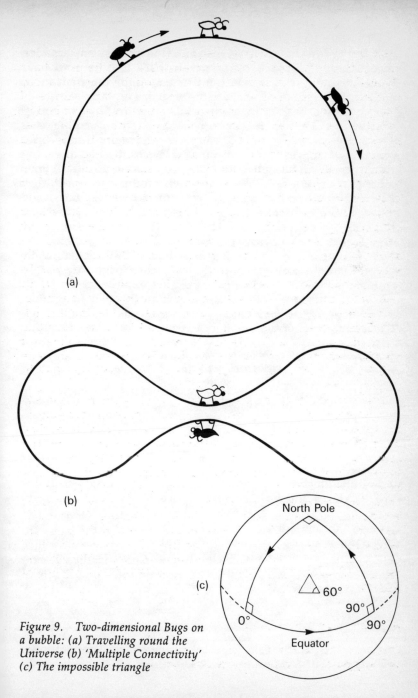

Figure 9.   Two-dimensional Bugs on a bubble: (a) Travelling round the Universe (b) 'Multiple Connectivity' (c) The impossible triangle

comprehensive and convincing than the 'equilateral triangle' described above. Deductions from Einstein's General Theory of Relativity indicate that 'space is curved', implying that a man looking through a telescope capable of seeing an infinite distance would see the back of his own head (providing that there was nothing in the way). This and other rather mind-boggling ideas are discussed in Appendix 3, and only mentioned here in brief. The theory suggests that our universe 'consists of' the three dimensional surface of a four-dimensional sphere (or hypersphere). When one asks the scientists what is inside or outside this sphere, one is told that question is 'not valid', in that the hypersphere is a convenient mathematical representation of something which cannot physically exist but which happens to comply with the calculations and observations.

This contradiction is carried to extremes. The attitude of Sir Herbert Dingle is discussed in the Appendix (page 256), but the problem is pin-pointed in a recent book: *The Arrow of Time**:

> A pristine piece of paper sitting on a desk top describes a flat space (it has no curvature). On the other hand, the surface of a sphere is curved.
>
> These two-dimensional spaces or surfaces . . . are easily illustrated because *they are embedded in the three-dimensional space with which we are all familiar.* With the possible exception of mystical experiences, it is not possible for us to visualise the geometries of dimensions higher than three. *Yet it is important to recognise that the property of flatness or curviness intrinsic to the space. No reference is needed to some putative higher-dimensional space.*

The weakness of this statement is evident in the quotation itself, and can be illustrated by reversing our previous analogies. If it is possible for a three-dimensional space to be curved without involving a fourth dimension, then it must be equally possible to construct (either physically or mathematically), a curved two-dimensional surface which does not require the existence of a third dimension. To the best of my knowledge, this has never been attempted, nor is it imaginable (pace Dingle). No appeal to higher mathematics or esoteric theories would seem to be valid, and unless such a surface can be demonstrated, the idea is unacceptable.

---

*Coveney, Peter & Highfield, Roger. *The Arrow of Time*, W.H. Allen, 1990.

So we may legitimately accept the concept of the 'curvature of space' derived on relativistic grounds as positive evidence for the existence of a physical fourth dimension, and dismiss this particular aspect of the opposition of science to the idea as illogical.

The analogy with our own case is quite explicit. It is quite possible (in the sense that the hypothesis cannot be disproved) that we cannot visit or envisage the centre of our hypersphere universe for the same reason that the bugs cannot dive or fly – because evolution has not provided us with the necessary organs or capabilities, so that our scientific exploration cannot keep up with our mathematical concepts, which are less limited.

The point is a vital one. If the shape of any physical object can be described in terms of measurements, then why is the reverse not true? Why can we deal mathematically with 'objects' like the hypercube and hypersphere, yet be unable to make one or imagine it? Could it be that mathematics is not subject to the limitations of the human senses, so that we can calculate and deduce in areas we cannot understand? There is no answer to this question, and we tend to accept the situation, and to dismiss any objection to it as being contrary to 'common sense', which may reasonably be defined as logic based on our own memories and the knowledge we have received from our ancestors. So we come to the next great imaginative leap:

Just suppose that this is really a four-dimensional universe, and that the apparent limitation to three dimensions is due to characteristics of the human sensory organs or the human brain.

Obviously, the idea has staggering implications for all aspects of human thought, and particularly for science, philosophy and religion. Some of these will be considered later, but one of the most disturbing consequences is apparent from the outset. It specifically suggests that our senses are so limited that we are oblivious to the vast majority of the universe we inhabit. In view of the complexity of the world as we know it, it certainly seems incredible that it could be infinitely more complex, but this attitude begs the question, since our criterion of complexity is based on our own ability to understand. To a mouse in a barn, the world as he sees it is sufficiently complex as to require all his knowledge, cunning and instinct just to survive.

Imagine that we could catch such a mouse and somehow introduce into his brain some simple items of human experience, such as a game of dominoes, a ride in a double-decker bus or a day at the seaside. What would be his reactions? The game of dominoes would be an incredibly complex exercise in incomprehensible mathematical concepts; the bus would be a terrifying and enormous monster, and the beach an unbearably naked and exposed area, stretching to infinity in all directions and bordered by a glaring, flickering, deafening horror, advancing inexorably to destroy the world. If we conclude that my supposition may be true, we may be forced to accept that there could be entities as far beyond us in capabilities as we are beyond a mouse or a worm. Perhaps Kipling was right when he wrote:

> A veil twixt us and Thee, Good Lord,
> A veil twixt us and Thee –
> Lest we should hear too clear, too clear,
> And unto madness see.

However, before we aspire to such heady concepts, there is much we can do without involving quite such excessive stresses on our imagination.

CHAPTER 4

THE EGG-HEADED PART*

*'It is becoming apparent that the universe is not only more queer
than we think, it is probably more queer than we can think.'*
J.B.S. Haldane

Despite our natural reluctance to assume that our senses are not
sensitive to the majority of the reality around us, there is a very
strong argument from basic principles that the universe (even in
our immediate surroundings) could be far more complex than we
can imagine. One has only to compare the amount of man's
knowledge obtained (or which could have been obtained) by his
unaided senses with the enormous increase provided by the development of such devices as telescopes, microscopes, radio receivers and X-ray machines, to realise how very limited we are.
Note that the purpose of each of these is to receive energy which is
too weak or of the wrong form to be detected by any of the senses,
and to amplify or convert the information in that energy to a form
or level which is within the capacity of one of them. Study of a list
of such artificial aids shows that they can be separated into two
distinct categories. Telescopes, microscopes and similar 'magni-
fying' techniques form a continuous and open-ended chain of
development. The urge to see farther and smaller has always
existed, and is fundamental to the extent of being instinctive. No
matter how powerful an instrument is built, there will always be
some object of interest which is barely visible, and so an awareness of things still beyond its range and an incentive to improve it.
This has encouraged the development of the necessary technology
(of lenses, etc.).

---

* For a deeper and more technical discussion of some of the subjects
referred to in this chapter, see the Appendices. Conversely, a reader
finding difficulty may pick up the threads again in the summary at the
beginning of the next chapter.

On the other hand, such developments as radio communication and X-ray examination required the positive discovery of radio waves and X-rays before they could even be contemplated. Only then could the requisite technology be developed so that they could be used to gain further knowledge. One would expect any 'extra' dimensions to come into this category, and there could well be other equally fundamental 'unknowns'. Until an initiating discovery is made, it is extremely difficult to conceive of their existence, speculate on their characteristics or imagine the consequences.

The particular cases of radio waves and X-rays are also excellent examples of the limitations of our senses in other ways, since they are two examples of electromagnetic radiation (henceforward abbreviated to 'e.m.r.' for convenience). Such waves have been used or studied with wavelengths extending over a range of 10^{16} (1 followed by 16 zeros), although our senses respond only to visible light*, which covers a range of barely 2:1 in wavelength, and outside this range we must rely entirely on aids. On a dark night, it is possible to see the light from a small torch bulb (radiating about a fiftieth of a watt of energy of visible light) at a range of about half a mile. On the other hand, you could stand within a few feet of an aerial radiating over a million watts of radio-frequency energy and be unaware that the transmitter is switched on. Other living things have different ranges of sensitivity. For instance, a bee can see ultra-violet light, while flights of migrating birds may be scattered and disorientated by the signal from a radar transmitter, both of which are undetectable to man without his constructed aids.

There are other known cases of the shortcomings of our senses. There is no way that a man can tell whether or not a piece of steel he holds is magnetised (except by experiments with electrical instruments, or known magnets), and Sir Alister Hardy has suggested[31] that if the surface layers of our earth had not contained any iron ores, it is possible that the existence of magnetism would never have been detected by man – although presumably some birds would still be able to navigate by the earth's magnetic field, and tiny snails respond to variations of it, as described by Lyall

---

* I cannot accept Prof. Taylor's argument[77] that man is sensitive to a wide range of wavelengths, believing that most of the effects he discusses, if they occur at all, do so only in very high radiation levels, and may be ascribed to heating of the tissues or other irrelevant phenomena.

Watson.[84] With such evident examples of the limitations of our senses, what justification can there be for maintaining that the fourth dimension cannot possibly exist, merely because no one can sense, imagine or describe it?

We can approach the same conclusion by a different way, using an idea derived from H.G. Wells's story 'The Country of the Blind'. Imagine that the human race was blind. Would a rainbow still be a real and physical effect? Of course. Would it still be visible by sighted animals? Of course. Would the laws of reflection and refraction of light still be valid physical relationships (although not expressible in words)? Of course. The analogy can be extended; suppose that some rare genetic mutation allowed a tiny minority of people to see normally, and these people tried to describe to their companions the process of seeing, the glory of a sunset, or the sparkle of water; could they succeed? Of course not. There would be no words, no metaphors and no comparisons which could provide a common ground for description (a limitation which is referred to repeatedly in later discussion). But suppose the sighted people demonstrated that they could communicate with each other over a distance (using lamps or flags), and set fire to hayricks or inflicted burns at a distance by making lenses and focusing the sun's rays – what then? Intelligent but blind scientists who had attended the demonstrations would realise that here was something outside their knowledge. They would cooperate with the sighted people in an attempt to learn more, but would be seriously hampered by the lack of a suitable language and such basic matters as their inability to recognise or imagine the difference between light and dark, or a transparent substance and an opaque one.

The majority of blind scientists would dismiss the whole thing as a hoax and absolute nonsense, insisting that the sighted people were liars and charlatans who signalled to each other by jerks on long cords (carefully positioned to avoid the investigators) or by high-pitched whistles, and who had practised throwing lighted matches over long distances. They would argue that since there were undefined times and conditions (i.e., cloudy skies or darkness) under which these people were powerless, and they could not reproduce their tricks down mines or in deep valleys, then it was obvious that the abilities they claimed were non-existent, and their ridiculous attempts to describe impossible sensations should be ignored. The ordinary people, motivated mainly by fear of the unknown, would accept this logic and either ignore sighted people or ridicule them, until some aspect of their activities became too evident, when there would be panic, accusations of witchcraft and sorcery, and consequent persecution. Sighted people would learn by bitter experience to conceal their gift except from those who shared it or those who showed genuine interest. The analogy with psychic abilities is obvious.

The last point illustrates another very important factor – the strong tendency of hidden or misunderstood aspects of natural phenomena to be attributed to supernatural causes. A flash of lightning is generated by the build-up of electrostatic voltage created by the movement of ice crystals in a cloud, but the ancients believed it to be the deliberate act of a powerful god; naturally-occurring magnetic stones were assumed to have been bewitched by wizards, and so on. There is adequate precedent to justify a search for new knowledge among legend, superstition and 'supernatural' events, and such thinking convinces me that, while my search may eventually be proved fruitless, it cannot logically be dismissed as stupid or without foundation.

Flexible Space And Other Universes

Let me return to the subject of multi-dimensional objects. If you think deeply of the implications of the hypersphere and the hypercube, and the limitations of three-dimensional models, it is not difficult to appreciate that the existence of a fourth dimension would radically upset all our concepts of space and distance based on three. Arthur Koestler, discussing the work of Professor John A. Wheeler of Princeton University, remarks:

> Wheeler's superspace [which has an infinite number of dimensions] has some remarkable features; one of them is multiple connectivity. This means, to put it into simple – and simplified – language that regions which in our homespun 3-D space are far apart, may be temporarily brought into contact through tunnels or 'holes' in superspace.[78] [Koestler emphasises that these are *not* the same as the 'black holes' to be discussed later.]

Despite the suggestion by some authorities that Wheeler's ideas are a little 'over the top', and his own insistence that they should not be used to justify a belief in the paranormal, this particular concept is relatively simple to support by analogies. Let me return to our bugs living on a large bubble. Now distort the bubble by pushing inwards two opposite sides towards the centre, as shown in Figure 9(b) (page 55). Even when the two sides are almost touching, the bugs will still be totally unaware that the other side of their universe is only a fraction of an inch away beneath their feet. Now use some third-dimension force to 'poke' one of the bugs through the two surfaces, and he will find himself half a universe away from his friends, having travelled a very short distance through a hole in an 'unknown' dimension.

As an alternative illustration of this very important point, consider two bugs living on a flat map of the world, one in New York and the other in London. Now fold or roll the map as shown in Figure 10, and the two could be within a very short distance of each other through the third dimension, and remain unaware of the fact.

This leads to a variation on the idea. Think of an atlas of such maps, with two-dimensional creatures living on each page. Now if one of those creatures could only penetrate the thickness of a sheet of paper, he could move from Westminster Bridge to the South Sea Islands or Antarctica by moving a fraction of an inch. Furthermore, each page could be of infinite size – a complete universe – and the paper of microscopic thickness. The analogies are clear:

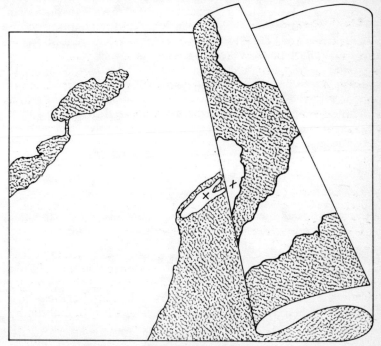

Figure 10.   Bugs living on a map. How far is a bug in London from his friend in New York? Answer: In two dimensions about 5000 kilometers; in three dimensions — 10 km? 1 km? 1 m? 1 cm??

a) If this is a four-dimensional universe, then any two points in our known universe, no matter how far apart they appear to us, may be separated by a very short distance through the fourth dimension.

b) There could be other three-dimensional universes, very close to our own, but separated in the fourth dimension.

There is an important alternative approach to the 'holes in superspace', but one which reaches a similar conclusion. The 'EPR paradox' and subsequent work related to it (discussed in Appendix 2) suggests that, in principle, it may be possible for an event in London to affect an object in New York *without any detectable connection or intervening phenomenon of any kind.* This conclusion is based in the first instance on an abstruse mathematical analysis of the behaviour of 'photons', the elementary 'particles' of radiation, but it does not give an explicit explanation of how such remote reactions may take place. It rather suggests that such 'action at a distance' may occur simply because both ends of the link exist in the same universe, which reacts as if it were a single organism! This explanation is no explanation, whereas the assumption of a fourth dimension specifically implies that an event in London may affect an object in New York *because the two points are in close proximity in the fourth dimension, or because there is a fourth-dimensional link between them.* There is obviously a relationship between the two approaches, which could possibly be revealed by a detailed analysis, but for present purposes the 'fourth dimension' is the more attractive to me as the more simply-expressed and comprehensive concept, capable of further extension as follows.

Why Is The Fourth Different?

Such concepts as the hypercube and hypersphere, and the existence of other universes, assume that the fourth (and fifth and sixth . . .) dimensions are all exact equivalents of the three 'physical' ones which describe our world, interchangeable in every way and mathematically indistinguishable. (Since these describe our 'space' – in the ordinary, not the NASA sense – they are conveniently referred to as 'Spatial' dimensions.) However, we must recognise that of these dimensions, three are, to a human being, 'special'. The eminent 19th-century mathematician and scientist, James Clark Maxwell, stated the problem in a letter to his friend and fellow-scientist, C.J. Monro, over a hundred years ago. He wrote:

The peculiarity of our space is that of its three dimensions none is before or after another. As is 'x', so is 'y' and so is 'z'. If you have four dimensions this becomes a puzzle, for, first, if three of them are in our space, then which three? Also, if we lived in a space of 'm' dimensions, but were only capable of thinking 'n' of them, then first, which 'n'? Secondly, if so, things would happen requiring the rest to explain them, and so we would be stultified or made wiser.

Maxwell's conundrum – if there are more than three mathematically-identical dimensions, why and how does the human body select only three of them? – has never been answered, but there may be a hint of a clue in our bug-on-a-pond analogy. The next chapter studies the changes in the bug's world if the water-level rises or falls, causing him to move in the third dimension without his realising it. But what if he moves and the surface does not? Suppose he is lifted off the surface by a gust of wind, or pushed under it by a falling twig or a raindrop? Under these circumstances the whole of his environment is drastically changed. This is obviously because the bug's world 'consists of' the surface between two different media – air and water. By analogy, it is possible that our universe consists of a 'three-dimensional surface' between two four-dimensional 'volumes' with different characteristics; as if, for instance, our hypersphere universe was filled with space of a different 'density' from that outside it. This could be the answer Maxwell was looking for – that the fourth dimension is unlike the other three *because it is not symmetrical*, movement one way meets different characteristics from movement in the other direction. However, there are considerable problems inherent in this idea, which are discussed in more detail in Appendix 5.

Time As Another Dimension

The possibility of an unsymmetrical dimension leads to another important concept, often (misleadingly) stated as 'Time is the Fourth Dimension'. The basis of this statement is usually traced to calculations by Hermann Minkowski, following up some of the conclusions from Einstein's Theories of Relativity. One of the important mathematical relationships he derived, now known as 'Minkowski's Space-Time Continuum', suggests the existence of a 'Fourth Dimension' of the form:

$$D = \sqrt{(-(cT)^2)} = (-c^2T^2)^{1/2}$$

where D is a distance; c is the velocity of light, and T is a measurement of time.

This mind-boggling possibility is discussed in more detail in Appendix 3, but it may be helpful to point out here that a mathematician can deal in 'imaginary quantities', which are recognisable in that they always involve the square root of a negative number – as in the expression above – and that where such a quantity denotes a length, it exists *at right angles to all 'real' lengths*. The Minkowski equation apparently achieves what we failed to do with our rod in Figure 7 on page 50, in that it involves *a measurement of length at right angles to all the other three axes*. Since, despite arguments as to its interpretation, the Minkowski equation is fully supported by experiment (as are most of the physical conclusions arising from Relativity Theory), it cannot be ignored or its implications overlooked. One of the other primary conclusions from Relativity is that measurements of distance and time are inextricably mixed, one affecting the other. As a result, and despite the objections outlined below, the concept of time as a fourth dimension is fully accepted in many fields of advanced physics. For instance, a recent TV programme discussed the work of Professor Stephen Hawking, Lucasian Professor of Mathematics of Cambridge University (and author of the recent best-seller *A Brief History of Time*). It showed the Professor and his students discussing the universe as 'a cylinder with time as its longitudinal axis'.

In fact, in some very simple contexts, the use of time as if it were a fourth dimension causes no problems. The method of describing the position of a point by reference to three axes at right angles can easily be extended to make statements about the past and the future. An Air Traffic Controller can say, 'Fifteen minutes ago, that aircraft was five miles North of the runway, eight miles East and six-thousand feet up.' This is such an obvious and simple procedure that there may be some surprise that the concept of time as another dimension is not completely acceptable.

The problem is that time is *not* 'the same as' or interchangeable with a spatial dimension. I can rotate my reference axes in any direction; I can move freely in any direction and return to the point I previously occupied; I can see and hear things at a distance from me in any direction. Apparently I can do none of these things in time. I seem to be doomed to travel through it at a fixed speed in one direction, and whereas my memory may enable me to recall happenings in the recent past, I cannot foresee happenings in the future. In fact, time has exactly that quality that I suggested could possibly, but with difficulty, be associated with the fourth spatial dimension – it is apparently unsymmetrical about the present moment. To us, Time Forward is not the same as Time Backwards.

If we try to think of time in the same terms as a spatial dimension, we need to envisage *the whole of it as physically existing at all times*, stretching from the infinite past to the infinite future, but only the present instant detectable (a concept completely consistent with the point made on page 48, that there is always one point in an 'unknown' dimension which is real and observable in other dimensions).

Perhaps the best illustration of this idea is given by Dunne. He pictures each individual as a lone traveller in a railway carriage, travelling through a darkened landscape, with no light other than the lamp in his own carriage. As he looks out of the window he sees trees, bridges and fences illuminated fleetingly by that light, but he cannot see approaching objects (in the future) nor those he has passed (in the past), *although all these exist at all times* – he is simply unaware of them. (This idea of the symmetry of time, with more evidence similar to that produced by Dunne, including precognition in dreams, is discussed by Alan Vaughan.[79])

On consideration, this is a frightening idea. If the future exists now, what price man's much-vaunted intellect, his questing spirit, his freedom of thought and action? The future for each individual and for mankind as a whole is fully predetermined and unchangeable. If this is true, there is not much point in existence and we are all victims of some cosmic practical joke. The situation is expressed more flippantly by Maurice Hare:

> There was a young man who said 'Damn!
> It appears to me now that I am
> Just a being that moves
> In predestinate grooves –
> Not a car, not a bus, but a tram.'

Hare's wit suggests an alternative to Dunne's concept, offering more hope. Suppose we are not travelling on a fixed set of rails (and since each individual experiences a different life, he must have an independent track), but rather each in his own motor car, which is destined to career at an uncontrollable speed across a darkened landscape. The car can be deflected from its course by slopes, rough ground, and by impact with rocks or other cars (representing all the chance occurrences which determine our lives), but we retain a basic ability to steer our car to some extent. Thus we have some freedom of choice over our course, but since we can only see our immediate surroundings, we cannot see where we are going and have no way of predicting the longer-term effects of our decisions. In this concept, there exists now an almost infinite choice of different future 'lives' for each of us, and the one we actually experience depends partly on chance, and partly on our own decisions and actions.

This vision of life as a desperate drive by a short-sighted man in a scarcely-controllable Dodgem car raises some massive problems, not least of sheer comprehension, but this does not automatically prove it to be nonsense. The often-quoted aphorism by Haldane which heads this chapter is a vital philosophical rock in a sea of contradiction, misunderstanding and argument. The essential point is that man's powers of understanding and imagination are as much a product of his evolution as any other part of him, and as such have been fabricated primarily to meet some requirements for his survival. There can be no guarantee that such powers are infinite, or even that they are capable of encompassing all the factors in his environment, however 'real' those factors may be.

It is very important to note that the evidence for time as a dimension is totally independent of that suggesting that there is a fourth spatial dimension. The idea that 'Time is the Fourth Dimension' is therefore misleading. The two possibilities must be considered independently, and with the inference that either or both may be true.

There are, I suggest, three separate major questions to be addressed:

a) *What physical evidence is there that there exists a Fourth Dimension of Space?* This question requires research into the physical aspects of the paranormal, notably poltergeist effects (particularly teleports and apports), psychokinesis (including the 'Geller effect') and possibly telepathy and clairvoyance.

b) *If any such evidence is found, then how and why does human consciousness ignore the Fourth Dimension?* This falls into the domain of biology in general, and particularly those life sciences concerned with the relationship between the physical and the mental (as in the study of the link between the 'conscious mind' and the physical brain – see in particular *Mindwaves*, edited by Colin Blakemore and Susan Greenfield, Basil Blackwell, 1987).

c) *What is the physical relationship between the 'pseudodimension' of Time and the dimensions of Space?* This question has been studied intensively for the last eighty years by specialists in theoretical physics, and particularly involves cosmology, relativity and quantum physics. It is unlikely that research outside these subjects will help, and it is a reasonable assumption that if an answer to the question is ever found, it will be virtually incomprehensible to a layman.

Throwing No Light On The Problem

Now I come to the second deep mystery raised by Minkowski's Continuum. What in heaven's name has the speed of light got to do with it? There is general agreement among physicists that the nature of light is one of the greatest scientific mysteries of today. It can be considered either as a continuous vibration of electrical and magnetic fields, or as a stream of 'bullets' of energy (the 'photons' referred to on page 34). In any one experiment or set of circumstances only one of these descriptions is applicable – there seems to be no case which can be described equally well in either terms. Furthermore, Einstein's famous equation $E = Mc^2$ (in which c, the velocity of light, is obviously a key factor) shows that these bullets can be converted into solid matter. No wonder that the dream of any up-and-coming young physicist is that he may find an explanation which will combine both these characteristics into a single description, despite Heisenberg's conclusion that this is fundamentally impossible.

Reference to 'light' in this context is, of course, merely a convenient shorthand for 'electro-magnetic radiation', or e.m.r., since visible light is only a very small sample (occupying a range of barely 2:1 in wavelength) from the tremendous range of such waves, ranging from Very Low Frequency radio waves, with wavelengths of sixty miles or more, to X-rays and gamma rays with wavelengths less than 10^8 (one hundred-millionth) of a millimetre. All these waves travel at the same speed of 300 000 kilometres (about seven times round the world) in a second. This velocity is one of the most fundamental of all natural constants, being apparently determined by the electrical and magnetic characteristics of a vacuum!!

The whole idea of 'nothing' having physical characteristics seems absurd, and the theoretical physicist will hasten to point out that these are just convenient concepts, 'symbolic expressions' which enable us to express observed facts in reasonably intelligible terms. Nevertheless, it is highly significant that this basic characteristic of empty space should be found so often in association with time – as cT in Minkowski's equation – and 'posing as' an additional dimension.

CHAPTER 5

FLYING SAUCERS AND FOOTSTEPS IN THE ATTIC

'Our soul is cast into a body, where it finds number, time, dimension.
Thereupon it reasons, and calls this nature necessity, and
can believe nothing else.'
Blaise Pascal

The previous chapter threatened to develop into a long slog through a scientific morass, and the postponement of the more obscure points to the Appendices has alleviated the problem rather than removed it. I now need (and I take it for granted that the reader will agree) to review and clarify the situation in order to establish a reasonably solid foundation for what follows. I see no necessity for repeating the many points which were inconclusive and left 'in the air', or those which are not referred to in future discussions. I propose to go ahead on the basis of the following statements and assumptions:

a) Ours is apparently a three-dimensional universe, in that objects in it have length, width and height or thickness, and it is possible to describe the position of any point from a given starting point in terms of no more than three measurements;

b) We can imagine hypothetical living and thinking creatures which are limited in their senses so that although they exist in a three-dimensional world, they may logically believe that their universe is limited to one or two dimensions. We can deduce some of the misconceptions and wrong conclusions they could reach as a result;

c) The objective of this book is to study the *possibility* that our universe is extra-dimensional (see below), and that the apparent limitation to three dimensions lies solely in the limitations of human organs and/or senses;

d) There is no logical proof that a fourth dimension cannot exist, and no undue difficulty in mathematical calculations and concepts involving four or more dimensions. Four-dimensional 'equivalents' of the cube and the sphere can be analysed and their geometry studied. Three-dimensional models of such four-dimensional objects can be constructed, although these are incomplete or distorted and do not comply with the theoretical requirements. Even large numbers of dimensions can be manipulated in equations or as abstract concepts;

e) If a fourth dimension exists, then any two places in our universe, no matter how far apart they may appear to us, may be in very close proximity through that dimension, so that our ideas of space, shape and distance may be misleading. This is referred to as the 'multiple connectivity' characteristic;

f) If a fourth dimension exists, then there could be universes other than our own and separated from us by short distances in that dimension, or on the other side of a 'fourth-dimension barrier'. It is probable that any such universes do not differ drastically from ours in the fundamental 'Laws of Nature' controlling them;

g) In addition to the possibility of other spatial dimensions (i.e., describing sizes and distances), there is a possibility that time itself, or something closely related to it, behaves in some ways like an additional dimension, but it would seem probable that this has characteristics not applicable to the spatial ones. I shall use the term 'Extra-dimensional' to include both time and the fourth (and fifth, etc.) spatial dimensions;

h) The nature of electro-magnetic radiations ('e.m.r.'), which includes light, radiant heat, X-rays and radio waves, is a mystery which seems to be closely tied up with extra dimensions.

This list summarises the discussion up to this point, and I can now go on to the next stage, in which I try to deduce, from common sense and by the free use of analogies and examples, some effects which could follow from the existence of extra dimensions, and to examine these in the light of reports of some apparently paranormal phenomena, beginning with 'poltergeists' (from the German for 'noisy ghost').

Things That Go 'Bump' In The Night

One of the best documented[33] and thoroughly studied poltergeist cases occurred in the offices of a lawyer in Rosenheim, in Bavaria, in 1967-8. The effects included a long series of totally inexplicable faults in the telephone and electricity supply systems, light bulbs exploding (while switched *off*), or being forcibly rotated in the holder, and pictures swinging wildly on the wall. Senior investigators from the telephone company, the electricity company and the local CID cooperated with Professors of Physics and Psychology from the Max Planck Institute in an investigation using all available technical and scientific resources. The final nineteen-page report concluded that it was a clear case of psychokinesis (physical effects at a distance, achieved by inexplicable and non-physical means) and poltergeist activity centred on a nineteen-year-old apprentice secretary. She was dismissed and all returned to normal.

I mention this case here to emphasise that poltergeist hauntings in particular have been very thoroughly investigated and documented.[39,53,61] and no reasonable and unbiased person can simply dismiss all of them as exaggerations, natural phenomena, hoaxes or old wives tales. In fact, the case is rather untypical, in that many of the phenomena were electrical in origin, and I am more concerned initially in mechanical effects, beginning with the relatively simple concept that an object may move in four dimensions and in doing so may enter, or break through, the world we occupy (as in the card-in-the-pond analogy). Our impressions of such an event can be predicted to some extent by comparing each situation with the effects on a two-dimensional water-bug of the movement of a solid object onto or through the surface of his pond. I will start by considering six simple cases:

a) A stone is dropped into the pond;

b) The falling stone strikes a twig and propels it some distance across the water surface;

c) The wind blows an overhanging branch, so that it dips and swings, occasionally lightly brushing the water surface;

d) A twig falls from a tree and floats on the surface. There is our little bug, minding his own business, when suddenly there it is, a real two-dimensional object which has appeared from nowhere;

e) A feather floating on the surface is blown away by a gust of wind, or a piece of water-logged newspaper finally sinks;

f) A bird swoops down to pick up a blade of grass out of the water, but after flying a short distance, drops it again.

While a stone is falling, it is travelling in the third dimension, undetectable by the bug until it hits the water, when it will rapidly disappear again below the surface. However, its impact with the water will create a variety of effects, from the energy of the waves created, or by the direct impact of the stone. Now transfer these conclusions to an object travelling through a fourth dimension and 'bursting through' a three-dimensional world. The possibility of the generation of 'ripples in space' (which could be e.m.r.) is discussed in Appendix 5, but here I am concerned with more direct effects. For note that, during its passage through the water surface, the stone would be a real and material obstacle to the bug, and in the same way the travelling object would be real and solid during its passage though our world. As such, it will displace a volume of air, and may also cause local heating of the displaced air by friction. In either case the effect will be to create a pressure wave radiating outwards, rather in the manner of a small explosion or a balloon bursting. (Such a 'step wave' or 'impulse' is one of the simplest and most fundamental of sounds.) Any large resonant surface, such as a wooden floor or a large piece of furniture, will 'drum' to the impact of the air wave, and the sound will be further modified by the acoustics of the room so that what is heard in an adjoining room will be a hollow bang or thump. As an illustration the sound of thunder is produced in exactly this way. The lightning stroke heats the air, causing a sharp 'crack' of sound, and the subsequent rumblings are repeated echoes from the surfaces of earth or cloud.

It may also be possible for such an 'instantaneous' materialisation to occur within a solid object. Michael Bentine describes loud bangs being heard from *inside the wood* of a table:

> There is no sense of the knocking being applied to one of the surfaces – top, bottom or sides – of the object being rapped. The sound appears to come from *inside* the wood and resembles the noise made by firing a .22 blank cartridge. There is no possibility of confusing this sound with the creaks and groans of wooden furniture drying out in a room . . . Creaking furniture is one thing and genuine spirit rapping, whatever its source may be, is quite different.[4] [Bentine's Italics]

The psychiatrist Carl Jung described in his autobiography an apparently paranormal occurrence when a sound, solid walnut, seventy-year-old table suddenly split from the rim to beyond the centre, with a loud noise like an explosion, (which could well have been an extreme case of the situation described by Bentine). A fortnight later the blade of a bread-knife stored in a cupboard with other cutlery shattered into several pieces. Bentine's observations are confirmed by experiments such as those by Wilson[88] and

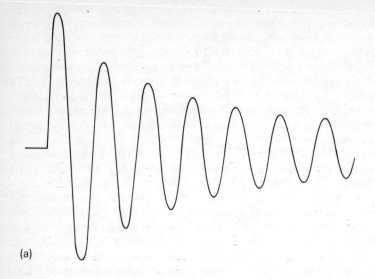

(a)

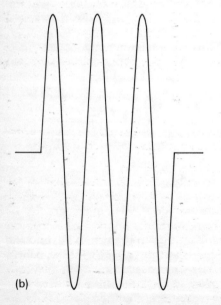

(b)

Figure 11.   Waveforms of 'rap' sounds: (a) 'Normal' rap (b) 'Spirit' rap

Puharich[70] in which raps and other noises heard at spiritualist seances and poltergeist manifestations were recorded and analysed. Both men report that in some cases the 'rap' was most unlikely to have been made by an impact on a solid object, such as by kicking or tapping a table. Such a process would produce a waveform rather like that sketched in Figure 11(a); after the initial deflection, the energy of vibration decays away as it is dissipated – like a single stroke on a bell. This is characteristic of the 'resonance' of a hollow object or an unsupported surface – the 'drum' effect referred to above.

Their descriptions are very explicit, and indicate that some recordings of 'Spirit Raps' produced a sound with a waveform that began and ended quite suddenly, with no decay of energy between – as shown in Figure 11(b), and only about a third of the duration of a 'Normal Rap'. I agree with Puharich that the latter waveform would be extremely difficult to simulate by physical means, requiring an 'explosion' as described above, followed almost immediately by an exactly compensating 'implosion'. Even to generate such an effect electronically would require quite sophisticated circuits. I would also observe – more as an interesting suggestion than as following from the discussion – that Waveform (b) is what I would expect to be generated by a *continuous oscillation* (see (b) below) travelling *through* the real world. To explain what I mean, imagine that you are within a building with thick, soundproof walls, standing directly opposite an open door, when a motorcycle travelling at speed passes close to the doorway. What would you hear?

Other Sounds

There are certain basic movements in nature which are conveniently visualised in terms of the sounds that they may cause:

a) An impulse or 'step wave' as described above;

b) A continuous vibration or oscillation, such as the moan of the wind in a chimney or the vibration of a wire. In its purest form this is known mathematically as a 'sine wave';

c) The sound generated by a large number of very sharp impulses occurring at random, such as the sound of a shower of rain on a wet road, the wind in a cornfield or the tide retreating on a pebble beach. This sound is known technically as 'white noise'. It is the 'hiss' heard in the loudspeaker of a radio set with its aerial disconnected, and its equivalent in e.m.r. is white light – hence the term;

d) Irregular (but not 'mathematically random') sounds, such as are produced by a stone rolling down a hillside, or two tree branches thrashing against each other in strong wind.

If any movement similar to these of an object in four dimensions should cause it to break through into our world, the corresponding sounds will be generated. In the context of mystery, fear or other strong emotion, such sounds could easily be grossly misinterpreted, sine waves being heard as whistles, moans or screams, white noise as whispering or rustling, and irregular movements as scratching, sawing or snorting sounds. Such sounds are characteristic of poltergeist hauntings, having been reported in the majority of cases.

Returning to our falling stone; in addition to its effect on space and on the air, the travelling object could well materialise at or very near to a 'real' object, in which case the impact could displace it – possibly violently (Case (b) on page 72). Again such effects are frequently reported in accounts of poltergeist hauntings, where pots and other objects may be hurled across the room, pendant light fittings set swinging, pictures swing askew or fall from hooks, and so on. In some cases the energy involved is considerable.

In subsequent chapters I will refer frequently to the experiences of Matthew Manning,[52,53,54] who has been described as 'one of the most gifted psychics of modern times', and who must certainly qualify to be considered for the title of the most thoroughly investigated. In 1967, at the age of 11, when he first began to be the centre for poltergeist activity, he was brought to the attention of Dr A.R.G. Owen,[61] Fellow of Trinity College, Cambridge (near to Matthew's home) and an internationally recognised authority on poltergeist phenomena. He rapidly came to the conclusion that both Matthew and his father were totally factual and reliable witnesses, and continued to investigate Matthew's ability for many years.

The poltergeist activity at Matthew's boarding school was well attested by his Headmaster, the Matron and a number of the boys, and was sufficiently severe to bring him twice to the brink of being expelled – not, as the Headmaster confirms, on account of any suspicion of deliberate mischief, but because of the fears of the other boys and the disturbance to school life. Those at his home were witnessed by his family (who were often closely involved), by Dr Owen and by professional friends of his father, who was an architect.

One episode with interesting implications occurred while he was lying in the bath (at school), when he watched as a spare bath plug rose into the air and 'shot towards the window as though hit forcefully with a bat'. It passed through the glass of the window, leaving it unharmed, and he later found it on the ground outside. Such paranormal movements are not always so violent. In the school dormitory a heavy steel bunk (without castors) was seen to drag itself across the floor, and he describes wooden chairs 'dancing and capering around the dormitory, colliding with anything that happened to be in the way'. Lying in his own bed at home, he watched a heavy wardrobe slowly advance about half a metre across the floor, while his bed (with him in it) was lifted several centimetres.

Probably the world's weight-lifting record for a poltergeist is held by one which infested a Paraguayan farm, and on one occasion moved a jeep (weighing about one-and-a-half tons and left parked in gear) uphill across forty yards of muddy farmyard, leaving no tyre tracks.[66]

This introduces another aspect of poltergeist effects. Most of those mentioned above, such as bangs, scratches and projected objects imply fourth-dimension movements that appear 'natural' (i.e., similar to those appearing in nature, as listed above), but others, such as the transport of the jeep, involve the apparently deliberate and controlled movement of a specific object – in fact every sign of *intention*. There are a number of phenomena in this category, including:

a) *Transportation*: The controlled and deliberate movement of an object;
b) *Teleportation*: The transportation of an object through walls, floors or other solid barriers (cf. Case (f) on page 72);
c) *Apportation*: An Apport is a solid, material object which apparently 'appears from nowhere', usually – but not always – in an unoccupied room (cf. Case (d));
d) *Disappearance*: An object disappears in circumstances which rule out loss or theft (cf. Case (e));
e) *Levitation*: An object floats unsupported in the air – apparently defying the Law of Gravity.

Manning describes the finding of a number of apports, including an old loaf of bread, a cigarette packet, geological specimens, and the pages from an old book (finally sufficient to reconstruct the whole book). Many of these he still retains, but others disappeared equally mysteriously, sometimes after several months. Some household articles, such as candles and handkerchiefs, also disappeared. He also describes a number of cases of Teleportation, such as the incident with the bath plug, and when a small table disappeared from his sister's bedroom, to be found later in the cellar (two floors down) with the books and ornaments on it undisturbed. On two occasions water was emptied from the U-bend of a sink or WC and appeared on the hall floor. Alan Vaughan refers to reports by Professor Hans Bender, Director of the Freiburg Institute for Border Areas of Psychology:

> Professor Hans Bender has reported a number of poltergeist investigations in Germany in which matter passed through matter: that is *teleportation*. Witnesses actually observed, for instance, the teleportation of nails from a basement cupboard to a few inches below the ceiling upstairs, where, forming in the air, the nails became visible and fell to the floor. A bottle put on the kitchen table materialised outside the house at the level of the roof and fell to earth in a zig-zag path.* Professor Bender's coat disappeared from a closet to be found lain neatly on the snow outside the house. There were no footprints. To one of Germany's most eminent physicists, Ernst Mach, genuine disappearance and reappearance of objects would offer the best evidence for the reality of a fourth dimension, a higher or 'other' space that allows for a fourfold freedom of movement. Although the concept of such a fourth dimension has been around since at least the 1880s, no-one has yet been able to demonstrate its actuality.[79]

The temporary levitation of a small object (sometimes as a preliminary to its being thrown across the room – as with the bath plug), is a frequent characteristic of poltergeist hauntings. Even more impressive are the many accounts of the controlled levitation of heavy furniture at seances with psychically gifted mediums, and despite the atrocious record of fraud in this respect there are a sufficient number of reports to warrant this being taken more seriously than it is at present.[39] A particularly fascinating phenomenon (to be studied later) is the levitation of the body of the medium him- or herself.

Movement In Other Dimensions

I will now consider more carefully some implications of the notion 'movement in the fourth dimension'. The concept is used glibly in

---

* This kind of movement has been described in a number of cases.

science fiction and pseudo-scientific discussion of the paranormal; the star-ship *Enterprise*, Dr Who's *Tardis* and the ghostly hooded monk are all presumed to be capable of it when the author or script-writer demands it, but the fact remains that movement in an imaginary dimension is even more difficult to comprehend than the existence of the dimension itself. Think first about normal movement. If I walk across the room I know that I have moved because my view of the surrounding objects has changed.* This change occurs because I have moved *and they have not*. If I were travelling at a steady speed in a railway carriage or a space ship, I would not know that I was moving unless I looked out of the window. It is evident that I cannot detect *movement* this way, but only *relative movement* between myself and something else.

There is no reason to believe that this concept does not apply to four-dimensional movement also. I and all my surroundings may well be travelling in the fourth dimension at this moment – but if so I am unaware of the fact. But if my desk or my trousers should travel without me (or vice versa), I would presumably soon become aware that something unusual was happening.

So can we predict the changes I would observe if I travelled in the fourth dimension and my surroundings did not? To tackle this question let me return yet again to the water-bug on his pond. Suppose that it has been raining, and the water level of the pond has risen slightly, causing the world of the little bug to change (see Figure 12). Some of the two-dimensional obstructions on the surface will have moved, some will have changed shape, some will have disappeared and some new ones will have appeared. He is aware of these changes, but since he is not aware of the movement that has taken place, he cannot explain them. In any case the laws governing his world remain unchanged and life goes on as before. The amount of change or movement that he sees in any object will depend on its shape in the third dimension, and whether or not it moves with him. A floating twig will not change; a vertical cylinder like a grass stem will change very little, while a flat-topped stone may change radically, appearing and disappearing for small changes in level.

Applying these ideas to our own world, I start to wonder what governs the 'shape' of an object in its fourth dimension – if it has got one . . . If it has got one?? . . . Deep thought . . . Light Dawns!!

---

* I am also aware of the muscular effort I have made, but this is irrelevant, and (for the physicist) I am ignoring acceleration effects – even Einstein found them too complex to start with.

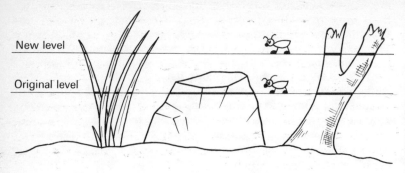

Figure 12. Bug's view of the change in water level

Think back to my Cockney engineer who said, 'If it aint got no fickness, then 'ah can you pick it up?' Since it is evidently true that in a three-dimensional world a truly two-dimensional object has no existence, then by unanswerable logic,

if ours is a four-dimensional universe there can be no such thing as a three-dimensional object. EVERYTHING, whether living or dead, dust, water, sun, star or atom must be four-dimensional.

To the cosmologist and the nuclear physicist this may be an awesome conclusion, requiring far more evidence before it can be taken seriously, but for the kind of broad-brush thinking in which I am indulging, it seems to be remarkably self-consistent, and to provide the type of universal principle for which I have been searching.

So suppose that an object, say a pencil on my desk, were to move slightly in the fourth dimension – what change would I see? That evidently depends on the 'length' of the pencil in the fourth dimension. If this is long, like its physical length, I may see little change, but if it is short, like its thickness, it could disappear altogether. If the fourth-dimension shape varies along the length of the pencil, I may see a change of shape.

Following the same logic, it seems that if I (alone) move in the fourth dimension, I may at first see very little change in my surroundings. Some objects may change shape slightly, some may disappear and some new ones appear, but such changes may be minor, and there is unlikely to be any sudden major change, or any radical change in the physical laws governing the world around me. These ideas are supported by noting that as I travel through the other extra dimension – time – (by just sitting still and watching the world go by) major changes seldom occur suddenly. The world ten minutes ago was very much the same as it is now, and it is unlikely to change catastrophically in the next ten minutes. (It is worth noting that my pencil has a shape in the time dimension – as it wears down and I re-sharpen it.) As I travel farther in either extra dimension, changes will tend to accumulate, and in the case of fourth-dimensional travel, I may find some aspects of the world getting most peculiar, but since I have no way of deducing or guessing the fourth-dimension shape of things, I cannot predict these effects.

But what about long-distance travel in the fourth dimension? Suppose that a child playing by a pond catches a bug, and carries it to another pond some distance away. How does this affect the bug? To him it is literally a new world, differing in size and shape from his old one, and possibly including some different species of insect and plant life, but probably including some members of his own or similar species and certainly obeying identical physical laws. By analogy, it would appear that travel through a fourth dimension should enable us to reach *new universes*, but if we do we may find each of them to be very similar to our own, in that the basic principles of chemistry and physics, etc., remain unaltered. This returns us, of course, to the bugs-in-an-atlas analogy of page 63.

Where Does The UFO Come From?

So much for static situations; but what happens while the movement is taking place? Let us go back to the pond and carry out the simple experiment shown in Figure 13. Dip a long garden cane into the pond and note first that as you alter the slope of the cane, the bug will see the shape of it on the surface change from a disc to a long ellipse or oval. Now hold the cane almost totally immersed and at a very shallow slope, then lift it slowly vertically, maintaining the slope constant. The bug will see the ellipse travel across the water at a high speed (much faster than the movement of the cane) until the end of the cane is reached, when it will suddenly disappear. Now, as I mentioned above, a four-dimensional object intruding into our world would be seen as a solid, material body. From the analogy, it is evident that as it moves through our world, its shape and proportions may change according to its shape in the fourth dimension, and it may finally disappear 'into thin air'. Now

I hate to mention the subject in a serious discussion, since it tends to invite ridicule, but is this not exactly the behaviour often ascribed to UFOs ('Flying Saucers')? Rapid change of shape, size and proportions, phenomenal acceleration, sudden appearance and disappearance – they are all there, and the luminescent effects and changes of colour are already accounted for in some of the technical discussions on the subject as being due to frictional heating and ionisation of the air. Such an explanation is at least as valid as the 'gravity-cancelling drive' so dear to the heart of some UFO buffs; they may indeed amount to the same thing! Note, however, that neither theory throws any appreciable light on their origins.

The reader may be rather disgusted at the previous paragraph, saying in effect, 'Does this chap really believe that UFOs are projections of four-dimensional objects into our three-dimensional world? He must be crazy!' My answer is quite definite. I undertook to look for possible explanations of unexplained phenomena in terms of extra dimensions, and my own beliefs or disbeliefs as to the reality of such phenomena or the accuracy of the reporting of them, are quite irrelevant to the discussion. I am merely pointing out that *IF . . . IF . . . IF* a fourth spatial dimension exists, then certain characteristics reported as being typical of UFOs may be simply explained in physical terms. Such a 'coincidence' is, in my opinion, worth considering. That is as far as I can

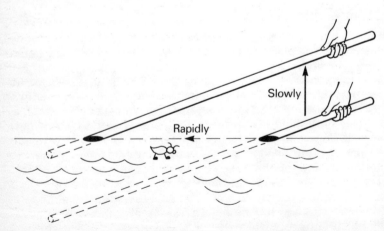

Figure 13. Exaggeration of speed in another dimension

go, or need to go in a book of this nature. This attitude applies to many of the phenomena in this book; having no personal experience to guide me, I refuse to be summarily dismissive of any reports having a reasonable modicum of scientific or well-informed support.

Poltergeist Energy

Now to another aspect of four-dimensional movement. Ever since Sir Isaac Newton advanced his 'Laws of Motion' it has been accepted that to move any material body requires the application of a force, and this normally requires the expenditure of physical energy.* There has been much discussion as to the source of such energy in poltergeist disturbances, traditionally resulting in either of two suggestions:

a) The energy is extracted from the air, causing a drop in air temperature;
b) The energy is extracted, directly or indirectly, from the body heat of one or more persons in the vicinity.

Either explanation could account for the feeling of chill which often accompanies or precedes psychic phenomena. If enough energy is extracted from 1 litre of air to cool it by 1 °C, and all of it converted to mechanical force, it could lift a load of 1 kilogram about 12 cm against gravity. One objection to this idea is that it offends against one of the fundamental Laws of Science, the 'Second Law of Thermodynamics', which states that one cannot extract heat from the coolest material in the vicinity without actually consuming energy (just as a refrigerator needs to consume electricity in order to transfer heat from its contents to the 'radiator' at the back).

The second explanation would not offend the law, since the human body is at a higher temperature than its surroundings, and again there is an appreciable amount of energy available. A man at rest is continually losing about 130 watts of energy to the air around him. If only 10 per cent of this were converted to mechanical energy it could lift a weight of 1 kilogram at about 1.3 metres/second. Either theory, however, is open to two major objections. The first is that in a few cases (such as the Paraguayan jeep), the

---

* In a later chapter I shall discuss the 'psychic energy' which seems to be necessary for a paranormal event to take place at all, but this is a totally separate subject.

amount of energy used would be so large that its source must have been evident. The second, and far more telling objection, is that one must assume the existence of some 'paranormal' method of extracting the heat energy, converting it to mechanical energy, and then directing it to some point, which may be some distance away or in the next room. Furthermore, either theory leaves similar phenomena (such as teleports and apports) totally unexplained. The alternative theory I am discussing, that forces may be applied in or through a fourth dimension and so accelerate an object, avoids many of these objections. Firstly, it is applicable (as this book tries to show) to virtually all of reported paranormal phenomena of this type. Secondly, if it proves to be true it will require a major revision and extension of most of the known 'Laws of Science', and in particular those involving physical movement and energy, to include the effects of the additional dimension. Thirdly, it does not – in the simple concept discussed so far – *require* the existence of any psychic powers, evil spirits, disembodied souls, or indeed any supernatural phenomena whatsoever. It simply supposes that our powers are limited so that the universe we experience is only a part of the true reality.

Energy From Nowhere

There is a second possible method by which energy may be transferred from an extra dimension (other than through the passage of a solid body). The fundamental and mysterious nature of e.m.r. has already been discussed, and it is no particular surprise to find that inexplicable sources of energy crop up in many aspects of cosmology, astronomy and nuclear physics – such sources always appearing, explicitly or implicitly, as e.m.r. An article in a Sunday magazine on modern research said:

> Among other things, the scientists in New Mexico are studying Quasars, vast sources of energy out in space which are known to be twice the size of our solar system. They seem to be radiating more energy than the average spiral galaxy . . . No known physical law can explain this vast outpouring of energy.

While in the TV programme on Professor Hawking's work it was said that:

> . . . a small black hole, about the size of an atom, would continuously emit radiation with a power roughly equivalent to six nuclear power stations. Such a source has not yet been found.

In the light of the suggestion in Appendix 4 that a black hole may be a point of contact between two three-dimensional universes, the latter quotation is particularly interesting. I do not find it unreasonable to suggest that such energy may originate outside our own three-dimensional universe and that e.m.r. may itself be capable of travelling through the fourth dimension (a concept that recurs several times in later chapters).

On a very much smaller scale, many paranormal phenomena include the occurrence of localised sources of radiant heat and light. Manning[53] describes the appearance of a patch of light on the wall of the school dormitory which, under the gaze of the matron and a dozen or so boys, slowly grew in size. The patch became too hot to bear the hand on it, and the warmth could be felt on the other side of the wall. On another occasion, while sitting at his desk, the rush carpet under his feet began to smoulder. There are reports (mostly older – I can find no recent cases) of poltergeist infestations limited entirely to outbreaks of minor fires.

More serious, and possibly in a different category, are the small number of well-attested cases recorded in relatively recent police and coroners' files, in which a person has apparently burst into flames spontaneously,[23,34] and the torso has burned to ashes at a very high temperature – sometimes without damage to adjacent objects. This has happened often enough to be referred to medically as 'auto-oxidation'. The only physical 'explanation' is the sudden release of a massive amount of thermal energy within the tissues of the body (usually beginning in the shoulders or the small of the back). Although Gooch suggests that some cases may be linked 'at least cautiously' with poltergeist activity, he does not elaborate this statement. If it is true, it is a notable exception to the general rule (discussed later) that while poltergeists may do considerable damage to property, they seldom do any serious harm to people. If body tissue is exposed to a sufficiently intense radiation of almost any wavelength of e.m.r., damage can result, due to the heat generated by electrical losses in the tissues (the principle of the microwave oven) or by other mechanisms. This may have some bearing on auto-oxidation.

If e.m.r. can be generated paranormally, then there is no reason why such radiation should be limited to the narrow band of frequencies around the infra-red and visible light. It is also feasible that such waves may be generated as a by-product of other psychic activities. Both Geller[21] and Manning[52] report cases in which the exercise of their 'psychic powers' in a TV studio or a laboratory has caused sudden and inexplicable failures in electronic and electrical equipment in the vicinity, in ways that suggest to me (speaking professionally) the presence of very strong electromagnetic fields. This raises a fascinating idea; I wonder if there are any records of poltergeist or other paranormal activity causing 'jamming' of, or interference with, radio or radar signals? If so, analysis of recordings of the jamming by competent communication engineers would probably yield invaluable information as to the nature and source of the energy involved.

Summary

To summarise this chapter: I suggest that our universe is four-dimensional. This means that *all material things, living and non-living*, exist in four dimensions and have a 'shape' in a fourth dimension in the same way that they have a shape in the other three. We have no means of measuring or deducing that shape. Objects may move, or be moved in all four dimensions, obeying laws of motion of which our known laws of mechanics are simple 'special cases'. A body moving in four dimensions may 'break through' into the volume of three-dimensional space of which we are aware and, through a number of quite predictable physical effects, this could account for many of the phenomena associated with poltergeist hauntings, including bumps, taps, scratching and groans, the movement of physical objects and the appearance of apports. The last would occur if an object travelled extra-dimensionally and came to rest in our world. If an object in this world moves extra-dimensionally, it may change shape or disappear altogether, possibly to emerge in another universe, or be transported through physical barriers to reappear elsewhere, (i.e., Teleports).

Acceptance of the idea that radiant energy (e.m.r.) may travel in the fourth dimension suggests an approach to the study of those paranormal phenomena which involve an increase or decrease in local temperature. It can also be applied to some puzzles in modern physics, whereby large amounts of energy seem to be emitted from no evident source. The same concept may ultimately point to a feasible explanation of the origin and nature of matter and of the universe itself (see Appendix 5).

CHAPTER 6

THE BRAINY PART – OR POIROT'S 'LITTLE GREY MATTER'

'If the human brain were so simple that we could understand it, we would be so simple that we couldn't.'
Emerson Pugh

The previous chapters have ranged wide and high, from the heart of the atomic nucleus to the infinity of space, from poltergeists to water-bugs, but none the less there has been a common approach, in that the discussion has been in terms of basic physical quantities such as length, time and energy, and physical phenomena such as sound and light. However, we must not lose sight of the fact that the majority of paranormal effects have two aspects, the physical and the mental. For example, there is very strong evidence that poltergeist attacks are in some way triggered off by subconscious processes in the mind of a young person, and while telepathy, the direct contact between two minds, is ostensibly a purely mental process, it is puzzling simply because it involves communication over a physical distance.

It is obvious that we must consider both factors, but we must not overlook the all-important link between the two – man's senses. The whole of man's knowledge is, so far as we are aware at this stage in the argument, strictly limited to evidence gained through one or other of his five senses of sight, hearing, touch, taste and smell, and so we are completely at the mercy of the accuracy and reliability of those senses. For example, it may be true to say in a literal sense that, like a camera, the eye cannot lie, since it consists of no more than a single lens throwing an image onto a light-sensitive surface. In practice, we know that the processes of perception within the brain are capable of manipulating and modifying that image to an alarming degree before it arrives in our conscious mind so that we 'see' it. It has been shown, for instance, that if a newly-born kitten is kept continuously in a box, the interior of which is painted with strong vertical stripes, when it is mature it is unable to 'see' horizontal lines. Its eyes have developed normally; it is the perception process in the brain which is incomplete, a point discussed in Chapter 1.

If it is thought that the brain is incapable of this degree of omission, distortion or falsification, consider the situation described by Lyall Watson, although this quotation only condenses facts fully accepted in the world of psychology:

> Perception is not just a passive reflection of external stimuli. What we actually 'see' is only a fraction of all the possible visual signals in our environment. The eyes, like cameras, may pick up most of what is there, but even they are selective because it is the brain that directs their attention and focusing. There is no simple one-to-one relationship between internal perception and external reality. The visual language of the brain is immensely complicated by processes of matching, comparing, analysing and *a large amount of creative synthesis*. The visual letters and words are shuffled around until they agree with *certain preconceptions about reality*. Someone who puts on inverting glasses will see the world upside down; but if he keeps them on for a while, the brain takes over and reorganises perception, restoring order so that he once again experiences things 'the right way around'. Construction and reconstruction carry on to a large degree *quite independently of what is actually out there*. Perception of all kinds is a function, not only of what is coming into the brain, but what is already there inside . . . 'I wouldn't have believed it, if I hadn't seen it,' has become a truism: but the structure and function of perceptual mechanisms suggest that it might be more neurophysiologically precise to say, 'I wouldn't have seen it at all, if I hadn't already believed it in the first place.'[83] [My italics]

The implications of the situation described by Watson recur throughout this book, but it is sufficient for the present to emphasise that the brain is perfectly capable of distorting or misrepresenting the sensory information it receives, and even, in extreme cases, of inventing completely spurious impressions or preventing the conscious mind from receiving genuine information. In many cases of 'faulty' operation of the perception processes, it seems as if the brain is trying to rationalise a situation that it does not understand into one that it does. It has to be confessed that we are not even beginning to understand all the 'motives' which guide this part of the brain's function.

This sometimes leads to the conclusion that we know very little about the brain, but this idea is misleading. The physical structure (the shapes and sizes of the bits and how they fit together) has, of course, been investigated in as much detail as any other part of the human body; the mode of operation of the basic components such as the nerve fibres and the Purkinje cells is reasonably clear; the areas of the brain dedicated to specific and easily-defined functions such as sight and muscular movement are also known. What is virtually unknown is the way in which the brain is organised, the way it 'works' as a unit. We do not know what 'consciousness' is, how 'memory' works, what is 'sadness'. We do not understand 'will' and we cannot define 'self'. We cannot find the reason why we sleep, and we are not even sure of the true fundamental difference between life and death. What is reasonably certain is that the answers to such questions – if there are any – are hidden in the 1.3 kilograms of grey (and white) matter we each possess, and that it aches if we try to think too deeply about how it works. In fact, Pugh's neat aphorism at the head of this chapter says it all.

The Brain

A very elementary idea of the physical arrangement of the brain can be gained by reference to Figure 14. For present purposes this can be studied in terms of three layers, both physically, in evolutionary terms and as 'layers of consciousness'. At the lowest level in the very centre of the brain, are the *medulla oblongata* and the other organs formed by modifications of the spinal cord itself. These control such vital and fundamental bodily activities as breathing, heartbeat, control of body temperature and other autonomous functions (i.e., those which operate independently of any conscious intention). Such organs are present in some form in all animals.

Surrounding this area are a number of irregularly-shaped organs often known collectively as the *limbic system*, the *animal brain* or the *reptilian brain* (since they developed in the very early lizards). The functions of these organs are difficult to investigate and are complex and ill-defined. They figure largely in subsequent discussion as being the possible site of the 'subconscious mind', and the 'administrative control' of the brain.

The upper and outer layers of the brain, surrounding the inner organs rather as a barrister's wig surrounds his head, form the *cerebrum, cerebral cortex*, or *neocortex*. This is the most recent development of the brain. It has grown at an enormous rate during the later stages of the evolution of man, so that it is now considerably larger (relative to body size) than in any other animal. This is

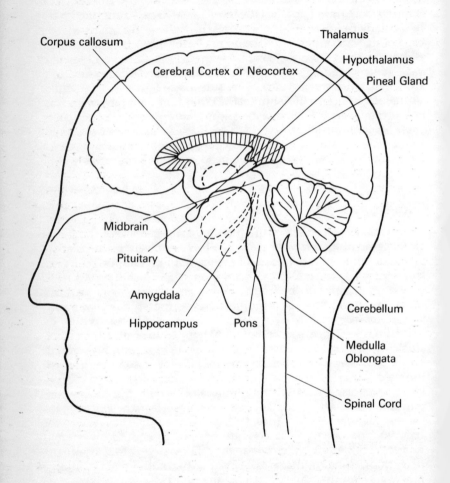

Figure 14. Section through the brain, showing the principal organs

the location of the 'conscious mind', interpreting and responding to the information provided by the sensory organs (eyes, ears, etc.) and controlling deliberate muscular movements. The whole of this upper region of the brain is divided into two by a deep cleft running from front to back of the brain, and the two halves are then connected at a lower level by a thick mass of neural connections – a kind of massive trunk telephone cable with thousands of wires – known as the *corpus callosum*. As is explained later, these two halves of the neocortex can act largely independently, and are often known as the *left brain* and the *right brain*.

The outer surface of the neocortex is subdivided (although not by any observable barriers or margins) into a number of separate areas (known as *cortexes*) each of which has been identified with a specific operation of the conscious mind. Communication between the various cortexes is carried out by streams of electro-chemical 'neural pulses' travelling along myriads of nerve fibres which form a dense mat below the neocortex and between the organs of the limbic system. Although each pulse is undetectable in itself, the sum total of the impulses in one area can be detected on an electrode attached to the surface of the skull, and the variations in activity recorded. These are seen as regularly-repeated 'brain waves' typical of the type of activity going on, and this process of 'electro-encephalography' (EEG) is the principal technique used in research into the neocortex, and has enabled the functions of the various cortexes to be mapped out with reasonable accuracy.

It has been found that many of these are symmetrical on either side of the head, but crossed over. For instance, the 'visual cortex' on the right interprets the information received by the left side of the field of vision seen by the eyes, the 'motor cortexes' in the left brain control the right hand and foot and deliberate muscular movements on the right side of the body, and so on.

The Sense Of Hearing

In studying the way that our senses operate, consideration of the functions of the various cortexes is most important, and I am particularly interested in the similarities and differences in this respect between our two most important senses – sight and hearing. Let me begin with the latter. Sound waves striking the membrane of the ear drum are converted to neural impulses to be conveyed through the auditory nerve into the brain. Sound coming from my left reaches my left ear directly, but has to go round the head (a distance of about 30 cm) to reach the right ear. This causes attenuation (reduction in strength) of the wave, and the time delay causes changes in phase or epoch of the waveform, and thus there are small differences between the signals received by the two ears. These are quite complex and vary with the pitch of the sound, but are sufficient to be processed by the auditory cortexes to give information as to the direction from which the sound comes.

Our whole impression of space around us, of distance and perspective, is closely bound up with sight, as will be described later, and all the required processing is carried out in a limited area on the top of the right side of the brain (the right parietal lobe). Hearing is subordinate to sight in judging direction and it is probable (I have found no specific information) that the *directional* information from the ears is dealt with in the same area. The recognition and generation of an *emotional* response is carried out in a different area on the right side, but interpretation of the *meaning* of words is dealt with on the left side of the head (Wernicke's area), so that it seems that the signals from both ears must be directed eventually to at least three different areas of the brain.

Such conclusions are important in studying what goes on inside the brain during a number of paranormal phenomena (leaving until a later chapter the question of how paranormal information gets into the brain in the first place). For instance, while most poltergeist noises seem to be true sound waves, most verbalised messages in paranormal events are of a different nature, being heard 'inside the head' and are inaudible to others.* This also applies to a non-verbal sound which has been described by a number of psychically sensitive people, including Mrs Rosalind Heywood. Mrs Heywood's books are for me among the most interesting and convincing of those on the paranormal, whether she is reviewing and commenting on the field in general,[36] or recounting her own experiences and opinions,[35] and I will make many references to them. She describes the experience she calls 'The Singing':

> It is best described as a continuous vibrant inner *quasi*-sound, to which the nearest outer analogy is the noise induced by pressing a sea-shell against the ear, or perhaps the hum of a distant dynamo. This sounds like tinnitus to anyone else, but to the experient it does

---

* There are exceptions, such as the 'Direct voice' phenomenon to be discussed later.

not appear to be heard by the ear or to be exactly located. Rather, like light, it pervades the whole atmosphere, though it is most clearly perceptible in a wide arc above and behind the head.

As many hi-fi addicts will recognise, this adequately describes the impression gained when a monophonic (single-microphone) source is heard through good headphones, i.e., when both ears are receiving identical signals. As for the sound itself, on page 75 I described 'white noise' as one of the basic sounds in nature, and it is what one hears in a sea-shell, since it is generated by random movements of the molecules of air against the ear-drum (although the sound heard is modified by the acoustics of the shell). The impression described by Mrs Heywood is exactly that which one would expect if purely random ('noise') signals were fed into, or generated by, the appropriate cortexes, *but not the cortexes which deal with directional information.*

At a spiritualist seance, the medium will frequently refer to voices being heard 'inside the head' in a similar fashion, and there is an interesting and subtle possibility that could account for some very puzzling features of psychic communications of this nature. Unless one is prepared to assume that messages are exchanged between various parts of the brain in words, which is unlikely, it seems inescapable that some parts of the brain must deal with abstract concepts, with 'meaning without words'. This is completely in accord with Freud's theory referred to in Chapter 1, that the brain stores independently the representations of things as ideas or concepts, and the representations in words. Somewhere in my brain at this moment there must be stored the idea of a 'cow' which does not involve the word C-O-W. If such an area is stimulated (through mechanisms yet to be discussed) by an impulse which forces the impression 'cow' into my consciousness, that consciousness will be unable to make sense of it without the associated words (as Freud emphasises). The rationalisation process in the brain, which is a basic part of perception, will be compelled to extract the word 'cow' from the verbal memory, and then, in order to account for the presence of the word in the conscious thought, may further rationalise it into the impression of a word or noises 'heard'. (See the case of telepathy between Mrs Heywood and her husband on page 102.) It seems quite possible, by this theory, that patterns of thought or emotion which may be initiated by an accidental or non-specific stimulus may be forced to be heard as 'voices in the head', although possibly in a depersonalised and detached form. One factor which supports such a theory is that it would account for the many cases in which the context or apparent origin of the message would lead one to expect it to be heard in a foreign language. Since its original introduction may be in a non-verbal form, 'translation' is automatic, being produced by the brain itself.

Where the text of the message is such that it is directly and emotionally associated by the hearer with a specific source (such as 'Hello Mary, This is Dad'), the rationalising process could go much further, attributing to the 'voice' the correct characteristics, accent and emotion. Going still further, if the apparent source of the words is visible – such as a vision of a face with moving lips – the voice could be interpreted as coming from that direction. The last effect can be simply demonstrated by noting that while watching the TV, the voice is apparently originating from the lips of the face on the screen, although the actual source is the loudspeaker, which can be moved some distance away before the illusion is lost.

In a later chapter will be discussed a phenomenon Mrs Heywood refers to as 'Orders', in which she experienced a strong compulsion to do some action which logic said was irrational, and Inglis[40] discusses a number of such cases in which the message constituted a very urgent warning – literally a matter of life or death. What is interesting is that in many of these cases the warning was heard as an impersonal 'voice in the head', but in two cases it had definite associations with a dead person. A lorry driver who had fallen asleep at the wheel was suddenly wakened by the voice of his mother calling him as she did when he was a child, and was just in time to avoid going through the wall of an overpass. The singer Tito Gobbi, when driving up a narrow and winding mountain road, suddenly heard the voice of his dead brother Bruno say 'so distinctly that he seemed to be sitting beside me . . . "Stop! Instantly!"' He reacted immediately, pulling onto the only stretch of grass verge wide enough to take the car, and a few seconds later an articulated lorry careered out of control around the corner just ahead of him. In such cases it is difficult to decide whether the personal characteristics of the voice were actually received, or were rationalised by the brain into the voice which would cause the most immediate reaction. Such cases are considered again in Chapter 14, in the context of the idea of a 'guardian angel'.

However, the ultimate case of a paranormal voice, in terms of difficulty of explanation, occurs on the occasions when a medium who is unacquainted with the original 'speaker' describes a 'spirit voice' as having a lisp, a stammer or a regional accent. 'Merely' telepathy from the mind of someone present (to be discussed later) is a weak suggestion, and there seems to be no alternative to the assumption of 'psychically received speech', i.e., a speech signal identical with that normally developed by one ear, being fed to the auditory cortexes, but not to the area dealing with direction.

There would seem, therefore, to be three stages of complexity in the communication of apparently verbal messages, but involving no physical sound waves. (All such processes will be referred to henceforth as 'pseudo-speech'):

a) A simple stimulus reaching a verbalising cortex triggers off a response which creates the impression of hearing sounds or a (usually simple and emotional) verbal message;
b) A more complex and continuous message is received by some means, and again stimulates a verbalising cortex to produce a 'voice in the head', but any characteristics of the voice other than the meaning of the words are added by the processes of perception or the ability of the brain to rationalise;
c) A voice, with all its normal characteristics, but with no indication of direction of the source, is 'heard' by the auditory cortexes.

Some suggestions as to possible mechanisms by which such signals may reach the brain are made later.

The Sense Of Sight

Having covered hearing and audible phenomena, let me now turn to the most important and in some respects the most complex of man's senses – that of sight. One would expect that there should be accounts of visual hallucinations directly equivalent to the three described above, and as an example of (a), I will quote an account by Mrs Heywood of her 'mental contact' (I can find no better phrase) with a friend Vivian Usborne, who had recently died. He had suffered from an incurable disease, and:

> . . . had come to feel, like me, that at death man snuffed out like a candle, and he lamented bitterly that all the many ideas simmering in his head would never come to fruition. [About ten days after Vivian died, Mrs Heywood went to his rooms to collect a gift he had bequeathed to her, and:] . . . I ran slap into 'Vivian' himself, most joyfully and most vividly alive . . . I felt 'Vivian' communicate inside my mind, and I shut my eyes and stood still to attend better. He conveyed in some fashion so intimate that the best word seems to be communion . . . that he had been entirely mistaken in expecting extinction at death. On the contrary, he now had scope, freedom and opportunity beyond his wildest dreams. [Mrs Heywood, prac-

tical as ever, asked for evidence to present to the Society for Psychical Research, of which she was a Member.]

Vivian's response to my question was emphatic and immediate, 'I cannot give you evidence . . . I can only give you poetic images.' At that, far, far above me, I saw – with the inner eye – an immense pair of white wings flying in a limitless blue sky.[35]

The verbal 'messages' show all the symptoms of pseudo-speech types (b) or (c), while the visual image of wings is equivalent to type (a), being generated as a response to a suggestion of 'supreme joy and freedom'. Visual images identifiable with the other types may also be found, but what is of greater interest is the possible occurrence of a visual equivalent of 'physical sound waves', but by a different mechanism.

The method by which we perceive space, distance, size and perspective, is similar in many respects to the auditory location of direction. If I look at an object – a tree for instance – a few metres away, my two eyes, being about eight centimetres apart, see two slightly different views of it. These minute differences are processed in the right parietal cortex to produce an estimate of range and an impression of solidity. Now apply this concept to the situation when one 'sees a ghost'. The example I quote here is given in some detail, since not only is it unusually clear and explicit, but it also includes a number of puzzling factors which will be useful later. It is the account given by Manning[54] of his 'meeting' with an apparition of Robert Webbe, a previous owner of the Manning's house in the 18th century. The Manning family were getting used to the psychic phenomena associated with Webbe. On one occasion Matthew had seen his 'ghost' on the staircase, and his father had had the hair-raising experience of sleeping 'in' it as described on page 148; various objects had appeared and disappeared, and there were frequent inexplicable noises.

One late evening Matthew was passing through the hall of the house when he noticed a strong smell of rank tobacco smoke (and none of the family smoked). He traced the smell upstairs and along the landing. His younger sister was in bed and reading, but she could smell nothing. He opened the door to his parent's bedroom and the smell was stronger. He stepped into the room, which was dark except for the light from the landing – the curtains were drawn. He saw the figure of Robert Webbe standing in the far corner. Manning twisted slowly around and switched on the light.

Webbe was standing there, seemingly unaware that anything was happening, or even that I was in the room. He stood, supporting his short portly body on a pair of sticks which looked as if they had not long been cut from a hedge, staring vacantly towards me, but not at me . . . Webbe was as real as the furniture in the room . . . I was quite unable to see through him. He was not shadowy or pale. He was, to all intents and purposes, a physical being . . . Then slowly his gaze moved from the area in which I was standing, to the bed. [Manning stepped towards the figure, which moved away.]

Now I seemed to have a heightened awareness of what I was doing, almost as if I was standing outside myself, watching Matthew Manning semi-mesmerised by this person . . . I took two steps forward with no hesitation, holding out my hand in front of me . . . For this move he took two steps back. [I said] 'I only want to shake hands with you.' . . . As soon as I spoke, it was as though a warmth kindled suddenly inside the worn figure. I saw that his eyes seemed to brighten, and he quickly, although with some difficulty, grasped two sticks in one hand, leaving the other hand free. He held out his hand . . . The next moment something inexplicable happened, and I was aware that I was no longer watching myself. I seemed to be one person instead of two. At the same moment I saw that my hand was shaking the air.

Robert Webbe had not vanished – he was still standing in front of me, but my hand passed straight through his. He may still have looked physical but he was like a mirage. Then for the first time he spoke, complaining of his "blessed legs", and rapping his stick on the floor. [Manning dashed out into his sister's room and told her that Webbe was next door, but she was frightened and would not come. He picked up the first thing to hand – a doll's wooden clog – and dashed back. Webbe was still there . . .]

. . . looking sorrowfully at the bed. Suddenly I was watching Matthew again, standing in front of Webbe. Both seemed wary of each other, like a pair of fighters. Matthew gingerly approached Webbe, holding the clog on the palm of his outstretched hand, and said, 'Here is a present for you. You can keep it.' I watched Webbe extending his fingers towards the clog lying on Matthew's hand and he quickly made a grab for it, as though catching a butterfly which had settled on a flower. My hand was empty, and I realised once more that as soon as Webbe had made contact with my hand, I had stopped watching myself from outside again. He looked at the wooden clog he now held in his hand – the same hand that only a few moments ago I had been unable to grasp. Then he put it in the pocket of his equally elusive coat, and I was unable to see it any more. He seemed to be growing impatient as he rapped his sticks on the floor . . . a most extraordinary thing began to happen . . . I noticed that the figure of Robert Webbe was losing its colour around the edges, so that his outer edges were greyish, while the main central areas of his body were still showing colour. [. . . and Webbe slowly faded to a shadowy grey and then disappeared.]

One could dismiss the whole of this account as a downright hoax and a load of nonsense, or treat it as an accurately observed and conscientiously reported incident. Seen in the light of the rest of Manning's writings, I take the latter view, and believe that any attempt to explain psychic phenomena should offer a reasonably coherent and self-consistent explanation of most (preferably all) of the effects he reports.

Now Manning saw Webbe quite clearly against the real background of the bedroom. Webbe moved towards and away from him (and in the other sighting he watched Webbe walk up the stairs). One could hardly imagine the fabrication within a cortex of two separate spurious impressions with the minute differences necessary to define position and movement with this degree of accuracy, and since the occurrence had no emotional significance for Manning there would be no undue urge to rationalise the impression. I am forced to the conclusion that an actual source of visual signals must have been situated in exactly the position in space at which Manning 'saw' it. In other words the 'ghost' was 'real' in the sense that there was *something* by the bed in that room.

The discussion can be widened by the introduction of two other visions which may be found to be comparable in some respects. They both form part of a single episode described by Michael Bentine, and although they break one of the requirements I listed in the first chapter, they bear his stamp of honesty and I find them very convincing. None the less, should they be considered unreliable in any way, I have no doubt that it would not be difficult to find equivalent accounts from other sources.

During the War, Michael's cousin Joan was a nurse at a London hospital and one night she was sitting in the Staff Room when she noticed that both her companions had fallen asleep:

> . . . opposite to her appeared the fully three-dimensional figure of her brother John, from the waist up . . . Joan adored her brother, and was deeply shocked. She only had time to notice that her brother was wearing an RAF shirt and a Mae West life jacket, but not the sheepskin flying jacket.
>
> She herself was wide awake, of that she was certain. Then she saw her brother run his fingers through his hair to show that it was dripping wet, smile his devastating grin at her and dematerialize . . . When I got the opportunity to come and see Pop [Michael's father, who had very pronounced psychic powers and had studied ESP for many years] at the end of my course he told me an even more remarkable story. 'The same night that Joan rang me I went to bed early and slept deeply. At first light I woke and, in that hypnagogic state between sleeping and waking, I saw how John died. I want you

to remember this Michael, because I feel that somehow this is very important evidence.'

'I saw cliffs surrounding a bay which was covered with low cloud. The stones of the cliffs were nothing like the sort of rocky coastline we have in this country. I felt that they were Mediterranean. I seemed to be viewing all this from above the sea, as though I was suspended below the cloud, facing the cliffs.'

'Suddenly, out of the cloud, came a German fighter – a Messerschmitt, I think – pursued by a British plane, a Spitfire. The British plane fired at the German and sent his plane into the sea. Then it seemed that the British pilot circled the foam-covered spot where the German had disappeared . . . While he was circling the area of the crash, a second German plane flew out of the low cloud and shot him down into the sea. The British plane sank immediately.'

'Remember what I am telling you, Michael, because that is how John died.'[3]

Later, John was officially posted as missing, and then, after Sicily was captured, his elder brother Alan was informed that John's grave had been found in a little cemetery there. He travelled to Sicily to see it and talked – through an interpreter – to the sexton and caretaker, who had seen the whole episode from the cliff top. At that time Alan had not been told about Pop's vision and it was not until after the war, when they met again, that the Sicilian's account as seen from the cliffs was compared with Pop's paranormal view from the opposite direction, when the two were found to be in complete agreement.

Four-Dimensional Light?

As a first shot at explaining the three visions (i.e., Manning's, Pop's and Joan's), let me return to our water-bug on his pond. Suppose that there is a tree overhanging the water. The bug is unaware of its existence, but when the light is strong, a reflection of the tree will appear on the surface of the water *in the same two dimensions as the bug*, only to disappear again when the sun goes behind a cloud. Note that the tree is a three-dimensional object outside the bug's world, while the reflection on the water is an illusion produced in his world by the normal operation of light rays obeying the laws of physics – there is nothing 'paranormal' about it, despite any impression the bug may get to the contrary.

A similar analogy which may clarify the concept is illustrated in Figure 15, which shows the action of a film projector throwing an image onto a screen. The fact that the 'real object' is now not a

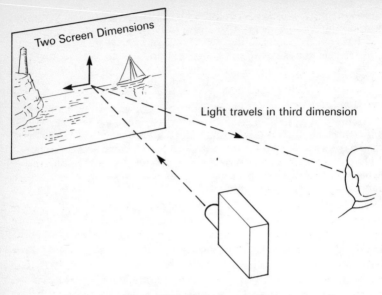

Figure 15. *Optical projection*

three-dimensional tree but a two-dimensional film (which itself carries a pictorial 'illusion') may confuse the issue, but it is not relevant to the discussion. The two significant points to be noted are:

a) The image on the screen is an illusion, which the eyes and the perception processes in the brain do their best to interpret in terms of real objects – and this action does not involve any hallucination, malfunction or mystery;

b) In order for the image to be projected on the screen, the light rays from the projector to the screen, and the reflected light from the screen to the eyes, must travel in a third dimension *which is different from those of the screen*.

Now step up the analogy by one more dimension, so that the 'screen' is now a three-dimensional space, (such as the Manning's bedroom). Let me assume that somewhere or other there is a solid, three-dimensional object (such as the body of Robert Webbe) separated from the room by a 'distance' in an extra dimension, and that somehow or other an image is projected over that distance to produce in that room a fully three-dimensional image which can move and turn, and is accurately located in space, but is an unreal illusion just like the image on a cinema screen.* Such an explanation would account for the characteristic observed in all three cases; each was fully three-dimensional and moved in a natural way, giving a convincing illusion that it was real.

There are some circumstantial factors which support the idea that light may travel extra-dimensionally to form projected images. If the light reflected (or emanating) from an apparition were of the normal kind, then it would be visible to anyone around and would be indistinguishable from that reflected from a physical object, whereas there is some evidence that a certain degree of 'psychic sensitivity' is necessary to see some apparitions, or a high level of personal significance. There are accounts (Manning's is a notable exception) which refer to unusual characteristics of the image itself, such as a strange luminosity or semi-transparency, which distinguishes it from its surroundings. There is a case, therefore, for suggesting that the light from such an apparition is distinguishable as 'extra-dimensional'. But if this is so, then either we have special organs to sense it, 'four-dimensional eyes' set close to our visible ones (otherwise perspective would be wrong), or – what is far more likely – our normal eyes are as sensitive to light arriving through an extra dimension as they are to the usual variety. Watson, discussing the hallucinations produced by the drug LSD (see later) writes:

> The word 'enlightenment' is an interesting one in this respect, because light seems to play a large part in transcendence. Visual hallucinations are the most characteristic aspect of the LSD state, and in several studies it has been discovered that the retinal cells are reacting entirely on their own. Without the stimulus of special light waves, they send signals off to the brain about *a whole galaxy of wavelengths and frequencies that apparently do not exist at that time and place at all*. The brain 'sees' those lights and colours as it sees the images in a dream . . . [82] [My italics]

The theory that light can travel in four dimensions may also account for another puzzling characteristic of a ghost, in that many reports refer to one casting a shadow. If the object exists physically in its own world, then it will cast a shadow in that world, and the

---

* The similarity to a holographic image is obvious, but I cannot see any easy or helpful comparison with the way such an image is obtained, although it is quite possible that a similar principle – the mutual interference between a large number of wave sources – may be involved.

projection process could well include part of its surroundings *including the shadow*. Two questions then arise: why are we not seeing such visions almost continuously? And why is it that some people may see them and not others? Both these are dealt with later.

Another problem with the 'optical projection' theory is to identify just where the 'object' being projected is situated at the time. Unfortunately, there is insufficient information as to the precise timing of the air fight and the two visions (particularly in view of the ambiguity of the phrase 'The same night that Joan rang me . . .') but bearing in mind that Pop's 'first light' would be fully daylight in Sicily, it seems possible that Pop's 'dream' was a view of the fight itself, projected from the Mediterranean through a fourth dimension (via a 'hole in superspace'?), in 'real time', i.e., while the fight was in progress. Webbe's apparition is more difficult to explain, and is discussed in a later chapter, as a possible case of 'optical projection over time', while Joan's offers the greatest puzzle of all, since what she saw *at no time existed in real life*, and this must wait for several more chapters.

Crossed Wires

Returning to the 'simple stimulus' (Case (a) of page 72), one could ask: if the stimulus is undirected, what determines which of the cortexes responds to it? In this context another account by Mrs Heywood is of interest. She describes her deliberate attempt to contact her husband by telepathy, when she was at a rather boring lecture and he at home in bed:

> . . . I blotted out my surroundings, pictured myself in my husband's room and said to him mentally, 'Frank, I'm here, I'm here with you. Do you see me?' Then I looked at my watch. The time was three minutes to ten. [When she questioned her husband he reported] 'I heard you unlock the front door and come upstairs and go into the kitchen . . . ' 'What time was that?' I asked. 'Just before the ten o'clock news.' . . . He insisted that he had clearly heard the sounds of my return, turning the key in the lock, walking upstairs, going into the kitchen, and so on . . . And once one has thought of it, it seems natural that his impression of my return, even if it was telepathic, would emerge as an auditory hallucination of the way I normally do so, rather than a visual one, *which would not make sense to him* if he had not heard me come in.[35] [My italics]

So, despite her attempt to communicate visually, the response was received 'audibly'. The situation is clarified by an observation made by Sir Frederick Myers in 1891, and quoted by Inglis:

> If a vague suggestion, say of *danger*, is conveyed to several hypnotised patients, to be developed after their awakening, each will realise the hallucinatory danger in a different way: voice of enemies – smell of fire – sight of a wild beast advancing.[38]

So it seems very likely that consideration of the other three senses (of touch, smell and taste) along the same lines as hearing and sight would lead to similar conclusions, and that an emotional impulse – implanted hypnotically or received by other means yet to be discussed – may stimulate any one or more of the sense cortexes, and produce a corresponding reaction. It would appear that the actual form of the experience, (whether one says 'I felt . . . ', 'I heard . . .', or 'I saw . . . ' etc.) may be dependent on a number of factors, such as:

a) Common sense or experience – as noted by Mrs Heywood;
b) Whether the experient is a 'verbaliser' or a 'visualiser'; (two categories of thinking habits recognised by psychologists);
c) The type of message or emotion – whether it is more easily represented in words or by pictures;
d) The clarity of the message – whether it appeals directly to a single sense, or is confused or incomplete;
e) Survival considerations; e.g., a very urgent message may produce an immediate muscular reaction, to be rationalised later – such as an instinctive 'duck' of the head, rationalised by an hallucination of a bullet passing over — or the type of Orders described earlier and discussed in more detail on page 117.

CHAPTER 7

MUMMY KNOWS BEST – SOMETIMES!

'Brain research and psychology must try to give an account of the mystery of mind in terms of the structure and organisation of the brain . . . To understand the world of physics, from the atoms to the stars, is wonderful. But to understand the organ that allows us to understand would be little short of a miracle.'
Colin Blakemore[6]

It is evident that the control of 'conscious experience' can be switched from one cortex to another or to several at the same time (one can see and hear simultaneously), but it is important to note that whole areas of the brain may be functioning without the conscious mind being aware of the fact. While one cortex may dominate the conscious thoughts, the rest of the brain is still fully functioning although *the subject is unaware of its activity*. Probably the most striking evidence for this conclusion is in the so-called 'split-brain' experiments, which warrant consideration in some detail.

Although the control of most muscles, and the less sophisticated interpretation of information from the eyes and ears, are symmetrical in the brain, and left and right are 'crossed over' as described, each side of the brain specialises in certain important functions. In a normal right-handed person (assumed in all subsequent descriptions) the right side of the brain is the subordinate side, referred to as the 'minor hemisphere'. It carries out most of the thinking based on complex visual analysis, such as recognising patterns and judging distance; its activities are closely bound up with non-verbal and 'absent-minded' activities, in that it controls intuitive thought and aesthetic appreciation, and the expression of emotion by the facial muscles (as in crying or frowning). Thus if you are listening to music, watching a football match or fuming after an argument, your right side is very active.

The left side of the brain is dominant (the 'major hemisphere'). It carries out logical or step-by-step thinking and – a very important function – it controls all aspects of 'verbalising', i.e., expressing thoughts in words, interpreting the meaning of speech received by the ears, and the control of the speech organs themselves. Thus if you are discussing your account with your bank manager, reading a newspaper or listening to a lecture, your left side is the more active.

There have been a small number of cases (most of extremely severe epilepsy) which have necessitated the drastic surgical operation known as a 'commisurotomy'. This involves opening the top of the skull, gently separating the two halves of the neocortex at the deep cleft previously described, and completely cutting through the corpus callosum, thus preventing all direct communication between the two halves of the upper brain. Amazingly enough, not only does the patient normally recover completely and quickly from this operation (which can be carried out under a local anaesthetic – the brain cannot feel pain), but he can then live what is to a large extent a normal life, although subject to certain rather peculiar restrictions which can best be discussed by describing some of the experiments which have been carried out on such 'split-brain' people.

First the patient is blindfolded, or in some other way prevented from seeing what is happening. A common object such as a teaspoon or a toothbrush is then put into his right hand and he is asked to say what it is. He has no difficulty in doing this because the sense organs in his right hand are connected to his left brain, which identifies the object and passes the message to the verbalising cortex (still on the left side) to put into words, which are then passed to the speech cortex which controls the larynx, tongue and other vocalising organs. However, if the object is put into the left hand, he cannot identify it. The sense of touch in the left hand is connected to the right side of the brain, which is capable of identifying it, but then cannot pass the information to the left side for verbalising because of the severed connections. The interesting fact is that the patient is not confused or frustrated, he is totally unaware that he is holding anything, but if he is now offered an assortment of objects to feel with his left hand, he can pick out unfailingly the one first offered.

This kind of experiment,[5,6] and many of much greater complexity, demonstrate that not only do the two halves of the neocortex operate to a large extent independently of each other, but activity in one cortex is not necessarily sensed in another part of the brain.

It has been shown that a split-brain monkey can deal with almost twice the amount of information compared with a normal animal, and that a split-brain human can carry out two tasks as fast as a normal person can do one.

Not only are the two hemispheres capable of a considerable degree of independent operation, but what also must be emphasised is that the individual cortexes in each hemisphere also have a large degree of independence, the whole system operating under some form of central control, which operates by manipulating the communication processes between the different cortexes.

The Telephone Exchange

This being so, it is evident that the method by which information is transferred from one part of the brain to another (i.e., the system of interconnections between the cortexes, and between each cortex and the 'control centre'), is as important as the cortex functions themselves. Most of the nerve fibres carrying messages into and out of the neocortex, and those coming up the spinal cord from the rest of the body, terminate in the *thalamus* (See Fig. 14 on page 90), which acts as a relay centre and 'telephone exchange' controlling communication between the neocortex, the other parts of the brain and the rest of the body. Intertwined with these nerves all the way up the brain stem, and particularly in the *pons* and the *midbrain*, is a lace-like network of fibres known as the *reticular formation*. It is believed that these fibres are capable of controlling the action of the nerve fibres, acting as 'switches' in the telephone exchange controlled by the thalamus.

An important demonstration of the way in which this control system works may be found in the psychiatric technique known as 'Primal Therapy'.[43] This operates on the principle that physical or mental stress (trauma) occurring very early in life – possibly before birth – may be 'locked up' in the lowest levels of consciousness and can cause severe neuroses in adult life. The 'control gates' block these experiences from reaching the neocortex and so prevent their being sensed by the conscious mind. It may take weeks of careful psychoanalysis, or regression under hypnotism (discussed later) to persuade the gates to open so that the memory of the pain and the fear may reach the neocortex. This experience can be very distressing to the patient, but once it is remembered in this way, the trauma can be verbalised and so understood, largely neutralising its effect on the individual. Janov writes:

Essentially it seems the responsibility of the limbic system is to integrate higher and lower centres and to filter out pains [physical and psychological] which cannot be integrated cortically. It is the limbic system, particularly the hippocampus and the amygdala with their direct connections to the frontal cortex, which acts as a 'gate to consciousness'.

In his book *Exploring Buddhism*, Christmas Humphreys sums up the same principle as follows:

We can at any time only affect our conscious life; psychology has proved how much more is unconscious, which must, that it may be brought under control, be rescued from that condition. This is one of the purposes of meditation, to release the forces of the unconscious into consciousness, and thence to control.[37]

The presence of these gates, and their ability to cut off or reroute messages between two parts of the brain (and particularly between the 'conscious mind' in the neocortex and the 'subconscious mind' – presumed for the present to be somewhere in the limbic system) is vital to any attempt to understand or explain paranormal events. There is strong evidence that they act as a 'censor' or 'Mummy-knows-best' system which prevents the conscious mind receiving 'forbidden' information, although just what criteria are used to judge what is forbidden and what is permissible is something of a mystery, and one which is very relevant to the subject of this book.

For instance, we can now see a possible answer to the questions raised on page 99 about 'extra-dimensional seeing'. Assume that the eyes can 'label' in some way those images produced by light which enters them from the fourth dimension, and that the censor mechanism in the brain will normally block that information and prevent it reaching the conscious mind. Then, for such an image to be seen, it would only be necessary for the censor mechanism to be disabled or weakened, and I will suggest in the next chapter that this is exactly what may happen in psychically sensitive people, or at times of extreme emotion. Note how Manning describes explicitly the way the apparition of Webbe slowly became colourless, then blurred, then faded to invisibility – exactly as a communication engineer would expect if the signal reaching the neocortex were slowly becoming weaker.

Hypnotism

A phenomenon which illustrates explicitly the ability of part of the brain to suppress or re-route sensory impressions, is Hypnotism. The hypnotist is capable of controlling certain functions in the brain of the patient. The description of the process in psychological terms is simple. Janov writes:

> The hypnotist has substituted his cortex for the subject's. That is, the subject's lower brain centres respond to the consciousness of the hypnotist instead of his own. So when there is an input, a suggestion, the patient reacts as if his own brain had perceived something.[43]

Gooch describes graphically the degree of control that may be achieved:

> The normal . . . human mind, under instruction from a hypnotist – that is, responding to purely verbal commands or requests – is able to fabricate an exact, true-life, free-moving duplicate of another person. Apart from being seen, this duplicate can be heard, touched and smelled by the subject. All the hypnotised person's senses are satisfied that this hallucinated person is really there, in the flesh.[23]

Pertinent facts of hypnotism may be summarised as follows:

a) The patient is in a condition of trance, and apparently totally insensitive to other happenings in the room – his senses ignore all information not originated by the hypnotist;

b) The instructions conveyed by the hypnotist may include incorrect sensory information (the subject 'seeing' things which are not there), the implantation of spurious 'habits' and the deliberate control of 'regression' (see page 142);

c) The events during the period that he is hypnotised are not remembered in the normal way. Instead, he may at a later time 'remember' imaginary events or respond to instructions implanted by the hypnotist. His memory is being activated entirely by the hypnotist, rather than by his own senses;

d) The hypnotic state can include not only the suppression of pain, suggesting that the part of the brain responsible for the sense of touch is disabled, but the hypnotist can 'instruct' the physiological functions of the body to suppress their normal reaction to physical damage – the patient's skin can be burned without a blister forming;

e) The process of 'common sense' – or judgment on what is rational – may be suspended under hypnotism. For instance, the subject will accept as normal a situation in which he can see a person in two places at once (one real, one hallucinatory) – and that person may be himself! Such a case is discussed on page 154;

f) The control exercised by the hypnotist may continue when the patient is out of range of the normal senses (i.e., out of sight and beyond earshot).

In short, the subject's sensations and the contents of his memory are controlled by the brain of the hypnotist, which does not seem to cooperate with, or to become part of the subject in any way, but rather it issues positive and dictatorial orders.

The situation can be expressed in terms of the censor mechanisms as follows: The hypnotist controls the message sent to the patient, and can also *instruct the censor in the brain of the patient to treat it as if it had originated locally*. One could compare the situation to that of a managing director who wants to give orders to a subordinate in a distant factory. He instructs his secretary to put through a telephone call to the secretary of the subordinate; each secretary switches through the call to the extension telephone at either end of the link, and the 'superior's' mind controls the 'subordinate's' actions. The location of the 'secretary' – the organ controlling communication within the brain – is discussed later.

Fooling The Censor

One characteristic of the censor has frequently been noted; it seems that certain kinds of thought-pattern or brain function can avoid its action more easily than others. Professor H.H. Price, Wykeham Professor of Logic at Oxford, writes:

> It looks as if telepathically received impressions have some difficulty in crossing the threshold and manifesting themselves in consciousness. There seems a barrier or repressive mechanism which tends to shut them out from consciousness, a barrier which is rather difficult to pass, and they make use of all kinds of devices to overcome it. Sometimes they make use of muscular mechanisms of the body, and emerge in the form of dreams, sometimes as visual or auditory hallucinations. And often they can only emerge in a distorted or symbolic form . . . [78]

This idea that paranormal information may be 'deliberately' modified to a form which has a better chance of avoiding the action of the censor is another concept which recurs frequently in the literature.

It is interesting to note that the reverse process to blocking of information can occur. Under the influence of hallucinogenic drugs (and possibly brain damage, trance or extreme religious experience) new or unusual connections may be made, and the senses cross-connected or distorted (a process known as 'synaesthesia'). Watson writes:

> If a nerve fibre from the tongue is connected to one leading from the ear to the brain, a drop of vinegar in the mouth is 'tasted' as a loud and startling explosion. This is how hallucinations occur, by drug- or stress-induced short circuits in the sensory system that allow music, for instance, to reach the brain as patterns of light.[84] [This idea of 'short-circuits' in the brain is referred to again later.]

Many research workers have described how some drugs can produce gross distortions of perspective, 'hearing colours' and 'seeing sounds'. Rosalind Heywood,[35] in experiments with LSD, refers to colours 'a thousand times more vivid and varied than a kingfisher's feathers' – while – 'for a fleeting moment . . . I appeared to climb out of my body up a Chopin Ballade.' Similarly, Carlos Castaneda,[9] under the influence of mescalin, describes violent and intense buzzing in his ears, the ability to see minute sand grains in the dark, and the impression of the whole world varying rhythmically from darkness to light in time with his own heart beat.

Where Is The Telephone Operator?

This concept of the action of the thalamus (and associated organs) can be clarified by direct analogy with the functions of a manually-operated telephone switchboard in a large block of offices, each cortex of the brain being equivalent to a telephone instrument (see Fig. 16 on page 122). A normal telephone operator can carry out three different types of operation:

a) He can connect any one telephone in the block to another in the same block;
b) He can isolate one telephone from all communication;
c) He can connect a telephone to an 'outside line'.

If this analogy is valid, it raises two questions:

If the thalamus is the telephone exchange, then where is the telephone operator? Is it possible that there exists an 'outside line', a communication link directly from one brain to another apart from the five physical senses (contravening the assumption made on page 16)?

The second question is dealt with later, but as regards the location of the operator, Stan Gooch gives a fascinating analysis of the question of where in the brain the 'unconscious mind' or 'subconscious' is situated, and this will be shown to be closely related to the same problem. Some of his preliminary comments are interesting, particularly in view of my later suppositions. He says:

> Some outstanding modern psychologists (such as Sir John Eccles) do not consider that even the conscious mind can be wholly reduced to a supporting physiological structure. Nevertheless, the extreme view that the unconscious mind has no location of any kind in the physical brain would be a giant philosophical assumption . . . We must begin with the assumption that the unconscious mind does have an identifiable seat somewhere in the nervous system.[23]

After considering in some detail the claims of various areas of the brain, Gooch finally settles for the *cerebellum*, an organ similar in shape and form to the neocortex, situated at the base of the skull at the back of the head, and wrapped closely around the brain stem (see Fig. 14). Although part of the reptilian brain, it continued to develop during the later periods of evolution, and although it remains considerably smaller than the neocortex it has, thanks to its far deeper folds and more complex convolutions, about three-quarters of the 'working area' of that organ. It is, according to Gooch:

> . . . not simply the second most highly evolved organ this planet has ever produced, but *the* most highly evolved . . . there are more cells in the granular layer of the cerebellar cortex *than in the whole of the rest of the brain put together*. [Gooch's italics]

The Purkinje cells (the 'computing elements' in the brain) of the cerebellum are capable of developing as many as one hundred times more connections than those in the neocortex. The cerebellum has its own neural connections to the sense organs (independent of those to the neocortex), and also extensive connections to the frontal areas of the neocortex, the so-called 'silent areas' which are thought to be the most recently evolved and the functions of which are not completely understood. It has long been known to play an important part in the control of the more deliberate and delicate muscular movements, such as handling tools and control of balance while walking, but more recent work suggests that it includes more subtle functions, such as establishing the individuality of handwriting. Gooch suggests that the function of the cerebellum may be even more fundamental:

The foregoing points together constitute a striking prima-facie case for the cerebellum as the seat of an alternative consciousness. It is a brain within a brain, a complete organism within the organism. Not only does it have informational access to all sensory and motor systems, *but full executive control if the situation merits.* That full executive control, *overriding any current conscious decisions or wishes,* is frequently exercised in states of fear, panic, anger, sexual arousal, deprivation and exhaustion – in short, in all kinds of emergency and extreme conditions. Why, in principle, should not the cerebellum exercise such control on other occasions also? [My italics]

The neocortex is known to contain the conscious mind and to control the personality of the individual while he is awake, but Gooch argues that the cerebellum may contain a totally independent 'subconscious personality' or 'alternative consciousness' which takes over during sleep (it is known that the cerebellum controls dreaming), and on other occasions such as during religious or artistic inspiration, under hypnotism, and in some psychic events. The transfer of the control of personality from one source to the other could account for symptoms of some psychological disorders, such as multiple personality and schizophrenia, and it may be the alternative consciousness which is brought to the surface during hypnotism.

Gooch's argument leaves many questions unanswered or unsatisfactorily answered, but the identification of the cerebellum as an organ with extensive powers of control of sensory information and motor functions, and with the capability of substituting an alternative personality, makes it the primary contender for the control centre of our communication terminal, particularly in view of its location. It is wrapped around the 'switchboard' in the midbrain and pons region, and very close to the hippocampi and amygdala, which Janov calls 'the gates to consciousness'.

Strong and direct support for the theory that the control of paranormal or psychic ability is located somewhere in this area can be found in the Preface by Peter Bander to Manning's book *The Link,*[53] describing the background to the book and his own observations of Manning's work. He recounts that Manning, together with a number of other people claiming psychic abilities, attended in June-July 1974 a conference on psychokinesis (see page 133) at the New Horizon Research Foundation in Toronto. A large number of scientific experiments were carried out under laboratory conditions, and in particular EEG recordings were made under rest conditions and again when the subject was trying to exercise psychic powers. The results were astonishing:

As soon as Matthew complied with the instruction [to attempt to bend by psychic power a key held in his hand] the electroencephalograph registered an unexpected and quite unique reading. To all but one of the scientists present, the brain-wave pattern, registered each time for a period of twenty seconds, was entirely new. One of the medical professors recalled having seen such a pattern once before in a patient to whom a severe overdose of a hallucinatory drug had been administered . . . The readings from the computer are interesting. According to the evaluation given in REM (rapid eye movement), Matthew had been in the fourth degree of deep sleep. It was quite obvious to the scientists present that Matthew had not been asleep – they could see he was wide awake.

The second significant observation was made when the ramp function [the brain-wave pattern discussed above] was traced back to the part of the brain from which it originated . . . The only statement available is that the ramp function has been traced to a part of the human brain *hitherto believed to be defunct and degenerated. The old 'animal brain'* of homo sapiens was one of the descriptions given . . . [My italics]

Confirmation of the cerebellum and limbic areas as being unusually active during some paranormal phenomena occurs in the Russian reports on the psychic Nelya Mikhailova (see page 162).

Summary

The conclusions of this and the previous chapter can be summarised as follows:

1) The brain does not operate as a single unit, carrying out a single task at any one time. Different parts of the brain can operate independently and simultaneously on different tasks.
2) Although we may 'think we know what we are thinking', in fact most of the processes in the brain – including the reception of information from the senses – are carried out by isolated areas operating without our deliberate control or knowledge.
3) Our senses (eyes, ears, touch, etc.) may respond accurately to our surroundings, but such sensations must go through a complex process of 'perception' before they are received by our conscious mind. The various areas of the neocortex are quite capable of 'inventing' complete and detailed sensations as a response to an unspecific stimulus.
4) This process includes the 'gates' controlled by a 'censor' mechanism in the limbic system. We have no clear idea of what governs the censor, or the rules by which it operates.

5) As an example, if e.m.r. can travel through extra dimensions, it may be possible for a three-dimensional image to be projected through space or time, but this will only be 'seen' by the conscious mind of the percipient if the censor mechanism allows the sensory information from the eyes to reach the neocortex.

6) Information which for one reason or another does not reach the 'verbalising' cortex in the brain may be totally ignored – in effect the brain can refuse to recognise its existence. (This very important point, and some of the evidence supporting it, was discussed in Chapter 1.)

7) Certain kinds of brain function (such as those which control muscular action, and those active during dreams), seem to be less affected than others by the action of the censor, and there is a distinct tendency for paranormal information to be expressed in these forms.

8) The actual sensations we experience depend on what particular part of the brain a stimulus reaches, and this is not necessarily governed by where the stimulus originated (i.e., which sense originally detected it).

9) Many of these effects are attributable to a kind of 'telephone exchange' system within the brain, which may be able to connect part of the brain to an 'outside line', via a 'sixth sense' which is the subject of the next chapter.

CHAPTER 8

LOOKING FOR THE BRAIN'S BACK DOOR

'I am only too aware that my own views are coloured by the conviction which my experiences eventually forced on me, that there exists permanent subconscious communication between other people and myself.'
Rosalind Heywood

The second question posed on page 110 must now be considered; my previous assumption that man has only five senses may be false. If there is a fourth dimension to which we are insensitive, there may equally well be a 'sixth sense' operating through that dimension and capable of introducing information, ideas or emotions into our conscious minds by a route of which we are unaware. As a preliminary to examining this possibility, let me describe one or two examples of phenomena which may support the assumption.

I will begin by considering telepathy, as offering the clearest introduction to the particular aspects of brain function I wish to discuss, and since the general principle is well known, I will not attempt a definition, but merely introduce specific examples as convenient. The phenomenon was completely accepted by our ancestors, and is still taken for granted in many present-day or recently defunct 'primitive societies', as in the well-documented telepathic abilities of the Australian aborigine and the Bushman of the Kalahari. During the 18th and 19th centuries the vigorous revolt against superstition and dogmatic religion in Western Europe demanded the acceptance of strictly materialist ideas and ridiculed any belief not supportable by controlled experiment, or explainable in purely physical terms. Telepathy was for many years dismissed as nonsense, but started to creep into scientific thought with the experiments by Mesmer and others into hypnotism. It became established as a serious subject with the experiments of Dr Rhine at Duke University in the 1930s – although these later became bogged down in arguments as to how far the probity of an individual should be accepted as a factor in scientific proof, and whether chance operates in the way mathematicians think it does.

It is now under active investigation in a number of countries, notably USA, Canada, Japan and, most intensively, in Russia. The limited accounts reaching the West indicate that the work has got well beyond proof of the reality of the phenomenon, and could quite possibly have resulted in reasonably reproducible effects and even some kind of an explanation. Unfortunately, this work, like much in the USA, has strong military overtones and remains largely unpublished. It is known, for example, that the American experiments include attempted telepathic communication to space vehicles and submarines.[84]

The published work available to the layman on research carried out in Universities and research laboratories in the USA and elsewhere is limited but impressive. Telepathy has been demonstrated quite convincingly and on a large scale.[16,33] It has been shown that many people have the 'gift', that distance is no barrier, nor is the most elaborate electrical screening (to prevent penetration by radio waves). There is strong evidence that it is encouraged if the receiving person believes it to be possible, and if the transmitted information is emotional in content. Repetition, boredom, apathy, tiredness and disbelief in the possibility of ESP (in the research workers or their subjects) all tend to reduce the likelihood of it occurring. The messages transferred can be as simple as a selection of one symbol from five or six possibilities, or as complex as quite detailed drawings or photographs or quotations from literature.

Mrs Heywood[36] describes a number of cases of spontaneous telepathy, particularly between herself and her husband, in which quite complex messages were passed, such as 'Take a taxi to the station to meet me, and get a porter', or 'Go home as soon as possible, and go in by the front door'. On page 102 I discussed her account of a deliberate – and successful – attempt to communicate mentally to her husband the simple message 'I am with you'.

Such accounts, and the reports of experiments, represent only a microscopic fraction of the total evidence for telepathy, which led Dr Matthews, Dean of St Pauls, to say:

> I believe it is foolish not to recognise that Psychical Research may have much to teach us about our mysterious selves. We should not rule out the possibility that the next great advance in our knowledge

will come in this part of the field . . . The case for telepathy is so strong that one is tempted to say that the only way to retain disbelief is by steadily ignoring the evidence.

This process, of 'steadily ignoring the evidence', has been adopted by what one may refer to as the 'scientific rearguard' to an almost farcical extent. The standards of 'scientific proof' demanded would not be tolerated for a moment in any other field of research, and are automatically revised to become more restrictive after each successful experiment, an attitude covered in Chapter 2.

More Orders

There are other phenomena which, although not often mentioned as such, seem to have at least some relationship to telepathy. For instance, I have already mentioned the phenomenon of 'Orders' (see page 94). Mrs Heywood describes a number of occasions on which she experienced a strong compulsion to do some action which logic said was totally irrational, such as to phone a stranger and pass on a cryptic message, or to offer to distant acquaintances the lease of her house – without any knowledge that they needed one. In each case where she complied, the result was beneficial to the other party, who were as amazed as she was. A number of such cases are also described in *The Cross and the Switchblade*.[86] The author, the Reverend David Wilkerson, describes the setting up and operation of a Youth Centre for drug addicts and outcast teenagers in a slum area of New York. Most of the money needed to buy and operate the centre was acquired by a succession of events which could, without any risk of exaggeration, be called minor miracles.*

As a typical example of his method of operation, and one relevant to this discussion, the book recounts how one morning there was no food for the twenty-five young residents and helpers, and no money to buy any (they calculated they needed thirty to thirty-five dollars). As usual in such a situation, they assembled in the Chapel and prayed. Now a Pentecostalist at prayer tends to be vocal and expressive, and twenty-five hungry and anxious Pentecostalists even more so, so that it was no wonder that no-one heard the lady who knocked at the door and, getting no answer,

---

* A scientist may prefer the term 'extreme coincidences', but this is stretching the term to its limit. A disciple of Jung would call them 'synchronicities', a change of title but equally unhelpful.

entered and stood somewhat disconcerted at the sight – and sound – of twenty-five assorted persons, all on their knees 'thanking God for the food He had given us in the past and thanking Him too for the food He would be giving us, somehow, in this emergency'. When Wilkerson eventually approached her, she wanted to know the purpose of the Centre and to hear about its work, and seemed particularly interested in the reason for the praying:

> 'When did you begin this prayer?' the lady asked.
>
> I figured up. 'About an hour ago.'
>
> 'Well,' she said, 'That is truly extraordinary. I knew very little about your work. But an hour ago I received a sudden impulse to do something that is totally out of character for me. I felt that I was supposed to empty my piggy bank and bring the contents to you. Now I know the reason.' She reached into her purse.
>
> She placed an envelope on my desk, and with an expression of hope that it would be of some help, she thanked me for showing her our Centre, and left. That envelope contained just over thirty-two dollars, exactly the amount we needed to feed ourselves for the rest of the day.

This example is an admirable illustration of a factor underlying many cases of Orders, in that the Order seems to arise from a real and physical need of someone unknown, or only slightly known, to the recipient of the Order, and who is *completely oblivious to the fact that such an Order has been given*. In other cases, the Order has consisted of an urgent warning of impending disaster (see pages 94 and 219).

Automatic Writing

Another phenomenon which has, for present purposes, a relationship to Telepathy, is the process of 'automatic writing'. This is described in a number of books,[36,53,54] and has been recognised for many years as a technique whereby a psychically sensitive person may apparently establish contact with an 'intelligence' outside his own consciousness, with the additional disturbing factor that in some cases the sourse seems to be 'related to' the mind of a person known to be dead.

The procedure is simple enough; the subject holds a pen or pencil in contact with a sheet of paper and allows his mind to relax into a receptive mood which may (but need not) approach trance conditions. After a time he may produce writing or drawings which are apparently controlled by intelligences other than his own. Some remarkable results have been achieved by this technique, and Manning was an extreme case. He began such experiments following a suggestion that they may relieve the considerable stresses he experienced from the poltergeist phenomena which surrounded him, and he found this to be so. A good automatic writing session would often prevent poltergeist effects for several days.

After a few sessions he found that he was producing drawings to an extremely high artistic standard (and certainly well beyond his normal ability), and in a very wide variety of styles. Many of them bore a remarkable resemblance to known works by great masters such as Durer, Picasso, Goya and Aubrey Beardsley, some of them even 'signed'! He also found that he could communicate both ways with 'discarnate minds' by this process; he would write a question, and after a short interval his hand would write an answer in a totally different handwriting, sometimes in a foreign language or with archaic grammar or spelling, and with a sense consistent with it having been written by a dead person. Over a period of years he produced many hundreds of pages of manuscript and drawings by these methods.

Many automatic writing 'conversations' were held with Robert Webbe, the 'ghostly' previous owner of the house. The particular session I want to quote (since it will also provide useful illustrations for points to be discussed later) is that held on May 15th 1977. Transcribed from the narrative in Chapter 9 of *The Strangers* to a more convenient question-and-answer form this went:

> M.M. Who do you think you are talking to?
> R.W. I think sometimes I am going mad. I hear a voyce in myne head which I hear talking to me and asking me what I do. But tell no one else they locke me away. Who is this voice?
> M.M. The voice is me. Who am I?
> R.W. You frighten me. Who are you? You talk to me in myne head and not in myne ears. Who are you? Are you the ghost this voyce talks of?
> M.M. I am alive, and I live in your house. You are dead.
> R.W. This is nonsense. I am alive because I am here. If you are the voyce you are the ghost and you are dead. I cannot be dead else I would not be here.
> M.M. You died in 1736. I read this in the Parish Registers. The Vicar writes that he buried Robert Webbe, Gent. in April 1736.
> R.W. Then the good man is deceived by his eyes. Why I saw him onley today. How is this if he buried me. I must have words with him.
> M.M. I think you are a ghost and you died 250 years ago.
> R.W. You are mistaken. I am no ghoste. I am here. You frighten me.

And who do you say you are?

M.M. My name is Matthew Manning and my family live in your house.

R.W. But this I cannot understand. Where came you from? I have not sold myne house.

M.M. We bought it in 1968.

R.W. Now you jeste. It is only 1726 and you tell me tis 1968. Tis a joke. Are you a ghoulle of tomorrow? Off with you. Rob Webbe is mad. Mad. Mad.

M.M. You have talked to me before. What do you think I look like?

R.W. I hear onley this voyce in myne head. I cannot see you. But I hear this voyce for many years now and I know I go madd. Do not tell others. You are me if you are in myne head.

Note that although this takes the form of a conversation – and indeed Webbe's sentences would be more appropriate spoken than written – both sides were written by Manning himself, in two different handwritings. I will postpone consideration of the text, and concentrate first on the implications of automatic writing itself. The first and most obvious suggestion (after outright fraud or hoax) is that the messages were derived from the subconscious mind of the writer himself. This would mean that Manning's brain contained somewhere within it (at the age of 14-17 years) the following abilities:

a) To reproduce at will a large variety of handwriting styles, usually appropriate to the age, era and education of the apparent originator of the message;

b) To write in a number of foreign languages he has never been taught, or had any contact with. These include a variety of Arabic scripts 'ranging from the handwriting of a near illiterate to some calligraphic artwork' (to quote an authority who was consulted), and (when Manning was in Japan), Bonji, 'an ancient Japanese script once used long ago in the Daikaku Ji temple by the monks';

c) To produce hundreds of drawings and sketches, often at high speed, in a wide variety of styles and subjects. Many of these bear a strong resemblance to a known work by a great master or are in the style of one. (As an example, his drawing of 'The Hanging Man' on page 133 of *The Link* is virtually identical to a sketch by Leonardo da Vinci and actually includes a very close approximation to da Vinci's notes in his own 'cipher' language, which consisted of mirror writing of mediaeval Italian).

If it should be thought that too much attention is being paid to the exceptional case of Matthew Manning, I will later discuss in detail a whole series of automatic writings which is diametrically opposed in many respects[36] – that of the famous Myers-Gurney cross-correspondences. Here there were a number of recipients, mostly women, living in countries as widely separated as India and America. The apparent sources were the minds of the deceased Sir Frederic Myers (who had been a Professor in Classics at Cambridge and a founder-member of the Society for Psychical Research), and some of his erstwhile colleagues at the SPR. The analysis of the messages was carried out with great thoroughness and impartiality by his successors in the Society. Many of the communications ostensibly from Myers himself took the form of esoteric riddles and cross-references to abstruse passages in Greek mythology (on which he was a world authority), which could only be solved when texts from different recipients were compared. The apparent objective was to provide convincing proof that the messages could only have originated in the mind of Myers himself, and so prove survival of his personality after death, and the correspondences are discussed in this context in later chapters.

It seems totally unreasonable to assume that the ability to write calligraphic Arabic or mediaeval Italian (in Manning's case), or a detailed knowledge of Greek mythology (in the recipients of the Myers messages), can be acquired as a child and then forgotten, and one is forced to the conclusion that under automatic writing conditions, the writer's hand is being controlled by something external to himself, and since it is equally unreasonable to assume that a hand can be moved in such a precise way without the active cooperation of the controlling muscles, it seems inevitable to conclude that *an external agency must be operating through at least part of the writer's brain.*

This is the common factor, the thread joining these phenomena. During automatic writing the hand is being controlled by an external source; a telepathic message passes between two brains situated miles apart; an Order enters a person's mind in response to the needs of a distant stranger. In all cases it seems that there must be a communication link, an access route into the brain other than by the processes of the five physical senses, and despite the differences in circumstances between the various effects, it seems logical to assume in the first instance that this mechanism is common to all such cases.

The Radio Link

This 'sixth sense' can be studied by analogy with the 'outside line' facility shown in Figure 16, and it will be convenient to consider it in terms of a radio-telephone system, such as is installed on a

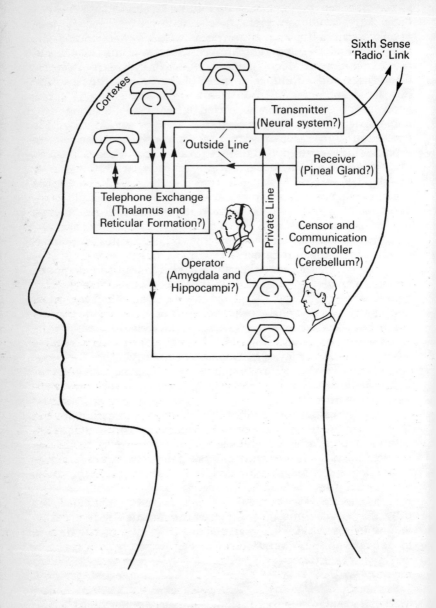

Figure 16. The 'Telephone Exchange' in the brain

cruise liner (or, in some respects, the VHF network between a Police HQ and its patrol cars). I have already identified the telephone instruments with the various cortexes of the brain, the telephone exchange with the thalamus and associated organs, and the telephone operator with the cerebellum. Before considering the situation of the 'radio equipment' I must look more closely at the communication medium itself, the 'radio waves' of our analogy.

First some technical introduction and a word of warning. The fundamental principle underlying the process of communication is the transfer of *energy* containing the information from one point (the 'transmitter') to another point (the 'receiver'), the energy travelling via some 'communication medium' such as a radio wave, or fluctuations in air pressure. Note that a random 'wandering' movement such as molecules follow in a gas or liquid, (rather like a swarm of midges), is not a 'vibration' in any real sense of the word, no matter how rapidly it is executed, nor can such movement convey information, for which energy must progress from the sending to the receiving point, and some degree of order or structure in the motion is essential. It seems futile to insist on using phrases like 'astral vibrations', endowing the word 'vibration' with mystical properties, without being able to quote a single characteristic to justify the term.

With this in mind, I can start by rejecting various similar *ad hoc* inventions such as 'thought waves', 'astral emanations' and 'psi fields', there being no evidence to support them and no recognisable characteristics to discuss other than those which require to be accounted for, thus effectively begging the question. Professor John Taylor[77] has studied a number of alternatives and reduced the contenders to one, a radio wave. Although it seems a large assumption, there seems no alternative but to begin by assuming that the communication medium is indeed some specific wavelength or band of wavelengths of e.m.r., used in a manner similar to a normal man-made radio link.

Although in my Preface I was at pains to deny that I had any particular qualification for writing this book, I think that this is one subject on which I may, with all due modesty, claim to be able to give an informed professional opinion. Discussion of the subject is of necessity rather technical, so details of my reasoning are included with other scientific and technical matters in Appendix 1. My conclusions are quite clear. After forty years in electronics, most of it spent in designing radio communication systems, all the training, knowledge and experience that I have supports the view that such a link is, even with the most optimistic assumptions, physically impossible, and this conclusion is in line with those of most of the research workers in the field.[31] Taylor, while admitting the force of many of the arguments that I advance, still insists that such a possibility is feasible, but I detect a note almost of desperation in his logic, which is apparently based on the dictum of Sherlock Holmes that 'when you have excluded the impossible, whatever remains, however improbable, must be the truth.' Such reasoning is unsafe unless it is certain that *all* possibilities have been considered, and I offer here one which seems to have escaped the notice of the Professor and other workers.

I was careful in my statement above to use the phrase 'a normal radio link'. But I have suggested in previous chapters that e.m.r. may be capable of travelling through extra dimensions, so what is the possibility of a link using such waves, but relying on this property? There are some aspects of the idea which support it. First, the 'multiple connectivity' of four-dimensional space has already been described, and shown to imply that any two points in our universe, no matter how far apart they may appear, may be almost in contact through the extra dimension. If this is so, then energy which can travel through that dimension will not necessarily get weaker when travelling over what is (to us) a long distance. Also, just as a teleported object may penetrate through a solid wall by travelling in a fourth dimension, so a fourth-dimensional link would not need to penetrate physically a barrier such as electrical screening. Such arguments support the possibility of a link of this type, but serve to emphasise the point that the operation of such a link must be predominantly extra-dimensional. If this is so, there is no point in carrying out interminable experiments to detect a radio link with all the usual characteristics. *IF* the link uses e.m.r., then it is the specifically extra-dimensional qualities of e.m.r., *in conjunction with the 'multiple-connectivity' characteristic of the fourth dimension*, which are involved, and the objections of Appendix 1 may be reconsidered with this factor in mind.

Although the energy may travel via the fourth dimension, it is reasonable to assume that it still retains other physical properties of e.m.r., and the particular characteristic I wish to use is that *a radio wave can only be radiated or received efficiently by a structure (an 'aerial system') which has at least one dimension equal to or greater than half a wavelength*. (For possible exceptions to this rule, see page 250). Taking tentatively a maximum size for such a system of about 1 cm (since anything larger would be evident in the physical structure of the brain), this suggests a maximum wavelength of the same order. On the other hand, it is unlikely that the wavelength will be shorter than that of visible light, as ultra-violet and X-rays can cause cumulative damage to human tissue. Frequencies between these limits (EHF to infra-red, See Figure 17) have a number of interesting characteristics in this context:

a) The highest frequencies used by man for communication in this sense are for the latest satellite communications systems, the so-called Ka-band. Efficient transmitters and detectors for higher frequencies have not yet been developed;

b) Roughly in the middle of the infra-red band are the waves which are emitted by any surface at about blood heat. Such waves are detected radiating from all parts of the human body (and head!) and study of them is the basis of the 'thermographic scanning' technique of medical diagnosis;

c) Any signals developed by the brain are likely to resemble such 'thermal noise', and if detected would be dismissed as being of thermal origin and so would not be investigated. (Possible methods of distinguishing between the two have been studied by the author.[72]);

d) The 'bandwidth' limitation discussed in the Appendix does not apply to such high frequencies. Almost any number of signals, each conveying complex information at high speed, could operate simultaneously without mutual interference;

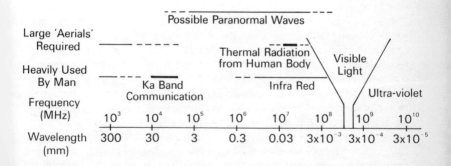

Figure 17. Suggested frequency band of the sixth-sense radio link

e) Although visible light cannot penetrate the skull, some infra-red waves can (although 'multiple connectivity' may make this unnecessary);

f) Such wavelengths are commensurate with their being generated and detected by structures about the size of small neural assemblies, or chains of large molecules. The detector system is likely to be electro-chemical in action (rather than purely electronic), possibly similar in principle to the 'rods and cones' on the retina of the back of the eye.

But Where Is The Radio Equipment?

The last point leads immediately to consideration of the whereabouts and nature of the brain's 'radio equipment' (Transmitter and Receiver). Gooch raises a very interesting point:

> . . . [the cerebellum] did once, in our pre-mammalian past, possess its own eyes. The additional pair of eyes was located on top of the head. In the course of further evolution, these eyes sank down into the brain, fused together, and became our pineal gland . . . The ancient Hindus, at any rate, referred to the pineal gland as 'the third eye'; and as such it is known to present-day mysticism.[23]

According to my medical dictionary, the *pineal gland or body* is:

> . . . A small protrusion from the centre of the brain [see Fig. 14]. Its function in man is not known. The pineal body has evolved from a primitive central eye. In a few reptiles it still responds to light . . . There is some evidence in mammals that chemicals concerned with *transmitting impulses in the brain* are formed in the pineal body. Descartes insisted that the soul resided in the pineal body. [My italics]

The *tuatara*, a lizard-like reptile of New Zealand, is one of the oldest species of animal still extant, having remained virtually unchanged for over 200 million years. Its equivalent to the pineal gland is a cavity high on the forehead, covered with a semi-transparent skin thickened to form a kind of lens. Its function is not yet fully understood, but the pit viper has two pit-like organs below its nostrils which are sensitive to a change in temperature of less than 0.6 °C and which it uses to 'home in' onto the body temperature of its prey. It is not unreasonable to suggest that the pineal gland in the tuatara may serve a similar function.

In higher mammals, including man, the neocortex has grown over the front of the organ, which has therefore sunk nearer to the centre of the brain. Nonetheless, one might reasonably suggest that some of its component parts still retain functions similar to parts of the eye, which, operating in conjunction with the visual cortexes, is capable of receiving and analysing a pattern of light, shade and colour conveying a large amount of information at quite a high speed.

This is very definitely food for thought. Here we have an organ which originated as an eye, but which over the millenia of evolution has sunk to a position where it is useless for that purpose. It was originally responsive to infra-red e.m.r. (a first-class communication medium for some purposes). It has not atrophied, but is still involved in communication within the brain, where it is very closely associated with an organ containing or controlling the subconscious personality. Its actual function is unknown, but it is traditionally associated with mystic powers and paranormal abilities. Is it too much to see the pineal gland as containing our 'radio equipment'?

It is technically feasible that a communication link could operate into and out of the human brain, the 'transmitter' and 'receiver' being situated somewhere in the limbic system, and using frequencies somewhere in the infra-red, or low infra-red bands. For long-range and extra-dimensional communication the waves would need to travel entirely or predominantly through the fourth dimension.

Tuning In To Another Brain

So, despite my homily on the misuse of the concept of 'vibrations', and my denial of the possibility of paranormal communication by a 'radio link' in the normal sense (neither of which do I withdraw), I am being dragged, almost unwillingly, into assuming that the sixth-sense link uses e.m.r., but in an abnormal way. It may be helpful, therefore, to consider further some aspects of radio technology (if only as an instructive analogy), beginning by examining the process by which a radio receiver distinguishes the 'wanted' signal from all the other signals which are received by its aerial.

It may not be generally understood that the electrons in any metal object, be it the chassis of a car, the girders in a bridge, or a wire fence, are continually 'receiving' (in the sense that they are responding to) countless radio signals originating over a large area of the globe and over a very wide range of frequencies. An aerial used for radio, TV or radar reception differs only in that its shape, size, position, etc., are designed to be inefficient in receiving most of these, and to transfer most effectively to the circuits of the receiver those signals which lie within a limited band of frequencies and/or which arrive from a specific direction. This rejection process is continued progressively in successive stages of the receiver circuits until, ideally, only the single 'wanted' signal remains. One could imagine the receiving mechanism in the brain carrying out a similar process of successive rejection and refinement, but with a very important reservation in the analogy. In a radio receiver, the tuning process by which we select the wanted signal is in almost all cases a matter of frequency, since the 'carrier wave' of each separate signal is (in principle) oscillating at a different rate. For the very high frequencies that I have suggested, such a process becomes infinitely more difficult, requiring the generation of extremely stable and accurately-controlled reference frequencies, which must be varied in order to select a specific signal. To the best of my knowledge, there is no evidence for such processes within the brain.

Theoretically, there are possible alternatives. I have perfunctorily studied a hypothetical link using techniques vaguely comparable to the known 'spread spectrum' principles, based on the idea that individual neural pulses in the brain modulate noncoherent thermal noise sources (as distinct from sine wave carriers).[72] The reception process could be remotely akin to holography. Such a system would seem to be marginally possible, but in my opinion extremely unlikely. The theory is very technical and is well beyond the scope of this book.

Despite the lack of evidence on the mechanism by which selection is achieved, some such function is necessary, and it is possible to suggest some of the factors which control it. To begin with there must be a 'coarse' selection process limiting the species of the sources that any one individual may contact (there is little point in having access to the cortex of a Patagonian anteater, and the animal would probably agree). Then it would seem that the process is heavily biased in favour of relatives and friends, those with similar social, ethnic and religious backgrounds (a point discussed in more detail later), and so on. There is obviously a strong emotional element also, with love, pain, grief, danger and the trauma of death considerably increasing the possibility of contact, then there is the pronounced tendency to contact someone who occupied the same space at some time past. Note one very interesting point, that most of these 'selection factors' (including the advantage of 'psychic sensitivity') seem to operate equally well *at either end of the link* – unlike radio communication, in which there is little that can be done at the transmitter to direct energy to a particular receiver (other than to project the signal in that general direction).

What About The Power Supply?

If our communication link involves the transfer of energy in any form (and I cannot envisage one which does not), there are two consequences:

a) The 'transmitter' and 'receiver' mechanisms will require a local source of energy on which to operate, and will absorb power from that source while they are operating;

b) The receiving system (or 'detector') will have an 'energy threshold', a minimum level of received signal energy below which communication will be inaccurate, unreliable or impossible. This threshold will be set by the 'thermal noise' generated by the random movement of electrons in the material of the detector, by noise-like signals from other sources, or by the reception of unwanted signals. The received signal must be strong enough to overcome all these three.

Paragraph (a) should not be confused with the effect discussed in Chapter 5, which studied the energy necessary to move or distort an object. What is under discussion now is the energy which seems to be withdrawn from the person experiencing a paranormal event, even a purely mental one. I am suggesting that much of this energy may be accounted for by the need to supply the power for the 'communication equipment' of the brain's extra-dimensional link. Any energy used in this way must be supplied by the body and so its excessive use will cause physical tiredness, just as a student will feel exhausted after sitting a stiff examination. This effect is fully accepted by spiritualists; many mediums comment on the mental and physical tiredness that they feel after a successful session. It is quite possible that, in addition to the causes of psychic sensitivity previously discussed, a psychically active person may possess an unusually powerful 'transmitter' which draws heavily on the energy of the body. Lyall Watson writes:

> Hereward Carrington, one of the old 'trouble shooters' of psychical research, described the condition of a psychokinetic subject at the end of her session as 'weak, drawn, nauseated, deeply lined about the face, physically and mentally ill – a broken shrivelled old woman'. He also noted that her expenditure of nervous energy was greatest when there were strangers present and her fear of failure, and therefore her degree of conflict, were also high.[84]

Manning describes in his books how he could feel this psychic energy building up in him, particularly if he was worried or exasperated, and he would use automatic writing as a means of dissipating it harmlessly and preventing poltergeist phenomena. A good writing session would exhaust the energy for several days, and he experienced no major phenomena for several months after his meeting with Webbe's apparition. He also tells how he could prolong or increase his psychic ability by drawing on the mental energy of cooperative friends, and a similar technique of concentrating the mental resources of helpers is commonly used by the 'psychic surgeons' of the Spiritist movement in Brazil.[66]

Interference And Jamming

Paragraph (b) above also has some interesting implications. The phenomenon of 'interference' or 'jamming' of signals is an all-too-familiar phenomenon in radio communication, consisting of the receipt of unwanted signals (accidental in the first case, deliberate in the second) mixed up with the wanted signal. The practical consequence is to raise the detector threshold, i.e., a larger signal is needed for satisfactory communication. Since we have no knowledge of how or under what circumstances the brain 'transmits', it is quite feasible that any particular link must compete with many others, and it is equally feasible that 'negative thoughts' – deliberate or accidental mental opposition to the communication – will act as jamming signals, requiring greater transmitter power or higher receiver sensitivity in order to overcome them, as is suggested by Carrington and many others.

The 'sceptic effect' is very well recognised in many branches of psychic research. Even the earliest workers noted that a spiritualist medium or clairvoyant who regularly achieved notable successes, was likely to fail miserably under test conditions in front of a critical investigating committee. This, to the sceptics, simply confirmed their suspicions that the claims were fraudulent, and this attitude is still prevalent, despite the many investigations which have proved that the effect is quite real, and very powerful.[16] Among the best-known of such reports is that by the American psychologist Dr Gertrude Schmeidler who asked the participants in her investigations into telepathy to fill in a questionnaire, one section of which dealt with their own opinions as to the possibility of ESP. Those who believed that ESP was possible she called the 'sheep', and those who were convinced it was impossible, the 'goats', and the results showed that the 'sheep' scored much higher successes than the 'goats' (and indeed the goats showed a tendency towards 'negative success', as if deliberately trying not to support telepathy!). This effect is not limited to the opinions of the participants themselves, but also to those conducting the tests, their assistants, and possibly even non-participating on-lookers. It seems that sceptical or over-critical opinions in the mind of anyone concerned can set up a background of 'interfering signals' which makes paranormal communication less effective and more prone to error.

A further complication in the concept was demonstrated in the tests carried out by G.W. Fisk on clairvoyance.[39] One of the procedures used was to send to each participant a card in an opaque and sealed envelope. The card would be marked with a clock face, showing a time selected from tables of random numbers, and the objective of the would-be clairvoyant was to 'guess' the time illustrated. The success rate was high, and then, as a variant, Fisk had half the cards prepared by Dr D.J. West, Research Officer of the SPR and a noted sceptic and 'psi-inhibitor'. The scores on the cards prepared by West (a fact not divulged to the participants) were notably poorer. As a second example, Inglis discusses:

. . . a report in the *Journal of Parapsychology* in 1973. A girl who had volunteered to prepare symbols for a clairvoyant test happened to be keeping notes of how she was feeling. At one stage of the work she had just received a note turning down her application for a job; at the same time she was suffering from a cold, and associated aches, so that she found it difficult to concentrate on what she was doing. When the trial was completed, although the overall results were negative there was a strong correlation between her moods and her subject's scoring rates.

The new factor in these two cases is that the jamming apparently caused by the 'negative thoughts' of West and the girl operated at a time when they were not involved, and were probably unaware that any attempt at communication was being made. Either there was a 'time shift', the thoughts at the time the cards were being prepared having an effect a few days later, or the effects of those thoughts in some way clung to the cards themselves. The first theory is investigated in more detail in Chapter 9, and the second, which is obviously relevant to the claim for Psychometry, discussed on page 213.

CHAPTER 9

THE INVISIBLE THREADS

'No man is an Island, entire of itself; every man is a piece of the Continent, a part of the main.'
John Donne

In view of the origins of the pineal gland, it seems hardly necessary to emphasise that the communication terminal under discussion is assumed to exist in some form within the brain of *every human being and animal*. Sir Alister Hardy, Fellow of the Royal Society and one-time Professor of Zoology at Oxford, remarks:

> It would seem to me surprising indeed if such an attribute [telepathy] were confined to just one species of animal . . . For me, at any rate, one interest in telepathy lies in the possibility that it may give a clue to a more fundamental biological principle.[31]

He goes on to point out that the assumption of telepathic communication between animals of the same species could explain much that is puzzling in the behaviour of animal groups and social insects such as ants and bees. The sensitivity of dogs to psychic phenomena has already been noted, and it is possible that the close rapport between dog and man may be due in part to one-way telepathy between them. I recall an old Sussex countryman recounting to me how his dog became restless and uneasy as a woman and her ten-year-old son (strangers to the district) approached the top of the lane leading to his cottage, and hysterical and uncontrollable when they reached his gate, so that he had to send them away without learning their errand. It was only some days later that he was told by a neighbour that the boy was mentally disturbed and had strong sadistic tendencies towards animals.

If psychic ability in animals is accepted, it follows that similar abilities in man are far more fundamental than is normally thought. The scientists witnessing the Toronto tests referred to on page 112 included Dr Joel L. Whitton MD, Consultant Psychiatrist at the Toronto Hospital. In their report the following passage occurs:

> The origin of the ramp function (and therefore the source of the psychic energy) in Matthew was found to be in the oldest part of the human brain; Dr Whitton suggests that psychic ability or energy is not a 'random gift' or a 'space-age ability', but an innate function and ability in homo sapiens that probably goes back to the earliest history of man . . .

This idea is supported by the many well authenticated cases of telepathy in so-called 'primitive' races such as the Australian aborigine, the Bushman of the Kalahari and many native tribes of central Africa in which the ability is accepted as a perfectly normal function. The absence of the equivalent strong and consistent telepathic ability in modern man can be accounted for by a factor previously noted in the description of the brain, that the neocortex of homo sapiens has grown at an enormous rate in a relatively short time (in evolutionary terms). Koestler writes:

> According to the theories of Paul MacLean, which are finding growing support among neurophysiologists, the unprecedently rapid growth in the course of the last five hundred thousand years of the human neocortex resulted in faulty co-ordination between this philogenetically new acquisition – the 'thinking cap' which governs rational thought – and the archaic structures of the brain, which we share with reptiles and lower mammals . . . [78]

Watson quotes Sir Alister Hardy as arguing that:

> . . . the development of language, important as it was for man, is unlikely to have produced extra-sensory perception as well, and . . . it might have had the opposite effect. Language undoubtedly assisted the growth of reason, the exchange of ideas, the initiation and spread of new inventions, and the enlargement of our cerebral cortex, but it might have repressed a more primitive form of knowing in favour of the more precise communication possible in a spoken system. [84]

It seems that the loss of telepathic and other paranormal powers may have been the price that humanity had to pay in order to be able to discuss abstract ideas with each other (as distinct from merely conveying facts, emotions or intentions). Many a proud dog owner has boasted that 'he seems to be able to read my mind', without considering why he himself is unable to carry out the

133

reverse process. The answer may be quite simple – he can talk but the dog cannot!

The occurrence of sporadic and limited telepathy between humans suggests that the loss may not be complete or irreversible; the requisite organs are apparently still there and functioning, but their operation is controlled by the censor mechanism. In most people the action of the censor is normally effective, although it may occasionally be weakened or bypassed by a number of factors such as illness, strong emotions such as love and fear, physical fatigue and so on. In a few it seems to be abnormally weak and more easily overcome, and such people may be able to respond psychically to the emotions of others. In some cases the censor may be capable of being deliberately and consciously controlled by the owner or by a hypnotist. There are some clues as to why these large differences in sensitivity occur. One of the most positive is found in another passage in Bander's Preface (see page 112). He refers to a questionnaire which was answered by all the psychics who took part in the Toronto experiments:

> Their answers to questions about personal experiences in early childhood showed several of the psychics had one experience in common. . . . [it was] that they had all suffered a severe electric shock before the age of ten. Matthew did not recall any such accident; it was only when we talked about this with Matthew's parents that we learned that Matthew's mother had suffered such a severe electric shock three weeks before Matthew was born that she feared she might lose Matthew.

Watson writes:

> In 1943 Peter Hurkos fell off a ladder, fractured his skull and found that he had lost the power of concentration, but had gained a new faculty instead. When asked to assist the police of The Hague, he had only to hold the coat of a dead man to describe the man's murderer in detail that included glasses, moustache and wooden leg.[84]

Similarly, Mrs Eunice Beattie began her career as an eminent psychic when, as a schoolgirl, the brakes on her bicycle failed and she was thrown into a brick wall, causing her to spend several weeks in hospital. There are many such references in the literature to the association of psychic ability with physical damage to the skull or its contents.

The implication that such ability may be induced by damage to the brain is inescapable, and to me (speaking from experience) there is an obvious analogy with a type of fault found in modern electronic equipment employing the technique of 'printed circuit boards', in which the interconnections between components consist of a network of very fine copper tracks deposited on a fibreglass panel. The spacing between such tracks may be as small as a few thousandths of an inch, and a minor defect in the production process or careless work by a technician may leave a 'whisker' of copper or solder bridging (or almost bridging) the gap between two tracks. In many cases, such a fault is intermittent, connection being made or broken in a random way, actuated by vibration, changes of temperature or supply voltage, and so on. When seen in the light of the structure of the brain, with its myriad of neural connections between cortexes, the mechanism of this type of fault is startlingly reminiscent of some symptoms of psychic ability.

It would be quite wrong to deduce from this that psychically able people are necessarily mad or mentally unstable. Certainly the mechanism could account for some of the symptoms of epilepsy, schizophrenia, hallucinatory tendencies and wildly irrational behaviour, and it is not unkind to psychics to note that many of them have suffered from mental breakdown in later life. But the brain is a wonderfully adaptable organ and many of us have quirks of individuality which could originate in similar processes in less critical areas of the brain.

Another View

However, although the more extreme cases of psychic sensitivity may be caused by some form of brain damage or abnormality, there is very strong evidence that some degree of paranormal ability is present in many people who have never had a psychic experience. A number of laboratory investigations into ESP (mostly telepathy and PK) are reviewed by Eysenck and Sargent.[16] These sought to relate ESP ability to sex, race, circumstances and character. The results fully support the 'sheep and goats' effect, and indicate that psychic ability is indeed related to such factors, but in highly complex ways which have yet to be clarified.

One very interesting facet of this work is the discovery that extrovert, socially active people tend to score higher in ESP trials than introvert 'loners'. It is known that the latter have a tendency to 'worry', and this generates a high background of brain activity. This supports the idea of 'jamming' of the extra-dimensional communication link by 'noise' generated locally in the brain itself, reducing psychic sensitivity.

There is in any case a serious weakness in the 'brain damage' theory. One would expect a single 'wrong connection', whether permanent or sporadic, to produce a specific effect each time it occurs. In fact, while each psychic tends to have his own 'speciality' (such as telepathy, psychometry or physical mediumship) this is often accompanied by a general sensitivity to a much broader spectrum of phenomena. The idea that a 'brain fault' bypasses a specific function of the censor would be misleading, and a more consistent picture is that in a sensitive person the censor mechanism as a whole is weaker, more prone to error, or more easily circumvented. This may possibly be due to weaknesses in the brain structure at specific points, due to the stresses induced by the rapid development of the neocortex. Despite these criticisms of the 'wrong connection' idea, it is still valid to discuss psychic sensitivity in terms of a tendency to allow forbidden information to reach the neocortex.

A Communicator's Nightmare

But if paranormal functions were present in the brain in the early animals, why was it necessary for them to be suppressed by evolution in the development of Homo sapiens? To tackle this question we must look again at our analogy with radio. The communication system which is the part of our sixth sense outside the skull does not operate as a simple telephone network does, with a separate and individual link between two subscribers, but much more like radio, in which each transmitter may be, quite unknowingly, 'broadcasting' thoughts and impressions which may, or may not be picked up equally unintentionally by another individual. Despite weaknesses in the analogy (such as my inability to offer ideas on the brain's selection system), it offers us a simple and specific model which should help us to envisage the problem. Just as any receiving aerial is (electrically speaking) floating in an infinitely complex sea of electromagnetic waves, both man-made and natural, deliberate and accidental, so we must regard the extra-dimensional side of our brains as being under constant bombardment by impressions and emotions generated by countless living things, and it follows that many of the mental impressions that we experience may be due to the 'background noise and interference' picked up by our sixth sense. Prof. H.H. Price writes:

> It is a plausible guess that many of our everyday thoughts and emotions are telepathic or partly telepathic in origin, but are not

recognised to be so because they are so much distorted and mixed with other mental contents in crossing the threshold of consciousness.[69]

This line of thought reaches its logical limit in the theory advanced by Henri Louis Bergson, which is best summarised in two quotations. Professor C.D. Broad writes:

. . . we should do well to consider much more seriously than we have been hitherto inclined the type of thing which Bergson put forward in connection with memory and sense perception. The suggestion is that the function of the brain and the nervous system and sense organs is in the main *eliminative* and not productive. Each person is at each moment capable of remembering all that has ever happened to him and of perceiving everything that is happening anywhere in the universe. The function of the brain and nervous system is to protect us from being overwhelmed and confused by this mass of largely useless and irrelevant knowledge, by shutting out most of what we would otherwise perceive and remember at any moment and leaving only that very small and special selection which is likely to be practically useful.[8]

Koestler, discussing the same Bergson hypothesis, writes:

In this hypothesis the brain acts as a protective filter for consciousness. Life would be impossible if we were to pay attention to the millions of stimuli constantly bombarding our senses . . . On our hypothesis, this filtering and computing arrangement at the same time shields us from the buzzing multitude of *extra*-sensory messages, images and impressions floating around in the psychic aether in which part of our individual consciousness is immersed.[78] [Koestler's italics]

It is quite clear from these comments that as the ability to communicate increased with the development of language, some such mechanism as the censor would be absolutely necessary to prevent the verbalising cortexes – in use almost continuously for normal communication and thought – from being swamped by an incredible amount of unnecessary information. The only alternative would be to allow the sixth sense communication organs to atrophy altogether, which would have involved the total loss of all psychic powers, and with them the very useful facilities they may provide in an emergency.

There is an evident parallel between Bergson's Theory, and the concept of the 'collective unconscious' advanced by Jung, which suggests that there is a pool of common mental activity and experience which is in some way shared by all living minds. It may be drawn on during sleep to provide material for dreams, presumably by-passing the censor in the process. This awesome concept is not just a metaphysical hypothesis. It not only has elements – tenuous and imaginative but not entirely imaginary – drawn from the physical sciences, but it would also seem to be supported by modern work in psychology and neurology.

Where Do We Keep Our Memories?

Bergson's Theory is reflected in some of the modern research on the location of memory within the brain. Penfield carried out experiments on patients undergoing open-brain surgery (which may be done under local anaesthetic).[5,43] Various areas of the exposed brain were stimulated by an electrode carrying a weak electric current, which produced reactions characteristic of the function of the stimulated cortex. Touching a motor cortex caused twitching of muscles, touching a visual cortex caused the patient to 'see' flashes of light or swirling colours, and so on. Stimulation of the hippocampus (see Fig. 14 on page 90) produced:

> . . . not mere fragments of movement or sensation. They were whole episodes of existence, plucked from the patient's previous life. The person would suddenly be transported into the past and would feel himself eavesdropping on a familiar scene.

This could be interpreted as showing that the hippocampus 'contains' the memories, but Watson disproves this. He writes:

> Epileptic patients are sometimes treated by surgically removing the entire temporal lobe. After the operation (which destroys the hippocampus), their IQ levels remain the same, they remember their past, their profession and their relatives, but they cannot hold new information for more than a short while. Articles may be read and understood, then completely forgotten; the death of a relative causes grief, but an hour later the news is lost and, if asked about the person in question, the patient will say he was fine the last time they had word of him. Without a hippocampus there are no fits it is true, but neither are there any new memories nor any dreams . . .
>
> One of the main stumbling blocks to any theory [of memory] that relies only on a static change in a particular nerve cell, is the difficulty of explaining why this localised memory is not altered by extensive brain damage . . . Huge sections of brain can be destroyed without the loss of any particular memories. There are records of brains extensively damaged by trauma, by tumours, by loss of circulation, by injury and old age. They may lose the ability to make judgements or to learn new things, they may lose physical sensation

or become profoundly psychologically disturbed, but the memory of past experience usually remains intact . . . There seems absolutely no evidence to suggest that memories are stored in any special part of the brain – or anywhere else in the body.[82]

So let us follow the clue suggested by Watson, and assume that the long-term memories are not held in the brain, but in some location or form accessible via the sixth sense. The hippocampus would then contain a part of the system controlling recording of memories but not their recall. Brian Inglis remarks:

> All Wilder Penfield's work on the human brain – half a century's work, which had won him an international reputation – had been based, he recalled at the end of his life, on the assumption that the mind is completely dependent on the brain, and had in fact been designed to confirm that proposition; but 'all of them had proved the exact opposite'.[40]

Note that such an extra-dimensional memory store would not be subject to the limitations of memory capacity discussed in the next chapter. This concept can be taken even farther. We can refer back to Gooch's hint on page 111 that the subconscious mind also may not be contained within the physical brain. Although the concept of a subconscious mind, repressed and separated by 'gates' from the conscious, has been accepted for practically a hundred years, even the most modern research has been unable to identify any one particular organ as the location of the subconscious itself. Combining Bergson's and Jung's theories with the idea of a sixth sense communicating with 'the unknown' leads inevitably to the idea that human memory and the subconscious mind may be part of that unknown, existing only at the other end of the link – a breathtaking concept indeed!

Summary

The picture emerging from the whole of this discussion is of a brain organised in three departments – rather like a factory or department store (and the list should be compared with the functions described on page 89):

1) The autonomous functions are the 'service and maintenance' department, responsible for keeping the building and machinery in good running order;
2) The neocortex (the 'conscious mind') includes the executive staff, carrying out routine day-to-day operations, assessing and

responding to the physical situation in the vicinity of the body, maintaining supplies of food and other essentials, and planning and carrying out fundamental activities such as procreation and self-defence;

3) The 'subconscious mind' is the 'Head Office', situated remotely and in contact only through a sixth sense link. Its 'local manager' is the Communication Controller (see Figure 16, p. 122), who manages the brain functions by his orders to the Telephone Operator. Head Office keeps all the files of past transactions (i.e., the memory) and is the only department which is fully informed as to the organisation, purpose, objective and future policy of the whole entity. It is in continuous communication with other entities but is well aware of the limitations of the physical part of the organism and so does its best to protect the 'staff' – other than the Controller – from knowledge of things which do not concern them and which may upset them. One factor which is particularly regarded as 'Confidential Information' is the true nature of the individual, and its relationship with the universe.

The last point is the vital one. Bergson's, Jung's and similar theories put the brain censor in a different light, dispelling any idea that it can be considered as a minor quirk of evolution, an *ad hoc* development to reduce the load on the neocortex and so leave the space required for language. Read in the light of the discussions in this book, they specifically suggest that the 'self' operates fundamentally in four dimensions, and the censor has evolved simply because the three-dimensional part of man is mentally and spiritually unable to cope with such a complex existence so early in his evolution. He must be protected from the infinity of knowledge which may ultimately be available to him, until such time as he has developed the required mental and spiritual capacity to handle it. The censor mechanism may be the only protection we have against being all-seeing and all-knowing, a God-like state for which we are patently unsuited and of which we are obviously unworthy.

CHAPTER 10

CAN THE EVER-ROLLING STREAM FLOW UPHILL?

'For tribal man space was the uncontrollable mystery. For technological man it is time that occupies the same role.'
Marshall McLuhan

The preceding chapters have concentrated on the possible consequences of a fourth spatial dimension, conveniently postponing consideration of the second possibility listed on page 65, that time itself (or something closely related to it*) may be another dimension. So, if two minds can be in contact by means of a telepathic link through a fourth dimension, is such communication also possible over a difference in time? There is some evidence, but the wide variation in circumstances can be confusing, and it is necessary to proceed circumspectly, clarifying concepts as they arise.

Many people have experienced the phenomenon usually referred to as *déjà vu*, a feeling that one has previously 'lived through' a particular episode now being experienced. Psychologists have produced a number of more-or-less convincing explanations for many of these, but there are some episodes, often involving dreams, which are less easily explained. I have heard at least three such accounts from friends and relatives, but in keeping with my policy of using only published reports, let me quote the one given by Tom Lethbridge.[50] He recounts how in 1964 he was visited at his house in East Devon by a BBC film crew to shoot a film for a TV documentary. The cameraman arrived first, and was astounded to find that he was thoroughly familiar with the house and its surroundings, having dreamt about it on five separate occasions

---

* For brevity, the precautionary phrase will be omitted in future discussion, but it should not be forgotten that a true spatial dimension will consist of time multiplied by a velocity (of light?).

(although neither he nor any of his relatives had ever been near the area). From the changes that he saw in the buildings from those in his dreams, it was possible to establish reasonably accurately that his 'memory' of the place dated from about 1929, about the time that he was born. It is possible to suggest several theories to explain this event, but the one I advance in this chapter is that in his dreams the cameraman was, for some unknown reason, in telepathic contact over a time slip with someone actually living in the house in 1929.

Reincarnation

Another phenomenon which may be associated with this type of *déjà vu* is that of 'regression under hypnotism', in which a hypnotist guides the subject back into his past, so that he experiences and describes in detail 'forgotten' episodes of his childhood. The process may be continued until the subject relives the trauma of his own birth (as discussed with reference to Primal Therapy on page 106). The explanation usually offered is that the hypnotist is controlling the gates to the subject's long-term memory and allowing deeply-buried experiences to rise to the conscious level. However, there is a bizarre extension of regression, which cannot be accommodated in this explanation. Here the subject is apparently regressed into a period *before he was conceived*, and describes episodes in a 'previous life'. Many of such cases have been reported, such as the famous case of Bridey Murphy in America.* A number were investigated by Jeffrey Iverson[42] for BBC TV. A particularly fascinating case was that of Jane Evans, a Welsh housewife and 'a lively and intelligent young woman' who was regressed by the hypnotist Arnold Bloxham into six different past lives, including one as a young Jewess living in York in the twelfth century, which ended in her murder in anti-Semitic riots, and another as a young servant living in the house of a French nobleman in the fifteenth century.

Another aspect of the subject is thoroughly explored in the

---

* After the Bridey Murphy book had proved a best-seller, the case was apparently explained in natural terms by an investigating team from another publisher. This report was itself questioned by an independent investigation, which suggested that it had been motivated more by commercial advantage than by a desire for truth. As so often happens in such cases, the first occasion was given great publicity and virtually closed the subject, while the second passed almost unnoticed.

books by the psychiatrist Arthur Guirdham,[26,27] in which he describes a fascinating and convincing case of apparent 'group reincarnation'. Over a period of years a young woman (a patient of Guirdham's) experienced dreams, 'memories' and compulsions by which she was able to build up a very complete and detailed picture of her 'previous life' as a member of the Cathar religious fraternity in the Languedoc area of France in the 13th century. Not only that, but she recognised Guirdham himself as one of her companions at the time and on visiting the area he also was involved in similar 'memories'. The accuracy of her recollections was confirmed by French historians, and in many cases she added to their knowledge, giving new details which were confirmed by later research. As time went on, a number of other people were involved, all of whom had apparently been members of the same sect at that time. Colin Wilson comments:

> . . . [Guirdham's story] presents a problem for the total sceptic, who is inclined to dismiss the whole thing as self-delusion or downright lies. Arthur Guirdham is an intelligent man; this was plain to me from his books, before I met him; if he is inventing the whole thing, why should he go out of his way to make this story unbelievable?[87]

Attempts to explain such accounts in terms of imaginative embroidery of stories read or heard as a child (as in the case of Bridey Murphy), or 'merely' telepathy between the subject and some hypothetical living historian who is the ultimate expert on the period in question, fail dismally to be convincing. Professor Ian Stevenson, of the University of Virginia, an acknowledged authority on cases of apparent reincarnation, is quoted by Watson as saying:

> ' . . . all of the cases I have investigated so far have some flaws, many of them serious ones. Neither any single case nor all of the investigated cases together offer anything like proof of reincarnation. They provide instead a body of *evidence suggestive of reincarnation* . . . To accommodate authentic cases of the reincarnation type that are rich in detailed statements and in unusual behaviour shown by the subject, with the hypothesis of super-extra-sensory perception, requires the extension of that hypothesis so that *it becomes no more credible than that of survival after death.*'[83] [My italics]

So Stevenson is prepared to consider, at least tentatively and in the absence of any better, the idea of reincarnation, the concept that some time after death the soul, personality or some identifiable and unique part of an individual enters into a new human life and is 'born again'. The relevant factor is that whatever is passed on must take with it all the long-term memories of its old life. These remain more-or-less permanently buried in the subconscious mind of the new one, only to be released by the hypnotist's control of the gates between the subconscious and the conscious mind, or by some damage or degeneration of the brain.

I confess to considerable difficulty in accepting this, mainly (surprisingly enough) on practical grounds. The first point is that there would seem to be no purpose, no evolutionary advantage, in retaining for an indefinite period the accumulated memories of life after life, normally totally disused and forgotten. Secondly, it implies that the subconscious must contain the complete memories of several lifetimes; all the sights ever seen, the sounds ever heard, the words ever spoken, the emotions ever experienced. Whatever the storage mechanism may be, whether physical, chemical, electro-chemical or molecular structure, it must have a finite capacity and that limit must ultimately be reached. Thirdly, and thinking on similar lines, it is often a source of wonder that the blue-print of the complete physical structure and personality of a human being can be carried in the DNA molecules of a single cell (male sperm or female ovum). How, then, can we accept that *within the same cell* is stored in addition the huge quantity of information I have listed above. It is logically and aesthetically unsatisfying to think of such a fundamental function of living things (for why should animals be denied the same process?) with such profound philosophical implications, remaining virtually unused and undetected for generation after generation, and being limited by simple physical factors such as memory capacity.

A Possible Explanation

While the theory previously advanced that the memory is external to the brain avoids the problem of a limited capacity, it does not address the explanation of inherited memories, which needs a different approach. One could argue that, if telepathy between two separate minds is possible with a time slip in the link, then why should it not be possible for a mind to communicate *with itself as it was at some time in the past*? In other words, the source of the mental images experienced by someone regressed into his youth could be his own long-term memory, but could equally well be his own conscious mind as it was on the previous occasion, contacted via a telepathic link through the time dimension. Similarly, apparent reincarnation could be accounted for in terms of one-way telepathy between a living consciousness and the mind of someone who is literally living in the past, and who may, but need not, be related to the experient by birth or in any other way.

This idea is supported to some extent by the nature of most of such communications. Unlike the Heywood/Vivian case, there is no evidence whatever that the source knows that he is dead, or attempts to deliberately convey a message. He is apparently totally unaware that the contact is taking place. Rather, the person being regressed actually 'lives through' the sensory experiences of the source *as if they were his own*. In effect, the sensory experiences of the source in the past are fed into the brain of the experient in the present in a way reminiscent in some respects to that occurring between a hypnotist and his subject – as if the 'dead' mind were hypnotising the live one through a time-slipped link.

Now apply a similar line of reasoning to the 'conversation' in automatic writing between Manning and Webbe (see page 119). Manning makes no mention of any sense of communication or 'presence' at any time (and indeed, if the occasion was typical of most such sessions, he was not aware of the sense of the messages while he was writing Webbe's words), so that it would seem totally unnecessary to imagine an invisible ghost of Webbe leaning over his shoulder and reading the words. It is far more likely that Manning's action in writing his own messages was a convenient way of verbalising them in his mind and so evading the censor. The verbalised messages could then be transmitted over time via the extra-dimensional link, to be received telepathically by a living Webbe as 'a voyce in myne hedde' or pseudo-speech. The reverse link, from Webbe to Manning, is even more interesting, since, if the 18th century spelling and grammar are accepted at face value, the verbalising cortex of Webbe, living in 1726, was instructing Manning's motor cortex to control his hand in 1977. The only thing that the two men had in common was *that they occupied the same room* (and, as discussed later, they were probably both psychic). The situation bears all the signs of two-way telepathy between two cortexes, with a 250-year time-slip in the link in each direction, with the interesting factor that the messages one way stimulated the motor cortexes to produce writing, while those the other way resulted in pseudo-speech.

The situation when Manning and Webbe met in the bedroom was obviously more complex than automatic writing. There was no question of either controlling the other; each was apparently in full possession of his normal senses. Webbe was as aware of Manning as vice versa; he looked towards him, moved away from him and 'shook hands'. However, Webbe was an insubstantial apparition, and if we accept my previous suggestion that he was an optical projection over time, such a projection would be unable to produce physical sound. It seems most likely, then, that the voice 'heard' by Manning was pseudo-speech received telepathically from the living Webbe over a time-slipped link, and attributed to his image as described on page 96. This idea is supported by the fact that Manning's younger sister, straining her ears in the next room, could hear his voice, and a rapping 'as though someone was banging on the radiator' but no second voice.*

Similarly, Webbe's image would not be able to hear Manning's voice, and I presume that the speech would again be transmitted directly from Manning's cortex to that of Webbe, over a time-slipped link, to be heard by Webbe as pseudo-speech in the same way. Manning's use of his voice merely served to help evade the censor, as described above for writing. One has only to assume that the image of Manning was projected through time to Webbe's bedroom to envisage a totally symmetrical situation, with Manning appearing to Webbe as a ghost just as much as vice versa, as shown in Figure 18.

Then, combining this concept with the text of the automatic writing, it is not difficult to imagine poor Robert, standing in his own bedroom in 1726 and daydreaming. He has for some time been subject to uncomfortable and inexplicable experiences ('I hear this voyce for many years now . . .'), holding imaginary conversations with people who do not exist, and seeing shadowy figures around his house. Now, the bedroom door opens and a young man comes in. Following a rather weird conversation, he pulls himself together with a start, and finds himself alone, but later he finds in his coat pocket a doll's wooden clog. (The clog is a major problem which I will deal with in the next chapter.)

Putting Life Into A Ghost

The implication from all this is that it is quite probable that Webbe himself was psychically sensitive, and that a complex and extreme paranormal event of this nature requires such abilities on both ends of the extra-dimensional link. There certainly seems to have

---

* The rapping, presumably of Webbe's stick on the floor, could be explained as an admirable illustration of an object travelling in an extra dimension and producing a real impact noise in our three-dimensional world, as described on page 73.

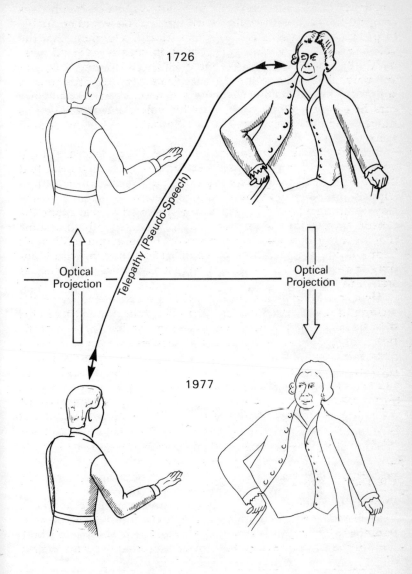

Figure 18. *Situation when Manning met Webbe's apparition*

been more than a passive acceptance of casual and accidental contact between them. Manning writes:

> The more I thought about it, the more convinced I became that Webbe's 'spirit' was some kind of incandescent light. A bulb will only light up when connected to a source of electricity, like a battery, and I came to the conclusion that I was the battery for Robert Webbe. I could not help thinking how he had looked wax-like and lifeless, until I had spoken to him. He had almost come back to life then.

One could theorise that an image may, on account of the psychic ability of its originator, be projected forward or backwards in time to an arbitrary period, but will remain there, undetected and unseen, or as a 'wax-like and lifeless image', unless there is a psychically sensitive person in the vicinity, who is not only capable of sensing its presence, but also of setting up the two-way mental contact with its originating neocortex and so 'bringing it to life'.

That term takes on a rather macabre meaning in another episode described by Manning, which could be interpreted in the same way as an 'image projection with telepathic contact'. It happened not to Matthew, but to his father, Derek Manning, who awoke in the middle of the night to find himself apparently 'inside the body' of another person, presumably Robert Webbe. He was looking out through Webbe's open mouth, with teeth silhouetted against the light. He could hear the rasp of the stubble on Webbe's unshaven chin against the pillow (even though he himself kept absolutely still), and he could feel a tingling sensation in his lower right leg – and Webbe suffered severely from gout. The important point for my present analysis is that he was sleeping in Webbe's room, and the layout was such that the bed must have been in the same position as in Webbe's day. As far as can be determined, his body was occupying the same point in space that Webbe had occupied nightly for many years. Then, following the same line of argument as Matthew's meeting, the 'optical image' of Webbe, projected forward in time, occupied the same physical space as Derek Manning (not an impossible hypothesis – note how Matthew's hand passed through Webbe's apparition; see also Appendix 4). At the same time, the sensory impressions received by Webbe (hearing his own whiskers on the pillow, feeling the pain in his leg) were transferred via the extra-dimensional link to the father's cortex, to become indistinguishable from his own sensations.

A word of warning; there seem to be two distinct categories of time-slipped mental contact. The first includes *déjà vu*, dreams and false memories. Such experiences are strictly temporary, and if the experient is not hypnotised or asleep, he retains his own identity. In the second, which includes regression, apparent reincarnation and the important phenomenon of 'possession', he actually takes on the characteristics and 'lives the life' of another person for a period ranging from minutes to months, or even indefinitely. One case as typical as any is that of Tony and the rabbi described in Chapter 13. Colin Wilson[89] discusses a number of such cases, including some in which a newly-born baby 'took over' all the characteristics of a person who had died, including his long-term memory, personal characteristics and even traces of body scars and birthmarks.

Objects Through Time

I have considered the cases of mental contact through space and time, and movements of objects through space. The next logical question is: is there any evidence in the phenomena discussed so far to suggest that objects may also move in time? There are certainly some pointers. Many of the apports reported by Manning were identifiable as originating in the past. The book pages were dated to the 18th century (Webbe's own time), the loaf was about 70 years old, the cigarette packet was a pre-war brand, and so on. Manning suggests that the objects may all have disappeared from the house at various times in the past, and then have reappeared in the present. One interesting factor which recurs in a number of accounts is that an apport which has mysteriously 'appeared from nowhere' has a habit of disappearing equally mysteriously some hours, days or months later (see pages 77 and 166).

It seems likely, therefore, that movement of objects through time may be possible; suggesting a parallel between apports (travelling in time but not in space) and teleports (travelling in space but not time). There is a notable similarity with mental communications in that either space or time dimensions may be crossed, although it is worth noting that occasions on which both dimensions are simultaneously involved seem much more rare.

Into The Future

Disturbing and controversial as the above discussions may be, there is a yet more contentious problem: the possible involvement of future events in paranormal occurrences; the possibility that time is on a par with spatial dimensions in being symmetrical about our 'real' world (see page 253). Dunne's accounts and the work described by Vaughan support the idea; Minkowsky's Continuum is identical for positive and negative time; and reports of predictions and premonitions by psychics and others appear by the hundred. If the symmetrical situation between Manning and Webbe in the bedroom is accepted as described, then Manning was seeing an apparition from the past, *but Webbe was seeing one from the future*, and indeed he refers to Manning in exactly those terms in the automatic writing session quoted. In 1863, Mrs Sarah Hall reported to the SPR that she was sitting in her dining room with her husband and two friends when all four of them distinctly saw an apparition of Sarah herself in a spotted dress, standing by a sideboard. She bought a dress of that pattern several years later.

Modern reports of sightings of a 'ghost of the future' seem rare, but Tom Lethbridge quotes a case from his own experience.[50] His house in Dorset was well known in the village for being haunted by a 'red lady', with many reported sightings dating from the period around 1916. The lady herself (habitually dressed in red, a resident in the village and well identifiable from the descriptions) visited him frequently from 1968 onwards 'in the flesh'. It is probably relevant that she was a psychic with a strong belief in 'astral projection' or 'Out-of-Body Experiences' (see Chapter 11) and claimed to have experienced them on many occasions.

There is evidence of a less anecdotal nature in a number of well-controlled investigations into telepathy which suggest that the information received may be anticipatory. Among the first and best-known are the experiments carried out by Dr Soal in 1927-9.[36] These were in the form of standard card-reading procedures, in which the percipient tries to identify which of a number of different cards is being studied by the 'sender'. The results were not conclusive, but were none the less published as such. Several years later, at the suggestion of Whately Carrington, the *same results* were analysed again, but this time with reference to the card before or after the current one. The results were startling:*

> . . . he was rewarded by the surprising discovery that two of his percipients had all the time been making significant scores. But not on the target card. One, a Mr Shackleton, had been scoring on the

---

* A suggestion that Soal may have 'massaged his data' was later publicly retracted.[11] In any event it does not invalidate this discussion, which refers to results published some years previously.

card immediately after it – precognitively. The other, a Mrs Stewart, had been doing the same thing on the cards both before and after.

The results of Soal's experiments, and others since, support to a considerable extent Dunne's idea that time is symmetrical, since telepathy of both past and future events has been demonstrated. In such experiments the time intervals involved were of the order of a few minutes or hours, but anecdotal evidence (some well supported) of precognition of weeks or months occur in many accounts by psychics, while Vaughan suggests the possibility of precognition up to several years, particularly in predicting events on anniversaries.

Reviewing The Situation

So where has this reasoning led me? If one is prepared to accept even the remotest possibility that a fourth spatial dimension exists, then there is mathematical and scientific evidence, and much paranormal evidence, to support that assumption. Then one must also accept the consequences that must follow, such as fourth-dimensional energy, apports, teleports and the consequences of 'multiple connectivity', the abolition of our accepted ideas of distance.

But for every phenomenon which apparently involves a fourth spatial dimension, there is *evidence for* (not 'proof of') an equivalent phenomenon in time. The ultimate problem is that if one accepts a similarity between time and a spatial dimension, one is faced with the idea of symmetrical time, that future and past are equivalent. By now the problems of conceptualisation are enormous, and it is frighteningly obvious that if there is any reality at all in such arguments, then man's view of his own universe is laughably inadequate. All one can fall back on is the dictum of Haldane's that 'the universe is not only more queer than we think, it is probably more queer than we *can* think'; or my own conviction that 'the fact that we cannot imagine it does not prove it untrue'.

And we have not finished our exploration yet!

CHAPTER 11

IF I AM IN HERE, WHO'S THAT OUT THERE?

'Man is to himself the most wonderful thing in nature; for he cannot conceive what the body is, still less what the mind is, and least of all how a body should be united to a mind.'
Blaise Pascal

The concepts developed in the previous pages shatter to pieces the whole idea of man as a bag of biological bits, self-contained and self-controlled. Instead, they visualise an individual body, complete with its senses and a neocortex to control and interpret them, as one terminal of a fantastic network of interconnecting links to other such terminals; that network encompassing the whole of life itself, present, past and future. Between the consciousness of each individual and the incomprehensible complexity of the network is the filtering process, maintaining sanity and preventing access to 'unauthorised knowledge' by blocking all information not required for survival, unless it is evaded by subterfuge, rendered ineffective by damage, or overwhelmed by emotion or trauma. For this picture to be convincing in physical terms, one must also assume that the communication links themselves employ a sixth sense which operates over the extra dimensions.

But if every material object has a shape in the fourth dimension, unseen by us, this must include the human body and brain, and paranormal events may occur as a result. There is a class of event which seems to offer some evidence on this subject: I am referring to the so-called Out-of-Body Experiences (abbreviated to OBE).

Let me begin with a simple case already described. In his account of his meeting with Webbe (see page 96), Manning describes how he sometimes felt 'outside himself', observing the scene from a separate viewpoint. He does not comment on any feeling of fear, surprise or frustration; it was simply as if his eyes were detached from his body and had moved to a different place in the room, but remained attached and operational through some invisible 'nerve fibre'. From that place he could observe his own body (including, presumably, his eyes!), and that body retained all its other faculties of speech, balance, movement, and so on, and remained the seat of his consciousness.

There are hundreds of such cases recorded, many of them far more complex, impressive and inexplicable than Manning's. One of those accepted as 'classic', and quoted by both Hampe and Puharich,[28,70] is the precise and detailed report of his 'death', given by Sir Auckland Geddes (a doctor) to the Royal Medical Society. He was alone in his bedroom when he developed acute gastro-enteritis and rapidly became too weak to summon help, but he continued to monitor, calmly and professionally, his own symptoms:

> My consciousness seemed not at all affected, the whole time. But I suddenly noticed that this consciousness was detaching itself from another one, which was also situated inside me. In order to describe it better, let us call it the A and B consciousness. In everything that follows my self was bound to the A consciousness. I noticed that the B personality belonged to my body. As my physical condition continued to deteriorate, and my heart hardly beat any more, I realised that the B consciousness belonging to my body was beginning to show signs of a complex make-up, that is to say it consisted of physical feelings deriving from the head, the heart and the viscera. These components took on an independent form and the B consciousness began to crumble, whereas the A consciousness, which was now myself, seemed to be completely outside my body, which I was able to see. I gradually realised that I was not only able to see my body and the bed on which I was lying; I could also see everything in the house and garden; and then I noticed that not only could I see things at home – I could see things in London or Scotland too, wherever my attention was directed . . . I then saw how the doctor was called . . . and I was brought back to life. I was very unwilling . . . I returned reluctantly to my body. And when I was back again, the clarity of the vision immediately disappeared. I had just a glimmer of consciousness still, shot through with pain.

The Journal of the SPR records many other cases, including that of an Army officer who was driving a scout car loaded with ammunition when it received a direct hit from a German anti-tank shell. He was blown over the hedge, and he describes vividly how, a fraction of a second later, a conscious, thinking 'he' hovered in the air watching with cold detachment his own body with hair and clothes aflame, rolling on the ground in terror and pain.

Puharich[70] also describes in detail the case of a man who experimented with glue-sniffing (inhaling ethyl ether and other solvents) and became addicted, experiencing some weird hallucinations under its effect. After a while he found that many such experiences could be initiated without solvents, but merely by an effort of will under semi-trance conditions. He found that he could will himself to leave his body (which he could see below him), float through the air, and fly (or tunnel through the earth) to places, sometimes of his own choice, and sometimes unknown. Such accounts could easily be dismissed as hallucinations caused by brain damage from the solvent vapours, but some incidents are more difficult to explain. On one occasion he 'willed himself' to fly to the house of a friend, who he believed to be ill in bed. As he approached the house (over a hill-top) he saw his friend and his wife walking towards the garage. He tried to talk to them, but they seemed unaware of his presence. On his return from his 'trip', he telephoned his friend, to find that he was feeling much better and had just been for a short car journey with his wife. He confirmed that they had set out at the time and in the clothing in which he had seen them. There are similar accounts in Carlos Castaneda's descriptions of the effects of mescalin.[9]

Controlled experiments have been carried out by Charles Tart[63] on a young girl who claimed that she frequently experienced OBE events. In the experiments she slept on a low couch, and was connected to EEG recording apparatus by wires (which also prevented her from raising her head appreciably). Several feet above her head was a shelf on which there was a piece of paper carrying a six-figure number (facing upwards). She was asked to try to read the number in her sleep and on the third such experiment she succeeded.

In another experiment,[83] Tart suggested to a deeply hypnotised patient that he was walking out of the room, out of the building, into the building and entering the room again. The hypnotised man, sitting all the time on a chair in the middle of the room, described accurately the whole of the journey, including events going on outside. Finally, he described the room as seen from the viewpoint of the doorway, including himself sitting in the chair. Furthermore, he insisted that *he himself was in both places simultaneously, and that there was nothing noteworthy or contradictory in that fact*.

There are a number of accounts of deliberate or accidental OBEs in books written by people who claim psychic ability, and at least one book is dedicated entirely to a description and discussion of all aspects of the phenomenon, written from the point of view of someone who claims to have experienced it frequently. Sylvan Muldoon claims to have had his first experience of an OBE at the age of twelve, and to have developed the ability to indulge in it almost at will. He says:

> Astral projection is not a gift to a chosen few; every living soul has latent forces at his disposal which merely require the proper manipulation. A prevalent idea is that one who is capable of projecting is one who is gifted with a peculiarly abnormal astral entity, much different from his fellow-beings; but I assure you that the physical body plays as important a part in the phenomenon as does the astral, and usually the abnormality is not existent in the astral body but in the physical body.[57]

He describes the exact process by which the two bodies separate, and then retain communication through an 'elastic cord' between the two heads. He defines two distinct ranges of separation:

> 'Cord-activity range'. Up to eight to fifteen feet – depending on the state of physical health. Within this range the cord exerts a physical force trying to pull together the two bodies, and reduces in diameter with increasing range from about half an inch at close ranges to the thickness of a fine wire at the limit. Movement of the astral body is at walking speed with the subject fully aware.
>   'Distant-point Projection'. Movement is 'at the speed of light' with the subject unconscious, becoming conscious at the destination. The cord remains at a constant diameter but must remain intact or death results. Distance and intervening barriers are no limitation.

Despite the thorough and apparently explicit descriptions, and the fact that many of the details (such as the 'silver cord') are confirmed in other references, perhaps it would be unwise to rely too much on a single book of this nature, particularly since it does not seem to have generated a vogue for Astral Body Flying Clubs at any time during the fifty years or more since it was first printed.

Sir Alister Hardy analyses 3000 cases of reports of spiritual or quasi-religious experiences, of which 179 (about 6 per cent) involved apparent OBE. In virtually all cases, as in those quoted above, the main characteristic of the 'floating body' (which I shall call the 'Detached Entity' or DE; Puharich calls it a 'Mobile Centre of Consciousness') is that it could *see*, and in particular it could see the abandoned body (referred to here as the 'Parent Body', 'Physical Body' or PB). Hardy writes:

When a person has the sensation of being outside his or her own body, their abandoned body appears to the person to be 'clearly seen' from a point some little distance away and often above the body left behind. It is because these cases involve the apparent seeing of the body that we class them among the visual experiences, and yet the eyes that are said 'to see' the body cannot, of course, be the physical eyes of the body itself; and this brings us to the most remarkable feature of so many of these surprising descriptions which are so consistent with one another, and so numerous, that they can no longer be dismissed as unworthy of serious consideration. It is this – the conviction of the person concerned that while the 'discarded' body is seen to have every appearance of reality, he or she has the feeling of being in a second body identical with the other and *equally real*; it is this aspect of the phenomenon which has been held by some to support the belief that there is a so-called 'astral' non-material body which is an exact duplicate of the physical one, and further that it is this 'astral body' which leaves the physical body at death.[32] [Hardy's italics]

Defining And 'Explaining' OBEs

The work of Hardy, Tart and many others, together with accounts from those who have experienced an OBE, allow one to propose, somewhat tentatively, a series of 'rules' by which it operates:

a) If the experient is psychically sensitive, he is often in a trance or semi-trance state, or, as in Manning's case, in what one could call 'a state of advanced psychical awareness';

b) If the experient is not normally sensitive he is often in a semi-coma (seriously injured or ill), or asleep (sometimes in a 'hypnagogic state' halfway between sleep and wakefulness), or hypnotised;

c) There is no feeling of fear, alarm, confusion or abnormality of any kind. The subject is often fully aware that his 'conscious mind' is handling sensory information from two distinct entities separated in space, but accepts this as quite normal;

d) Despite (c), the total sensory capability of the 'whole person' remains fixed; if the DE can see, the PB is blind; if the DE can move, the PB remains immobile, and so on. I will refer to this very important characteristic as the 'Total Capability Limitation'.

As a first attempt to 'explain' OBEs, consider an analogy. Let me return for the moment to our little bug on his pond. Near to him, a heron is standing on one leg, its neck outstretched above the water, where its single pair of eyes can see the whole of the bug's environment and its own. The bug 'sees' the bird as a single circular obstruction (where its leg enters the water), and, having no concept of the shape of the bird in the third dimension, he cannot possibly understand that even if he moves some distance from that obstruction, a pair of eyes which are part of the same object may be just above his head. There is a problem with this analogy, in that it is difficult to conceive of 'sight' without the image-forming mechanism (of lens and retina) of an eye, and Hardy makes the specific point that the physical eyes remain in the PB, but visual images are seen from the point of view of the DE. Hardy and others are quite emphatic that this is not only typical, one could say it was essential. The first suggestion is obviously a complete duplicate pair of eyes. Then if there is only a single visual cortex to interpret the images from both sources, the censor mechanism in the brain must select which of them controls the cortex and so provides the image 'seen' by the conscious mind.

One could suggest a minor variation on the same idea, noting that since we have no knowledge of the shape of an object in the fourth dimension, the eyes themselves may be extended. Nonetheless, it is probably easier to visualise some kind of connection (something like the 'elastic cord') joining the real to the extra-dimensional, than the concept of the organs being 'stretched' extra-dimensionally, and at our present state of ignorance, and by my present standard of speculation, the two suggestions are equivalent.

Seeing Through Time

A suggestion already made is applicable to the discussion; the idea that time is another extra dimension, so that if the astral body may travel in four-dimensional space, it may also be capable of travelling in time. This leads to some fascinating possibilities as to the 'explanation' of some cases of retrocognition: seeing events which have happened in the past, such as Mrs Heywood's experience on the Great Dyke, a prehistoric structure, of being 'surrounded by busy skin-clad figures'.[35] A more complex case, but with distinct similarities, is that of the 'Versailles Ghosts' described by 'Miss Morison and Miss Lamont' (pseudonyms for Miss Moberley and Miss Jourdain).[58] Although their accounts have been criticised[41] there is sufficient doubt, and sufficient similarity to the less complex cases, to use it as an example, and some details of the report make it of particular interest in the present context.

The two ladies, exploring Versailles for the first time on a very hot day in 1901, lost their way and seemed for a matter of several minutes to have travelled back in time to the late 18th century. They saw, spoke to, were seen by, and addressed by a number of people who they later 'identified' as Marie Antoinette, etc. Some of the experiences were shared by both ladies while others were sensed by one or the other.

'Explaining' this in my terms, the DEs of both ladies were simultaneously extended back over about a hundred years of time (remaining coincident with their physical bodies in space), and 'reported back' the sensory information received (sometimes incompletely and incorrectly), while their physical selves maintained normal contact, walking and talking in a desultory way. They describe a feeling of detachment, of 'walking in my sleep'. There were no effects of light and shade, and 'even the trees . . . seem to have become flat and lifeless'. Such an impression can be explained by reference to the 'total capability limitation', which implies that when one cortex has to deal with information from two different sources, it must exercise some form of priority. Normally, the information from the physical senses will be preferred, since that from the DE must run the gauntlet of the censor mechanism. In this case, real and astral eyes were at the same point in space and so saw similar scenes, but with minor variations caused by the passage of time, and this would be very confusing for the 'selection' system, but a large degree of rationalisation could have been achieved by rejecting most of the detailed information of light and shade from either or both sources. It makes sense that under such circumstances the sense of a dual identity would be absent.

The fact that the apparitions they saw reacted to the two ladies in a normal fashion, and some conversation was exchanged, leads to a symmetrical situation not unlike the Manning/Webbe meeting, the two ladies communicating with each other by normal speech, but hearing the 'ghosts' by pseudo-speech (see page 146). The implication is that on a very hot afternoon near the end of the 18th century, Marie Antoinette and some members of her staff (one or more of whom may have been psychic) may have been rather perturbed by the intrusion of a couple of rather strange middle-aged ladies. Both of the ladies had previously experienced minor psychic events, some similar in essence to the Versailles episode, but they had nothing in common with the French Queen other than what Manning had with Webbe – they occupied the same position in space but at different times.

'Precognition', the ability to foresee the future, has already been described, and where this takes the form of a 'vision', it is possible that such cases may also be attributable to an OBE.

Clairvoyance

In such cases, the paranormal information is quite specifically interpreted by the visual cortexes: the experient 'sees' visions. There are other phenomena in which sensory information is gathered from a distance by apparently paranormal means, but differ from more conventional OBEs in that the information simply comes in to the mind from an unknown source. How far such phenomena can be attributed to an astral body is very debatable, but there are some hints. An effect which may be considered in these terms is Clairvoyance, in which the experient reads messages or identifies objects in closed boxes or sealed envelopes, where the circumstances are such that he could not know the contents. This has been studied in the laboratory in 'double blind' experiments (in which no-one knows the correct answers until the results are analysed), and it seems to show characteristics similar to telepathy itself.[16] There are also many recorded instances of spontaneous clairvoyance. The relevant factor is that from what I have concluded of extra dimensions, the concept of 'size', in a three-dimensional sense, no longer applies, so that the DE may, in principle, penetrate into very small enclosed spaces, and physical barriers need present no obstacle.

Other Senses

If the eyes can be extended extra-dimensionally, resulting in a 'true OBE' as described, can we find evidence of other organs being extended in a similar way? There have been a number of investigations on people with abnormal senses, such as the young girl who, while heavily blindfolded, could read a book held close to her nose or her left ear, *and could smell with her chin and the back of her foot*.[88] Hyperaesthesia is an abnormally acute sensitivity of one or more of the senses, such as the ability to hear conversations through the separation of two or three rooms with solid walls. Sceptics sometimes quote the phenomenon as an explanation of telepathy, in cases such as Sir Gilbert Murray, who, to entertain his friends, would leave the room for a time, then return to identify (often amazingly successfully) a complete quotation, or a scene or a person, decided on in his absence.[36]

Then again, the 'glue sniffer' investigated by Puharich reported some weird experiences. He found that when he was in a semi-trance he could develop 'imaginary' limbs which he could deliberately manipulate while at the same time his 'real' arms and legs were quite visible. The extra limbs appeared semi-transparent and he could push them through the floor, and yet he could feel the sawdust and loose nails on the sub-floor. One could easily dismiss these as hallucinations, but it is worth noting that the 'total capability limitation' applied, in that while he was moving his extra arms, the real ones were folded immobile across his chest. One would have imagined that a' true hallucination would have been more likely to provide him with four movable arms. It is also worth noting that while a person is dreaming, the muscles of his limbs are 'paralysed'. Could the motor cortexes be in use operating 'imaginary' limbs?

Dowsing

A phenomenon not usually associated with OBEs is Divining or Dowsing ('Water-witching' in the USA). This has a long and respectable history, and is often omitted from studies of the paranormal, although it is not explainable in physical terms (if we ignore vague references to 'magnetic earth currents', whatever they may be). The mystery of dowsing is multiplied a million-fold in the case of Map Dowsing, or Distance Dowsing, in which the position of underground water, oil or mineral is pin-pointed on a map or sketch plan at a range of several thousand miles! If this claim is dismissed as ludicrous, the opinion of Major General Scott Elliott ex-President of the British Society of Dowsers and an experienced geologist and archaeologist, is worth noting:

I believe the trained and qualified dowser 'knows' the answers to his questions in his mind. How this is done and how it works I do not know. One has to face up to the fact that most of the dowser's work is near miraculous in relation to present day knowledge and physical ability.

For myself I am prepared to accept this and get on with the work of using this ability for good and useful purposes. Personally, I do not believe we shall know how dowsing works until very much more is known about the workings of the Mind in general.[15]

This view is supported by the fact that many professional dowsers (and some psychics such as Uri Geller) work for large oil prospecting and mineral mining organisations – often for large fees – and the list of practical successes is impressive.

One could follow a similar argument to that used for clair-voyance, and suggest that 'astral eyes' could be extended to search for an underground stream, a lost ring, or dead body. Distance dowsing would then be only slightly more complex, the dowser guiding the DE by reference to the map or sketch. It seems logical that where direct communication of information between the DE and the neocortex is impractical for any reason, the information can be transformed into a symbolic or mechanical form (by affecting a pendulum or dowsing rods) in order to bypass the censor, as discussed on page 109.

But which of the senses could be used to identify iron ore, oil-bearing shale or water-bearing strata, or to provide an accurate estimate of the flow in gallons per day of an underground stream? One wonders in how many cases these abilities are possessed by the parent brain! Dowsing is an enigma, in that it is arguably the commonest, most accepted and least 'supernatural' of the phenomena discussed in this book, and yet if it works to the extent that Elliot and others claim, it is among the most puzzling. It is amazing that no serious large-scale scientific study has been made of it.

Psychokinesis

In applying the idea of an astral body to such phenomena as Clairvoyance and Divining, the roving DE is envisaged as simply observing, gathering information, and feeding it back to the parent body, but in the very important case of Psychokinesis (abbreviated to PK), physical forces are applied at a distance from the person apparently controlling them. So is it possible that a DE may produce a physical effect? After all, it is assumed to have 'astral limbs' and presumably 'astral muscles' to move them. All that seems necessary is a means by which that force may be applied across a fourth-dimension gap, and this could be as follows.

All objects have a fourth dimension, and this may be large enough to extend from this world into the world of the astral body. If so, it will be real in that world also, and so can be grasped and moved, the 'whole' object, in all dimensions, moving together (as the cane in Fig. 13 moves in the two-dimensional world of the bug). Such a mechanism could explain the ability of some people to levitate objects (furniture, etc.) without touching them, to influence the fall of a die to favour a particular score, or even to influence electronic counters (although this again implies that the

DE has knowledge and abilities that the complete body and mind apparently lacks).

One of the outstanding performers in controlled PK experiments is the Russian woman Nelya Mikhailova, who can cause matches, glass tumblers or pieces of bread to move across a table.[84] She has been very fully investigated over a number of years, and her most famous feat was carried out under close observation by cameras and while she was attached to EEG and ECG recording equipment. An egg was broken into a salt solution in a glass tank about six feet from her, and then, by sheer concentration and with every move recorded, she 'forced' the yolk to separate from the white. In view of earlier discussions on psychic ability, a number of factors are relevant. Firstly, at the age of fourteen she was fighting with the Red Army when she was seriously injured by artillery fire, and while recovering in hospital she discovered her strange ability. Secondly, she found any exercise in psychokinesis exhausting. During the half hour of the 'egg' experiment, her pulse rate soared to four times its normal value, she lost over two pounds in weight, and at the end of the day she was very weak and temporarily blind. Thirdly, she had 'an unusual brain-wave pattern, with fifty times more voltage being generated at the back of the head than at the front' – and the cerebellum is at the back!

Psychokinetic forces are not always projected to a distance from the body. Combining the idea of applying a force to the fourth-dimension extension of an object, with the glue-sniffer's account of 'extra' arms and hands capable of penetrating physical barriers, provides a potential explanation for the 'spoon-bending' feats demonstrated (with a great flair for publicity) by Uri Geller, and which Manning has agreed could be quite authentic, and in his opinion not particularly noteworthy. Professor John Taylor,[77] Professor of Mathematics at Kings College, London and previously Professor of Physics at Rutgers University, New Jersey and at Southampton University, investigated Geller and went on to study a number of 'mini-Gellers', children who were able to bend wire paperclips or aluminium strips contained in an almost-sealed glass globe or a plastic tube.

PK Through Time

Continuing the exploration of all variations, we must consider the possibility that an astral body may extend through time, and exert a physical force on an object in the past or the future. One possible case already discussed can be reconsidered in this context; the meeting of Manning with the apparition of Webbe.

Manning offered Webbe a doll's wooden clog, which Webbe grabbed and put into his pocket, where Manning specifically states that it could not be seen. The clog disappeared from this world, to be found on the bed in the same room a considerable time later. From the discussion above, it seems at least a possibility that the DE of Robert Webbe was extended over the time dimension so as to be in that room with Manning, but separated by a narrow gap in the fourth dimension. When the two hands touched, Webbe grasped the fourth-dimension 'projection' of the clog and pulled it into his own time, from 1977 to the identical point in space in 1726, in the same way that I have suggested that objects may be moved by a DE operating over a distance. Manning describes his change of mental state at the instant of contact, and his own psychic ability would be sufficient for him to see Webbe's DE across the fourth-dimension gap, and hear it via telepathically-received pseudo-speech as previously described.

Elsewhere in the book, Manning taxed Webbe (via automatic writing) with the disappearance of a number of household objects, and Webbe admitted he was responsible. He also claimed that apports which appeared in the house from time to time were gifts from himself to Manning. Manning makes the very interesting point that the age of these apports suggested that they had been collected by Webbe (presumably from previous residents) during two or three limited periods in the past. I have already suggested that Webbe himself must have had psychic powers but he may only have been able to effect such transfers if there was a second source of psychic power in the house at that time. Again this raises the suggestion that difficult effects such as apports need a supply of psychic energy on both sides of the dimensional barrier.

Identical Twins?

By the time one has considered extended sight, and the ability of 'astral muscles' to apply a force, one must ask whether the astral body is indeed, as Muldoon and others claim, a complete duplicate of the physical body, but with the additional capability of extra-dimensional travel. It would presumably normally coincide with the real one in the three-dimensional world, and when it is exteriorised would be extra-dimensional and so invisible to the normal eye. However, by my previous reasoning, it could be seen by anyone with heightened psychic powers, or when conditions force the censor to allow the information through to the visual cortex. This would include the 'owner' himself, as in the Manning/Webbe encounter on page 96. This effect could account for the legends of the 'Doppelgänger', one's own wraith, in German mythology.

My instinct suggests that the concept of the 'silver cord' joining the two should be retained, since complete separation of the two bodies, even in four-dimensional space, seems very hard to swallow in view of the mental 'double identity' required (see below). I also have an aversion to accepting the idea of a *complete* duplicate of the physical body. It is difficult for me to envisage astral warts, bunions, cancers, digestive and excretory organs, and if the astral body is such a complete organism in itself, then why is it agreed by all authorities on the subject that communication must be maintained between the two, otherwise death occurs? I prefer an argument which suggests that the astral body and the physical one are two similar but not identical parts of a single person, and there is a line of reasoning which supports this. To begin with, since all parts of the body are assumed to have a 'thickness' in the fourth dimension, in a world very close to our own the astral must appear almost identical to the physical. But then, since we have no logical basis for knowing the shape of any object in the fourth dimension, some organs may be thicker in that dimension than others. It follows that as the viewpoint travels further in the fourth dimension, the shape of the body may change, losing those characteristics which are 'short', retaining others which are 'long', and possibly gaining others which do not extend into 'our' world (cf. Fig. 12, p.80). It only remains to suggest that 'physical' organs have a very small fourth dimension, while 'astral' organs are those which may extend a long way extra-dimensionally. By this reasoning, the distinction between real and astral bodies may be more a question of degree than of kind.

So, despite assurances that the astral body is a duplicate of the physical one, it seems more logical to assume that the PB and the DE have different characteristics, provided that it is implicit that the division is somewhat arbitrary. From the accounts of OBE and similar experiences, one can compile tentative lists of those organs and functions which *tend to be extended* extra-dimensionally, and those which are normally retained in the PB. There is evidence for the following:

164

Part of the Physical Body:
The physical, material body, with any physical defects.
The organs of breathing, digestion and others directly associated with the maintenance of physical life.
The brain functions controlling those organs (i.e., the 'autonomic functions'. See page 89.).
The control of the movement of the physical body and limbs.
The sense organs of taste, smell, touch, pain and discomfort, and hearing by sound waves.
Most emotions (including fear) and value-judgements, (but see page 178).

Part of the Detached Entity:
The sense of sight.
The sense of hearing *by pseudo-speech only* (cf. Moody[56] page 52).
An 'astral body' similar in form to the PB, required to contain and carry those functions.
The control of the 'astral body' and 'astral limbs'.
The ability to think logically and consecutively.
The identity, or feeling of 'self'.
The long-term memory.

The functions of the neocortex seem to be shared between the two, and capable of serving either, but not both simultaneously.

Vague, sweeping and contentious as these lists may be, it is interesting to compare them with the divisions of the brain functions on page 139, and the organisation of the brain on page 89. Other aspects, discussed in subsequent chapters, consider the separation of the astral and physical entities at the time of death, and the spiritualist concept of life after death.

Limitations Of The Astral Body

So, pursuing the idea of an astral body bearing at least a nominal resemblance to its physical counterpart, there arises a very important question. If the two are so similar, to what extent may the former replace or simulate the latter, appearing to others or carrying out physical activities at a distant point? A possible answer may be approached by considering again the analogy of the water-bug and the heron. Suppose the bird bends forward until its beak enters the water. Now the bug sees two separate objects, but has no way of understanding that they are two parts of the same body. Note: two *different* parts. The same part of the bird cannot be in two places at once (and I suggest that this is a fundamental law applying to universes of any number of dimensions). Now apply this idea to the astral body. If it extended to a distance and then re-entered the physical world, it would then exist as a physical entity, complete in itself in the real world, yet part of a distant physical body which was itself complete. In effect, the original body would have duplicated itself within its own universe – like an amoeba splitting, except that the process is reversible. This seems an unreasonable supposition, besides contradicting the Total Capability Limitation. It seems to me to be very probable that, while an astral body may approach very closely to any point in our own world, it cannot re-enter it.

Artificial Mediumship

In discussing physical phenomena involving real objects (whether attributable to astral bodies or otherwise), one must take into account an extremely significant discovery which has been made independently at several research establishments during the last few years. Reports have been published describing how a number of 'normal' people (i.e., none of whom claimed or showed psychic ability) deliberately set out to produce paranormal physical phenomena. After a few months of meetings and group sessions they were able to duplicate many effects previously believed to be limited to psychically gifted physical mediums. The number and status of these reports, and the detailed descriptions and analyses of the effects observed, render any accusation of deliberate hoaxing or self-deception of very doubtful validity. As an example, Watson discusses the work of Kenneth Batcheldor, head of the Psychology Department of a hospital near London. Working with a group of colleagues, Batcheldor found it relatively easy to produce 'paranormal' raps and bangs, and has investigated the mental conditions required:

> In the end, he and his group were able to levitate heavy tables and even a piano, without touching them at all . . . As the group became more adept, other unintended phenomena began to intrude. Small foreign objects began to fall out of nowhere like classical 'apports'. One stone four inches in diameter was sent to a London museum for analysis and never heard of again. Batcheldor got a bewildered note from museum officials saying the rock had disappeared.[83] [Cf. pages 77 and 149]

Accepting these and similar reports at their face value (as one must), the first reaction is to suggest that the whole concept of 'psychic' or 'paranormal' events is destroyed. If sane, sensible, responsible people can, merely by applying their knowledge of psychological principles, produce such phenomena, then where do the concepts of 'astral bodies' or 'etheric spirits' come into it? Indeed, in some books one comes across such opinions as: 'These effects are not paranormal, they merely demonstrate the immense and unknown powers of the subconscious mind' (or 'the power of interaction of mind and matter', or some other appropriate phrase). Such reasoning is premature and unsound, since it effectively throws out the physical baby with the psychic bathwater. Put it this way: if mental processes can cause a table weighing forty pounds to float in the air with no detectable means of support, then there are only two possible explanations:

Either (a) The Law of Gravity can be controlled by a mental process, so that it no longer operates on that table;

or (b) There is an upward force of forty pounds controlled by a mental process and being applied to that table by undetectable means.

Any attempt to explain the occurrence must opt for one or the other and must either advance a new Law of Gravity (which must account for all the known effects of the Newtonian version), or it must explain how the upward force is applied. Despite the EPR paradox, Bell's Theorem and conclusions therefrom (see page 64 and Appendix 2), 'action at a distance' in such direct and physical terms is as unacceptable today as it was to Newton's contemporaries. If minute electro-chemical or biological changes going on within a virtually totally-enclosed bone sphere can generate a strong physical force and apply it to an object some distance away without any detectable process in the intervening space, then such a process fully deserves the epithet 'paranormal', in that it is totally inexplicable by behaviourist or materialist principles. The theory of an astral body, contentious and improbable as it may be, at least offers some vestige of logical explanation.

The decisive phenomenon in this argument is the appearance of apports. I can see no manipulation of the 'powers of the mind' or any function of the subconscious capable of fabricating a solid object from thin air. If the Batcheldor report is not a stupid, mindless and short-sighted hoax, then there is a definite case for discussing the possibility that the mind may *control* events and objects in another dimension (via the astral body or by other means), and so provide a causal link between the brain and a physical event some distance away.

Batcheldor himself seems to support Muldoon's opinion. He writes:

> I think it possible that 'mediumship' is no more the prerogative of freak or abnormal personalities than is hypnotic behaviour, which was originally thought to be confined to hysterics . . . The rarity of behaviour often suggests a rare personality, but it later turns out that it is the conditions for the occurrence which are unusual.

This comment is supported by other authorities, and the opinions of many of the psychics themselves. Psychically sensitive people are not a different breed. Their abilities may be initiated and facilitated by the type of brain modification or damage previously discussed, but a major factor must be that once these powers have been recognised and exercised to any appreciable extent, the subject consciously or subconsciously learns how to control the mental attitudes and conditions that make them possible. It is also to be expected that acquisition of such ability by a non-psychic person involves careful study of the mental conditions necessary to by-pass the censor, and requires considerable mental preparation and practice. It is therefore extremely unlikely that such abilities could be acquired by a casual, diffident or sceptical approach. The few desultory experiments that I have made into Dowsing have convinced me that the effect is a very real one, and not easily explicable, but that control of it for a specific end would require considerable application and practice.

The Astral Mind

Having considered all aspects of the gathering of sensory information by an astral body, and the generation of physical effects, there is a third factor to consider. How many purely mental functions may be extended in the astral body? The list on page 165 includes the very closely-related factors of the feeling of 'self' or personal identity, and the long-term memory. This recalls the discussion in Chapter 9, suggesting that the long-term memory and the subconscious mind may be external to the body, and accessible via the sixth sense. This re-affirms the suggestion already implied, and which may now be stated more explicitly.

There is an extremely close relationship between the sixth sense, the subconscious mind and the mental attributes of the astral body. At our present level of ignorance it is impossible to advance clear-cut distinctions between the three functions, and it is possible that they are one and the same thing.

Summary

Summarising the general conclusions of this chapter; the concept of an astral body is attractive, in that it could explain many paranormal personal experiences, but it is probably less convincing in such contexts as Clairvoyance, Apports, PK and Divining. In particular, it would be a mistake to force it into explanations of cases which are open to simpler interpretation. For instance, Pop's account of the air battle (see page 98) suggests a projected vision rather than an OBE experience, and similarly, Mr Heywood's aural illusion that his wife had returned (see page 102) is far more convincingly explained as a hallucination invented by the auditory cortex in response to the simple telepathic message 'I am with you', rather than in terms of the DE from Mrs Heywood making physical sounds with the door lock and the kitchen utensils – quite apart from the fact that she presumably remained fully conscious at her meeting and the 'total capability limitation' would apply.

Similarly, it is possible that astral projection could form the basis of an explanation of many poltergeist and seance phenomena, including apports, teleports and levitation, and it would account for the close control of many such movements, as discussed by Wilson[88] and others, who describe how an object thrown by a poltergeist may turn sharply in flight to avoid being intercepted, or stop in mid-air and drift gently downwards, fragile objects coming to rest without breaking (see page 78). However, there are valid objections. In most such phenomena the 'controlling source' is not evident, and is usually unaware of the effects he is producing. The term 'PK' should be reserved for the exercise of deliberate control over a distance. Similarly, the concept of astral bodies is probably best reserved for those cases in which the experient consciously receives information or exerts a force at a distance.

What any such concept (extra-dimensional optical projection, extra-dimensional communication links or extra-dimensional extension of astral bodies) does allow is a simple categorisation of most mental paranormal phenomena according to two criteria:

a) Whether one neocortex is involved, or two;
b) Whether the extra dimension involved is spatial, or time-related.

The result is the simple table opposite, but this must not be taken too literally. It is obvious that we are far too ignorant of the phenomena and the underlying causes, to lay down hard and fast definitions. Indeed, I would suggest that the strenuous efforts that have been made in the past to distinguish between the various effects and to attempt to treat them as separable have been largely counter-productive. If the effects themselves are inexplicable, then the relationships between them must be even more so – unless they have a common origin. The essential point is that most of these phenomena breach the 'Laws of Nature' which are the foundation of materialist and behaviourist philosophies, and if only one of them in that category is incontrovertibly proven, those philosophies have been falsified and all the effects become potentially believable.

The second major point to emphasise is that all of them are explainable (at least in principle) by reasoning originating in only two assumptions:

a) This universe exists in more than three dimensions;
b) Human consciousness is normally unable to respond to more than three of them.

Table of Paranormal Events

Extra Dimension Involved	Number of Neocortexes Involved	
	ONE	TWO
Fourth (Spatial)	OBE Psychometry Clairvoyance 'Time of Death' Vision* Dowsing	Telepathy Communication with the Dead (See later) ? Pseudo-speech
Time (Backwards)	Memory Regression (Own Life) 'Ghost' Vision* Retrocognition*	*Déjà Vu* Regression (Other Lives) ? ? 'Reincarnation' Pseudo-speech
Time (Forwards)	Precognition*	? Pseudo-speech

* Can involve one or two cortexes, depending on circumstances.

CHAPTER 12

THE END OF THE BEGINNING

'Death in itself is nothing, but we fear
To be we know not what, we know not where.'
John Dryden

Of all the paranormal phenomena mentioned so far, the most
difficult to discuss dispassionately is the apparent communication
with the 'soul', 'spirit' or 'personality' or a person known to be
dead. This is the argument that makes the fur fly, in which
preconceptions, prejudices and bigotry are far more evident than
judgment or logic. It is noteworthy that the violent rejection of the
idea is a relatively new invention and peculiar to Western thinking. Elsewhere in the world, and in all 'primitive' societies, it is
largely taken for granted. Mrs Heywood writes:

> I heard not long ago of an anthropologist who asked a tribal
> medicine man whether his people believed they could speak with
> the dead. 'Of course,' said the man, as if it were as simple as
> telephoning to Brighton. 'Then why do you tell us nothing about
> it?' 'Oh. That is not the kind of thing one would talk about to white
> people.'[36]

Even in the Western world, outside the boundaries of academic
science the opposition is less frenetic and in many cases more of a
face-saving exercise. A man who has experienced paranormal
phenomena, even of a milder variety, will often flatly refuse to
acknowledge this publicly for fear of ridicule and its effect on his
professional career. Inglis tells how:

> Myers [while alive] lamented that valuable evidence had been lost
> to the SPR in this way, citing the case of a Fellow of the Royal College
> of Physicians with a striking instance of clairvoyance which he
> would not allow to be used. Scientific progress would be impos-
> sible, he agreed, if everyone behaved as he did; but he did not dare

face the risk of professional injury he would suffer if he were believed to defend 'opinions at variance with general scientific belief.'[38]

Evidently, when Science cracks the whip, Medicine, together with the other para-scientific professions, sits up and begs. Nevertheless, there is a hard core of acceptance of the reality of communication with the dead that cannot be wished away by those for whom the belief is inconvenient. They may safely (and with some justification) ridicule traditional 'old wives tales' and the proceedings at most run-of-the-mill spiritualist* seances, but the belief is well supported from personal experience by a number of men and women of undoubted probity and intelligence (as witness the books by Michael Bentine,[3,4] Rosalind Heywood,[35,36] The Revd Kennedy,[45] and Bishop James Pike,[65] to name but a few).

However, the number who are both willing and able to offer this kind of public affirmation with any degree of conviction is small. Many more nurture in their own minds the hope of survival on religious grounds, but for the majority of people the public profession of this kind of belief is irrevocably associated with superstition, crankiness or unthinking religiosity. If I am to make any sense of the rag-bag of evidence I have, I must at all costs try to avoid such dogmatic dead-ends and wish-fulfilling fantasies. I will try to stick to down-to-earth physical terms, concentrating on what, where and how, rather than why. Following the policy I have laid down, I am not going to be drawn into the question of proof of any particular event or assertion, but will take as honestly written one or two of the many published accounts, trying to use extracts which exemplify or summarise the consensus opinion of the type of level-headed author described in Chapter 1.

The first step is to clarify the problem. I have already dealt with two cases which might loosely be referred to as 'communication with the dead', and concluded that neither justifies the term. I suggested that the Webbe apparition (see page 96) used here as an example of a conventional 'ghost', was either an optical projection over time of an image of the living Webbe, or his astral body extended through time. The second case, regression into past lives under hypnotism, I suggest is achieved by one-way telepathy over

---

* The word 'spiritist' or 'spiritualist' (without a capital letter), implies one who believes in survival after death, and the practicability of communication with the dead. This belief is combined with more orthodox Christian principles in the teachings of Spiritualism and the Spiritualist Church (with capitals).

time. Now I will consider cases which will not allow this kind of interpretation.

The Heywood/'Vivian' encounter on page 95 demonstrates two-way communication between cooperative and intelligent minds which were obviously in complete spiritual and emotional accord, with no question of either controlling the other in any way. What makes the situation so totally different from either of the other phenomena is that *Vivian was fully aware that he was dead and appreciated the implications for his friend*. If the event happened as Mrs Heywood says it did, it was either a most complex and sophisticated hallucination, or existence after death is undeniable. One could argue that the whole episode was merely a natural reaction on the part of an imaginative and warm-hearted woman who has just lost a dear friend. I am sorry, but for me that simply will not wash. I regret that I have never met the lady, but I will happily bet a month's income that she is *not* a vague, fey old granny who chats to the dear departed over tea and muffins. The reader may reach his own conclusions (after, not before, having read her books). For me, I must accept the episode as written and there is no ducking the issue.

Even if the reader rejects this subjective opinion, the fundamental problem still remains, since there are very many cases in which such communications have been received by a detached and uncommitted third party. A book which illustrates this most directly and unequivocally is *A Venture in Immortality*, by the Revd David Kennedy. The author's wife Ann suffered from advanced heart disease and at the time of their marriage was given only a few months to live. However, she recovered sufficiently to live an almost normal life until she died in 1970, after 25 years of a close and happy marriage, during which David gave up his job as a consultant engineer in electronics, and was ordained in the Church of Scotland. After Ann's death he continued his ministry and the interest in spiritualism which they had shared.

Fifteen days after her death he had a sitting with a medium, Mrs Findlater, who was a stranger to him. She described to him his brother (a rear-gunner killed in the war), his father and father-in-law, who were helping 'a young lady who passed over about two weeks ago and is still too weak to communicate'. The accompanying messages included a wealth of personal details, including some items known only to Ann and which David confirmed for himself later.

Over the succeeding years, messages from Ann herself were received through a number of different mediums and provided very convincing evidence of her continued existence. Some of the best material came through Mrs Findlater, and a medium named Albert Best. The messages were astounding in their immediacy and directness, and showed that not only was she constantly with her husband and observing his minute-by-minute life, but also that, benefiting from their investigations together of the problems of psychic research, she was deliberately choosing to send messages which could not reasonably be attributed to telepathy. Of the many described in the book, two will suffice.

Communion Sunday in the Church of Scotland is a tiring day for a Minister. After about six hours of continuous services and interviews, David would come home exhausted about 4 p.m. and collapse on a couch. Ann would awaken him about 5.30 for a hasty meal and to prepare for the evening service. On the first such occasion after Ann's death (about eight weeks after it), David returned to the empty house and unwisely allowed himself to fall asleep. He was awakened by the telephone; it was Mrs Findlater calling from a town 40 miles away:

> Your wife is impressing me strongly that I have to telephone to you now. I have tried to write a letter and put off this feeling but I am being told that I must telephone you now, now. She is so insistent, yet I have no idea why. Your wife is simply saying: 'Get out now and use your old notes.' I don't know what it means but I had to do this.

David barely had time to grab the notes of an old sermon and get to the church. Three days later he was trying to wash a woollen jumper:

> I knew the general rules about washing the woollens carefully and gently in warm water and soap flakes. I'm afraid I was over indulgent with the soap flakes. Anyhow, in a short time I had the basin overflowing with soap suds in a rich lather while I squeezed away at my yellow pullover. Just then the telephone rang. Albert Best at the other end. 'Are you shampooing, I mean, not your hair, something woollen? I see lather, suds overflowing and something woollen in the basin. Your wife is saying she is watching you do this . . . [She is saying] 'Put in the black pullover while you are at it, the one with egg stains on it . . . [and] for Heaven's sake get yourself an alarm clock, and don't sleep in again at the end of the week.'

In most such cases, the recipient quite consciously 'receives a message', hearing it within the head as pseudo-speech or by other means. There is another phenomenon, often referred to as 'possession', in which this is not so; where it seems that part or all of the neocortex of the recipient is controlled by the source of the message, in a manner similar in many respects to that described by Janov as applying between a hypnotist and his subject, and having factors in common with regression (see page 142). The 'secondary personality' which controls the conscious mind may be recognisable as a specific person, sometimes one who is alive, but more often one who is known to be dead.[89] It is the latter which are of immediate interest, and in many of these cases the experient is in a condition of trance.

An explicit case I will quote as an example is described by Michael Bentine.[3] He was about fourteen years old at the time, and Neville, a thirteen-year-old Jewish friend of his, had been giving his father considerable trouble and distress by interminable arguments and rebelliousness. The old Jew came to Pop (Bentine's father) to ask his advice and Michael himself was called in to see if he could help. During the discussion, Michael's elder brother Tony came in from cricket practice and, after having a cup of tea, fell asleep on the sofa. Tony had been developing mediumship for some time, and in a few moments was in a deep trance. He suddenly addressed Neville's father in a guttural, sonorous language totally unknown to the Bentine family, and the old man replied in the same language with obvious amazement and emotion. A long discussion then ensued between the two of them, after which Tony stood up:

> ... seeming to radiate power and benevolence. With a flow of guttural and at the same time musical words, the phrases spoken in a sing-song cadence, he obviously gave the now kneeling Mr B. a blessing.

Then Tony sat down, closed his eyes and a few minutes later opened them and, rather embarrassed, began to apologise for falling asleep: he had no recollection at all of what had happened. When Neville's father (who had been weeping with emotion) had recovered, he said that the language was Hebrew, and that the character speaking to him was undoubtedly his rabbi, who had been a friend of his father's and who had died some years previously.

As I said, the implications of this event are very clear. Tony stood, spoke and reasoned exactly as the rabbi would have done in that situation. Most of the mental functions of the dead man: his memory, his reasoning, his character, verbalising, language, the lot, had taken over the equivalent functions in Tony's brain. If the account is accepted, there could not be a clearer case of the control of one cortex by another, and the factor which makes this case (and those similar to it) so startling is that the neocortex which was controlling every function of Tony's consciousness *had been physically dead for some years.*

'Merely' Telepathy?

So it seems that we can identify at least three different forms of communication from the dead:

a) The receipt of a mental message, recognisable as such, by someone who is emotionally involved and for whom the message is intended;

b) The receipt of a similar message by a detached and disinterested 'third party', the message including specific instructions that it be relayed to a specific destination;

c) 'Possession' of all or part of a neocortex by an external source which takes over some or all of its functions, with or without the cooperation of the percipient.

There seems little point at this stage in distinguishing between these cases, since the important common factor is that the message would seem to originate within the mental processes of someone known to be physically dead, but who nonetheless seems fully aware of the current situation. Hardy writes:

> Few dare to mention it for fear of being branded spiritualists, but there is in the files of the Society of Psychical Research some very remarkable evidence (I am referring to the best of the cross-correspondences) which, I believe, if examined in a court of law, would be held to demonstrate one or other of two things; either the survival of some part of a personality, or a degree of telepathy with living agents, which is quite beyond anything yet demonstrated by the experimental method and, indeed, of quite a different kind.[30]

The rational caution and reasoned reservations in such a statement are in stark contrast to the dogmatic and apoplectic reactions it may arouse, although these are somewhat mollified by mention of the word 'telepathy'. The reality of telepathy is normally hotly denied by the sceptics, but it is welcomed with open arms when offered as an alternative to accepting survival after death. Telepathy would certainly account for many of the phenomena at spiritualist seances, but there are some cases in which it is not acceptable. One such is the Myers/Gurney cross-correspondences referred to by Hardy. (See also page 190.) In some of these a message consisted of an erudite riddle only solvable by combining clues received by three different widely-separated mediums working at different times. In some cases the telepathy theory is stretched to assuming that the medium has extracted long-forgotten trivial facts from the memory of someone who was hundreds of miles away at the time, who had had no contact with the deceased or the sitters for many years, and no current interest in any of them. As an extreme case, the suggestion of telepathy (or, a favoured alternative, 'the power of the subconscious') in possession cases such as Tony and the rabbi verge on the ludicrous. In such cases the normal ploy is the Hansel/Price solution (see page 27): 'They are all lying.'

The views of Sir Alister Hardy, with reference to the cross-correspondences, may also be taken to represent the more balanced and dispassionate view on mediumship generally, while for those who have been directly involved there is no doubt. Rosalind Heywood and David Kennedy are typical in that they insist that, although they cannot claim that their own experiences constitute proof of survival in the scientific sense, they themselves have no alternative but to believe unreservedly.

What Survives?

Following my policy, then, I will assume without further argument that some kind of entity (referred to henceforward, with deliberate vagueness, as the Remote Entity, or RE) survives a human being after his or her physical death, and I shall now consider what kind of characteristics that entity may possess. From the accounts given through such messages of the 'life style' of the deceased (see Chapter 13) these include a body similar to its previous physical one, its long-term memory, emotional attachments, and so on. I will avoid much discreet hedging and equivocation if I suggest outright that these characteristics are very reminiscent indeed of those attributed to the DE in the previous chapter. So much so, that it is worth considering the possibility that the RE contacted in post-mortem communications is virtually the same thing as the DE which detaches from the body in OBE events; that the RE is no more than an astral body which is completely detached from its defunct physical body and operating independently.

There are, of course, observed differences between the cases, but these seem to be capable of being explained in terms of the differing circumstances. For example, accounts by those who have experienced OBE stress a feeling of detachment and lack of emotion, whereas the RE of a dead person seems fully able to experience emotions – as Vivian experienced happiness and freedom, and others have expressed regret or remorse. Now in an OBE event the information from the DE has to compete with that from the corresponding organs of the physical body for the control of the appropriate parts of the neocortex, in which competition the DE is handicapped by the need to overcome the control of the censor. The emotions of the physical body are normally powerful, with an immediate control of the conscious mind, so one may safely assume that corresponding reactions of the DE find it difficult to prevail, to the extent that the censor may continue to favour the physical 'emotion-centres' *even when the physical body is moribund*, resulting in a feeling of cold, emotionless detachment. On the other hand, the RE of a dead person has undisputed use of the whole of the astral neocortex (and there seems no basis for any assumption that this is limited in any way compared to its physical counterpart). This could account for the difference between the two cases, and emphasises what would be apparent in any case from deeper study, *that death removes the need for the censor mechanism, which consequently may be assumed to die with the autonomous functions in the physical body*. There may be other differences between the DE and the PB, to be discussed as they arise, but the advantages in assuming that they are the same are considerable, allowing a unified and logical approach.

The idea of an astral body which leaves the physical body at the time of death is as old as mankind itself. The *Tibetan Book of the Dead* (often referred to as the *Bardo Thödol*)[15a] is arguably one of the oldest known books, showing evidence of pre-Buddhist beliefs and having much in common with the pre-Dynastic *Egyptian Book of the Dead*. In a footnote, the translator, a Tibetan lama and scholar, states specifically:

> The *Bardo* body [which leaves the physical body at death], formed of matter in an invisible or ethereal-like state, is an exact duplicate of the human body, from which it is separated in the process of death. Retained in the *Bardo* body are the consciousness principle [similar to the Christian 'soul'] and the psychic nerve system (the counterpart, for the psychic or *Bardo* body, of the physical nerve system of the human body).

I confess that I have reservations about the concept of an 'exact duplicate' of the living body. It would seem to lead to complications, for instance, in cases where a dying person is physically deformed or disabled, or when the body was badly damaged at the time of death.

Take as examples Uncle Arthur, who lost a leg in the War, and was a martyr to gout in his other foot until he died, and poor Cousin Millie, killed in a car accident in which her body was badly burned. I am quite prepared to consider the possibility that the astral body may, at about the time of death, have extended itself into the fourth dimension and then severed the connecting cord, but if the RE is a duplicate of the living body, what shape is it now? It is hard on Uncle to have to hop about for another existence (even if he feels no pain), and it is uncomfortably gruesome to picture the disfigured body of Millie being reproduced with 'life' in it.

For guidance on this question, one must obviously refer to 'the horse's mouth' (if our astral friends will forgive the phrase) in the form of the many descriptions received via mediums of 'life on the other side'. The provisos surrounding the acceptance of such information are discussed in the next chapter, where examples are given in more detail, but anticipating a little, I quote here as typical some of the comments apparently received from Raymond Lodge, a young soldier killed in the First World War. The messages (apparently recorded verbatim), change rather bewilderingly between third person and first, as the medium either relays a message or Raymond 'speaks through him':

'My body is very similar to the one I had before. I pinch myself to see if it's real and it is, but it doesn't seem to hurt as much as when I pinched the flesh body. The internal organs don't seem constituted on the same lines as before. They can't be quite the same but to all appearances, and outwardly, they are the same as before. I can move somewhat more freely.'

'He knew a man who had lost an arm, but he has got another one. Yes, he has two arms now. He seemed as if without a limb when he first entered the astral, seemed incomplete, but after a while it got more and more complete, until he got a new one . . . When anybody's blown to pieces, it takes some time for the spirit-body to complete itself, to gather itself all in, and to be complete.'

One has the feeling at first that it is all too glib, but note how the descriptions tie in with the assumed characteristics of astral and physical bodies, in that basic physical functions such as digestion and the sensitivity to pain have been left behind.

Following the suggestion previously offered, let me assume that the physical characteristics are 'short' in the fourth dimension, while the astral characteristics are long. Then diseased cells, such as cancer, may come into the former category, and violent injury may also be limited to the physical world, so that in either case the composition and appearance of the RE are relatively unaffected. Now consider the situation immediately after a very sudden and violent death. The DE is separated rapidly from the physical body (or may even remain in 'the same place' as far as the physical world is concerned) but the communicating cord is ruptured, leaving the RE as a free agent, *but he* may be unaware of the fact*. All the physical objects around him will have their fourth dimensions, so there is no argument in favour of a major change of surroundings, and his senses are still apparently operative. Here, perhaps, is an answer to the question raised on page 98. If the vision of John the RAF pilot, seen by his sister Joan, was an optical projection, just where was his body at the time? His physical body was undoubtedly dead, drowned in his cockpit, but I suggest that his RE was detached, trying to make sense of his surroundings, *and still running with the water of the Mediterranean which had clung to it during its short 'trip' through the fourth dimension*.

Ridiculous? Of course! Until you consider this story along with the many other similar 'Time of Death' visions, hallucinations and communications. Take as a second example, and one with even more breathtaking implications, the account by Paul Brickhill in his book *The Dam Busters* of the famous bombing raid by 637 Squadron on the Moehne and Eder dams. The latter was a particularly difficult target, in a narrow steep-sided valley. Several attempts failed, then:

> Maudslay said he was going to try once more. He came slowly over the ridges, turned in at the last moment and the nose dropped sharply into the gloom as he forced her down into the valley. They saw him level out very fast, and then the spotlights flickered on to the water and closed quickly and he was tracking for the dam.
>
> His red Véry light curled up as Fuller called 'Bombs Gone!' but they must have been going too fast. The bomb hit the parapet of the dam and blew up on impact with a tremendous flash; in the glare they saw 'Z Zebra' for a moment just above the explosion. Then only blackness.
>
> Gibson said painfully, knowing it was useless: 'Henry, Henry – Hullo "Z Zebra!", are you all right?'
>
> There was no answer. He called again and, incredibly, out of the darkness a very faint voice said, 'I think so . . . Stand By.' They all heard it, Gibson and Shannon and Knight, and wondered that it was possible. After a while Gibson called again but there was no answer. Maudslay never came back.

---

* Despite hair-splitting arguments which may ensue, it is much easier to personalise such an entity and regard him as an individual, rather than insist on referring to him as 'it'.

So we have an aircraft flying at about 60 feet above the detonation of 6000 lb of high explosive on impact with a concrete wall; a tremendous blast which must have shredded everything vulnerable within a hundred yards. Half a minute or so after the explosion a voice, composed and coherent, is heard independently by three pilots over three different radio receivers. Either Maudslay had survived comparatively unhurt for that length of time – *and not only Maudslay but his radio transmitter, the generator which powered it, the engine which drove the generator, his microphone, the aerial and all the interconnecting cables* – or (my theory), those items had functioned for long enough in the Fourth Dimension for the message to go out, and the radio waves had crossed the dimensional gap to the other aircraft.

The suggestion that material objects may survive in the fourth dimension even though badly damaged in this world, is a startling one, but again there is some support, this time in reports of experiments with Kirlian Photography, which claims to photograph the 'aura' of an object. Watson writes:

> In Moscow a Kirlian machine has been used to take photographs of an intact leaf, then a third of the leaf is cut away and more photographs are taken. For a short while after part of the leaf has been removed, an image of that part remains as a 'signal', making up a complete sparkling outline of the whole original leaf.[84]

Could this also explain the statement made by 'Raymond', quoted above, that where a body has been damaged at death (such as someone 'blown to pieces') it may be reconstituted – by drawing on undamaged material still further in the fourth dimension? To illustrate this, consider an old fence post in damp ground. It will have rotted most at the level of the surface of the soil (where oxygen and moisture are both available), and remain sound above and below this level. The post may then be 'renewed' at that level by sinking it further into the ground.

It is worth noting that if, under exceptional circumstances, material could be transferred from the fourth dimension into our world in this way, it could account for some of the stories of 'miracle cures' of cripples and deformities (see, for example Watson[85]), and such miracles as the feeding of the five thousand. The idea is attractive, and would solve many problems, although it leaves the situation as regards long-standing injuries and congenital deformities in a rather vague state, to say the least.

So, returning to the main thread of the discussion, despite the problems involved, I feel justified in assuming tentatively that the

RE retains after death a strong resemblance to, and many of the characteristics of, its 'earthly' body, and that damage to living or inert matter is limited initially to three dimensions.

What Can An RE Do?

I can now move on to the situation of the Remote Entity a little later in time (shortly after recovery from the immediate trauma of dying). He is now free in four dimensions *but there is no basis for assuming that he is immediately aware of the fact.* If the person was not psychically endowed, then for all his earthly life the DE has been the 'poor relation', contained for most of the time within the confines of the physical body. On its occasional excursions (during sleep or illness) its sensory impressions and emotions were suppressed by the censor or heavily modified by the rationalisation processes of perception. Now it has a totally unnatural freedom which it cannot comprehend. The world is still apparently three-dimensional and 'normal'. Many 'near-death' OBE accounts[56] emphasise that he can see his own body and surroundings, and the people around that body. They are oblivious to him, and are only interested in his corpse, for which he feels no affinity.

The *Bardo Thödol* has already been mentioned, the *Tibetan Buddhist Book of the Dead*[15a] which must be read over and over again by an officiating priest into the ear of a dying man (and daily for 49 days after death!). It gives clear instructions as to what will happen to the *Bardo* body (or 'soul') after death, and what action should be taken. It says:

> When the consciousness-principle [or 'soul'] getteth outside the body, it sayeth to itself, 'Am I dead, or am I not dead?' It cannot determine. It seeth its relatives and connexions as it had been used to seeing them before. It even heareth the wailings.

Probably the first of the new powers to be appreciated, judging again by the accounts of near-death OBEs, is that he now has the freedom to levitate, to travel rapidly over long distances and to pass through solid obstacles. Again these conclusions (and Raymond's assertions as to the 'man blown to pieces') are confirmed, with surprising clarity, by the *Bardo Thödol*. Defining some of the terms he has used, the priest tells the dying man:

> O nobly-born, again listen. 'Endowed with all sense-faculties and power of unimpeded motion' implieth that although thou mayest have been, when living, blind of the eye, or deaf, or lame, yet on this

After-Death Plane thine eyes will see forms, and thine ears will hear sounds, and all other sense-organs of thine will be unimpaired and very keen and complete.

O nobly-born, 'unimpeded motion' implieth that thy present body being a desire-body – thine intellect having been separated from its seat – is not a body of gross matter, so that thou hast the power to go right through any rock-masses, hills, boulders, earth, houses, and Mt Meru itself without being impeded.

O nobly-born . . . Thou art able in a moment to traverse the four continents . . . or thou canst instantaneously arrive in whatever place thou wishest; thou hast the power of reaching there within the time it takes a man to bend.

Given the situation in which the new RE finds itself, one would naturally expect him to try to contact the only source of help and advice that he knows – his bereaved family and friends. To do this he must somehow reach them across the fourth-dimensional barrier. It is important to draw precise distinctions between what one may regard as three stages of ability in overcoming this barrier:

a) He may *see* across the fourth dimension, as one looks through a window;

b) He may *communicate* through the fourth dimension, as one shouts to a friend on the other side of a river, or pushes a letter through the letter-flap in a door;

c) He may himself *move through* the fourth dimension, as we move through our own three.

As I have shown, there is evidence that light can travel in the fourth dimension, and since the astral eyes and cortexes of the RE are presumed fully operational, he is able to achieve the first stage immediately, as confirmed by the accounts of OBE previously quoted. I have suggested that the second stage is more difficult. His friends cannot see him, hear him or touch him since their censors are operating, but suppose that he should try to touch one of them, or to move a physical object?

It is interesting that in most of the accounts of OBE experiences of the living, such as an Army Officer, the 'glue sniffer' and the Doctor there is no reference to the ability of the DE to create physical effects. Physical phenomena associated with a recent death are sometimes observed about ten to twenty days after it occurred (cf. Jim Pike and Ann Kennedy) but they are usually minor movements of objects (such as the 'falling picture' syndrome) or the teleportation of small objects. If my previous suggestion is correct, the RE is unable to intrude physically into this world, and so is unable to handle familiar objects in the way that he used to (as Manning's hand passed through Webbe's). On the other hand, he would be able to grasp the extension of any object through the fourth dimension into the new world that he inhabits (as described on page 163) if that extension is long enough, and *if he knew that such an extension existed*. It may be that untutored efforts of a new RE, bewildered by its change of circumstances and trying to cope with totally new dimensions, could, almost accidentally, result in physical movements. Events requiring closer control or more practised ability, such as apports, or the levitation of heavy objects, seem to be limited to seances in the presence of experienced mediums, supporting the concept that these phenomena may require psychic power to be available on both sides of the dimensional barrier. There is a definite tradition, and considerable literature to support the idea that some advanced paranormal phenomena require 'organised effort' on the part of a number of RE's, and such effects are discussed in the next chapter.

Telepathy From The Dead

Finally, what is the possibility that he may attempt direct telepathic contact with the neocortex of a living person? On reflection, this may be possible, but is likely to be difficult. Even if he had experienced OBE in his lifetime, communication between his DE and his physical brain had always been direct and 'instinctive', operating without his awareness, and he thus has no precedent to suggest to him that mental communication with another brain is possible, or how to achieve it. Furthermore, should he attempt it, he finds himself thwarted by a mechanism in the brain of the receiver of the message which exists for that purpose – the censor. His own may have died with his body, but those of his living friends are still functional. These difficulties may only be overcome by a high level of emotional need on the part of the RE aided by a degree of psychic ability in the recipient. Mrs Heywood writes:

> I have had several other experiences connected with the recently dead . . . They all had one thing in common, either a sense of contemporary purpose on the part of the dead, or an urge to action on my part, and in this they differed from my experience of the phenomenon known as haunting, in which, whatever causes it, the sense of urgency is usually lacking.[35]

It is small wonder that in the accounts of this experience received via mediums, the RE tends to linger for some time in the vicinity of the scene of his death, or to follow any movement of his friends and relatives or the body itself, although the emphasis seems to be on feelings of bewilderment and disorientation rather than distress. This concept is embodied firmly in the traditional views of death found in world-wide mythologies, superstitions and religions, which are discussed in Chapter 15 as possibly reflecting instinctive or subconscious knowledge. The ideas of the 'lost soul' who cannot accept that he is dead, the ghost haunting the place of his sudden death, hoping for release, and the 'watchers by the dead' – possibly to assure the RE, who would be familiar with the ritual, that his friends were satisfied that he had died – are all consistent with the concept of an entity which has not yet lost its human qualities, and which will need time to adjust to a totally new environment.

Where death terminates a long illness, and particularly if the dying person has held religious or spiritualist beliefs, one would expect the RE to be more quickly aware of his passing, and for there to be fewer such problems. Then the next stage, in which the new RE is welcomed by friends and relatives 'on the other side', may take place relatively quickly. Indeed, there are many accounts of dying persons greeting unseen friends with surprise and delight, and it is significant that statistical analysis shows that most such visions are of persons known to be dead, and very few are of living people. There is a strong inference in spiritualist writings that such a meeting cannot take place until the RE himself has accepted the situation – which would naturally occur more rapidly after an anticipated death than a sudden one – and that fear and apprehension are conspicuously absent.

Summary

Summarising the above discussion:

1) The human body extends into the fourth dimension by variable amounts; predominantly 'physical' organs extending a short distance while predominantly 'astral' organs extend farther;
2) Injury, disease or deformity affects mainly the physical body, the damage so caused not extending far;
3) At death, the physical body remains in this world, but the rest of the system is detached to form a Remote Entity (RE, 'astral body',

'soul', 'spirit', etc.), which is a four-dimensional entity substantially similar in form to the physical body, but no longer subject to its restrictions, and in particular being free from the control of the censor mechanism in the brain;

4) Any damage or disfigurement of the physical body which is transferred to the RE may be repaired in time by calling on material which is even farther into the fourth dimension (and this may also be true of inanimate objects);

5) An RE wishing to contact someone still living may possibly be able to do so by telepathy, but this is likely to be thwarted by the censor mechanism of the living person, unless he is psychically gifted;

6) Immediately after death, the senses of the RE are still programmed to operate in three dimensions only, so he is not immediately aware of his change of status. There is therefore some degree of bewilderment and disorientation, which will take time to assimilate;

7) Although he may unwittingly move in four dimensions, the RE is still subject to the restriction that he cannot re-enter the 3-D world he has just left;

8) Similarly, he cannot touch or move objects in the world he has just left, other than by any fourth-dimension extension into his own world. This is a totally new situation to him and will be difficult to understand, so such movements are rare, and when they do occur, may be unintentional or uncontrolled.

So we form a picture of our RE in the period immediately following a violent or unexpected death. He is disorientated by sensations never before experienced and the feeling of abilities he does not understand and cannot control. He is in familiar surroundings, with friends and recognisable people about him, but he cannot touch anything or communicate with anyone. He is bewildered, and, until he has understood and accepted the true nature of his situation, alone.

CHAPTER 13

THE SPOOKY PART – WITH NAUGHTY LITTLE DEVILS

'At some future day it will be proved – I cannot say when and where – that the human soul is, while in earth-life, already in an uninterrupted communion with those living in another world; that the human soul can act upon these beings, and receive in return impressions of them without being conscious of it in the ordinary personality.'
Immanuel Kant

Before investigating in any great depth the kind of life led by an RE after death,* it is advisable to consider more carefully than I have hitherto the evidence on which such discussion must be based. Postponing until the next chapter any contribution from traditional beliefs, superstitions, mythology and religious doctrines, and reiterating that I have no personal experience to offer, I consider first the primary source, i.e., published books quoting or discussing messages said to been received by spiritualist mediums of one kind or another 'from the other side'. Such literature is available by the ton, ranging from long accounts of twee and cosy chats with swarming relatives of everyone concerned (with a garnish of the famous and infamous to add flavour), to 'scientific' statistical analyses and probability calculations, based on some of the more serious or accepted publications.

The situation has considerably improved since the halcyon days of spiritualism a hundred years ago, when any unprincipled person with a good understanding of human nature, a quick mind

---

* I apologise to the reader yet again for such ghastly and ridiculous abuse of the English language, but such phrases seem to be inevitable in discussing this subject. The only alternative seems to lie in such studied and painfully pedantic circumlocutions as to make the book almost unreadable. My main concern is to make my meaning plain, at the risk of causing distress to the literal-minded.

and a gift for histrionics could set up as a medium (as did Browning's Mr Sludge, a cruel lampoon of D.D. Home), and there were enough gullible or unhappy people around to keep the business flourishing. Even in those days, however, it was more profitable to run bogus seances than it was to write books with bogus claims, so while some modern books by mediums or their friends may fall into the 'twee and unconvincing' category, the claims made are unlikely to be completely unfounded.

This does not mean that such accounts can be taken completely at face value; there are certain factors which must be taken into account. Having specifically rejected the possibility of deliberate hoax or fraud, one must first consider the possibility that a message did not originate from 'the other side', but was received by telepathy from the mind of a living person or was generated in the mental processes of the medium himself. As I stressed in the previous chapter, telepathy is a reasonable assumption in many cases, but one which can be stretched too far. What is a much greater menace is a mixture within the brain of the medium of self-delusion, wishful thinking, the desire to convince and the urge to please. These pressures must be particularly severe in the cases of public seances or Spiritualist religious services using a paid medium (who none the less should not automatically be condemned as spurious). Lyall Watson referring to the majority of the seance material he has collected, says:

> The content of the material is almost unremittingly banal, consisting mostly of pious sentiments, couched in woolly language, entirely consistent with those providing the information. There are the expected examples of cultural bias, and an interesting tendency for those concerned to get what they want to hear . . . In short, there is nothing there that would not be available to those involved, or to someone near to them, or which reflects beliefs markedly different from those they themselves hold.

Although a psychologist would have no hesitation in pronouncing most of such utterances to be the product of living minds, a possible explanation for this characteristic is discussed below. Unfortunately, one has to accept that this type of honest self-delusion can rapidly deteriorate into fraud, and it is all too easy for someone who is determined to deny the existence of the paranormal to justify that assumption. Mediums tend to be neurotic and highly-strung people, and many have suffered mental breakdowns at a later stage in their lives. After middle age, the gift of psychic sensitivity often seems to deteriorate, just when the

189

reputation and the resulting demands on the medium have reached a peak. Inevitably there is a pressure to repeat old formulae, to pad out weak impressions, and ultimately to cheat. It is a historical fact that a number of famous mediums who were exhaustively studied by professional investigators at an early stage in their career, were later caught out in trivial and elementary frauds which would not have remained undetected for an hour in their heyday. (It is also an unfortunate fact that the publicity following such exposure usually undermined, and often totally destroyed, any contribution the early investigations may have made towards serious psychic research.)

Speak Up, Please, It's A Bad Line

Even if one takes for granted the honesty and psychic ability of the medium, this does not mean that one can automatically assume that he will always receive a message clearly and completely. There are many accounts of the difficulties of communication as seen 'from the other side', which apparently include at least three categories of problems:

a) Limitations of the knowledge of the RE's themselves;
b) Difficulties in communicating into the subconscious mind of the medium;
c) The difficulty experienced by the medium in expressing those ideas in words or by other means.

This aspect of spiritualist communications was a recurring subject in the Myers-Gurney cross-communications referred to on pages 121 and 177. Sir Frederic Myers was a founder-member of the Society for Psychical Research, and one of the most noted and respected names in the field in the late 19th century. He had been involved in psychic research for about thirty years before his death, and had established a reputation for absolute honesty and insistence on the highest standards of evidence. It is hardly surprising (if one accepts the possibility at all) that after his death in 1901 he was apparently very active in trying to prove the reality of his survival by an almost continuous series of communications over nearly twenty years through a number of mediums in widely-scattered places. Many of the messages were in automatic writing and some bore his 'signature'. Many included 'coded' references to Greek and Roman mythology (in which he was a world authority) to prevent their being dismissed as telepathy between the medium and a living person.[36] This is the material referred to by Sir

Alister Hardy (see page 121) as the strongest available evidence for survival. If we are to put any trust at all in such communications, then those from Myers (and by association his friends) must claim first consideration.

On the subject of the difficulties involved, Myers and his colleague Gurney, another 'RE contact', are both quoted by Walker:

> Thus we have Gurney interjecting the following remark during a session: 'You never seem to realize how little we know . . . Sometimes I know and can't get it through, but very often I don't *know*.' So also had Myers remarked on a previous occasion: 'Remember there is as much room for knowledge in some ways here as with you, and many mysteries remain mysteries only to be approached from other and higher standpoints.'[80]

In other words, there is at this stage no reason whatever for assuming that an entity after death is any more knowledgeable and reliable than he was when he was alive. G.L. Playfair writes:

> Once we manage to make contact with discarnate entities under controlled conditions, we will not solve any of the world's major problems overnight. We shall find that the spirit world is as confusing as our own, and that a great many of its inhabitants are no more intelligent than they were down here.[66]

The problems of the communication link itself are frequently referred to, one of the more popular quotes occurring in another message from Myers:

> The nearest simile I can find to express the difficulties of sending a message – is that I appear to be standing behind a sheet of frosted glass which blurs sight and deadens sounds – dictating feebly to a reluctant and somewhat obtuse secretary.

The basic causes of this difficulty are not made clear, but I would suggest that they must include those suggested in (b) and (c) above. Firstly, while the medium's censor mechanism may not be fully operational, it is often sufficiently active as to cause difficulty in 'reception', and can only be bypassed by modifying the form of the message, as discussed earlier. Communication by symbolism or muscular movement (in the form of ouija board, automatic writing, etc.) seems able to resist such suppression. Secondly, if the message is not in itself verbal, it may only be expressible as abstract ideas, leaving it to the verbalising cortex of the medium to express in words. This restriction would particularly apply to discussion of the circumstances surrounding the RE. One must accept that the conditions in a fourth dimension are beyond our experience and largely beyond the bounds of our vocabulary, so that any attempt at description, even by an experienced RE, must be fraught with the possibilities of ambiguity and misunderstanding. This point is made implicitly by Myers (quoted by Colin Wilson):

> Asked about the problems of communication, he explained that their method was to 'impress' the 'inner mind' of the medium with the message, and that the inner mind would then send it on to the brain. 'The brain is a mere mechanism. The inner mind is like soft wax, it receives our thoughts . . . but it must produce the words that clothe it.'[89]

– and more explicitly by Lord Balfour, (quoted by Walker):

> The suggestion seems to be that the subliminal self of the discarnate being uses categories which are beyond the reach of the incarnated [Sic!] mind, much as the categories employed by the human mind are beyond the comprehension of animals.[80]

These statements are extremely significant, when seen in the light of the discussion on page 93 in which it was suggested that part of the brain handles ideas as raw concepts, as 'meanings without words', and Freud's theory (discussed in Chapter 1), that they are subconscious, and cannot be 'thought' by the conscious mind until words are available to describe them. If those ideas themselves, or 'categories' as Lord Balfour calls them, are beyond the concepts normally handled by the human brain, there is a double difficulty, first in the understanding of them, and secondly in finding suitable words to express them. The compulsion in the mind of the medium to find such words, however inadequate, could account for much of the banality, repetition and ambiguity in many seance accounts, the strong reflection of the medium's personality, and the 'cultural bias' mentioned by Watson. Bishop Pike (see later) was evidently fully aware of this effect. He writes:

> I would repeat my emphasis on the fact that whatever words come through a medium, whether one accepts the survival hypothesis or not, are fallible and finite, stemming from human personalities.[65]

All in all, it is no wonder that the accounts of some seances read very much like a verbatim transcription of one side of a telephone conversation with a mentally retarded, fulsome old lady over a very bad line.

Life After Life

After accepting, and paying due regard to, all these factors, I still have little alternative to the policy already stated, which is to quote mainly from a small number of references which I find convincing, which are referred to with respect in the literature, and which seem to represent typical or consensus opinions. These I will accept as being honestly written, with no further attempt at establishing truth or falsehood.

One of the earliest, the most detailed and the most respected of the accounts of the after-life is found among the works of Emanuel Swedenborg, Swedish philosopher and mystic, who died in 1772. He was also a scientist and engineer of international reputation, who initiated advances in such varied fields as mathematics, cosmology, magnetism, metallurgy, anatomy, neurology, and so on. He was probably the last great scientist to claim and publicly demonstrate advanced psychic powers, before the advance of materialist philosophy made the breed extinct (or, more likely, drove it underground). Arthur Ford writes:

> At the ordinary levels of the after life Swedenborg matter-of-factly reports a world having much in common with our own. He found a natural terrain and population centres containing men and women with all the habits and aspirations of familiar humanity. Everyone is busy in some pursuit for the general good, and all are both learning and teaching – learning from souls who have gone to a higher wisdom, teaching the befuddled and confused among the newly arrived.[18]

This basic concept of Swedenborg's is repeated over and over again in more recent reports. One book which includes a long series of question-and-answer sessions with various REs is Sir Oliver Lodge's *Raymond*, a classic of its type and frequently quoted by other commentators.[18,36] The origin of the book is of interest, in that it involves the post-mortem activities of Myers.

The two men were friends, sharing a common interest in psychic research for 16 years, before Myer's death in 1901. In August 1915, the famous American medium, Mrs Lenore Piper, received a message for Lodge from Myers which was interpreted as meaning that he (Myers) would do his best to shield Lodge from 'a blow'. Five weeks later Lodge's son Raymond was killed in Flanders. Eleven days after his death, Mrs Lodge accompanied a friend to a sitting with a remarkable medium, Mrs Osborne Leonard, who did not know her identity or the circumstances, and they were not introduced. A message was received from 'Raymond' saying: 'Tell father I have met some friends of his.' Mrs Lodge asked for a name and the answer was 'Myers'. This was only the beginning, and the subsequent long series of 'conversations' with Raymond, through several mediums and over a number of years, are among the best documented in the field. The general consensus of the messages regarding Raymond himself are typical of those concerning someone who has died suddenly or unexpectedly: initial shock and confusion, slow recovery and reorientation over a period of weeks and months, and finally happiness and fulfilment in the job of helping newly-dead to adjust. (A very similar process is described in the messages from 'Jim Pike', see page 210.) Ford summarises:

> By the middle of November, two months after his death, Raymond is in full possession of his faculties, at home in his new surroundings and fully able to describe them in detail. He is far more sure of himself in handling the difficult communications problem in getting messages through to earth-side minds through mediums. Here he gives us a strongly personal, subjective, impressionistic account of how things look and feel *to him*, without the complex analysis of whether his world is wholly mental, quasi-physical, real or dream, and the other considerations so dear to the hearts of psychical researchers.

Some of the messages received from Raymond have already been quoted, and others are particularly appropriate to the present discussion. As before, they are expressed in a confusing mixture of first and third person:

> '[Raymond's grandfather] lives in a house – a house built with bricks – and there are trees and flowers, and the ground is solid . . . The night doesn't follow the day here, as it did on the earth-plane. It seems to get dark sometimes . . . What I am worrying about is, how it's made, of what is it composed. I have not found out yet . . . for a little time I thought one's thoughts formed the building and the trees and solid ground; but there is more than that.'
>
> When asked if Raymond could see ahead, the reply came 'He thinks sometimes he can, but it's not easy to predict. I don't think that I really know any more than when on earth.'

I cannot resist one more quote, irrelevant though it may be:

> Raymond makes the interesting literary observation that books have already been prepared on his plane, awaiting an opportunity to be inserted into the minds of congenial authors and ultimately published on earth. [This author, congenial or otherwise, refuses to comment!]

The pictures of the after-life drawn by Raymond, Myers and many others show a remarkable degree of consistency with that of Swedenborg. Each individual has retained his own personality and outward appearance, but has recovered from any illness or injury. The surroundings are outwardly physical, but there are frequent references to reservations and incomplete understanding, both as regards the material of which objects are constructed, and the construction and needs of their own bodies. This is puzzling until one realises that (according to my theory), the physical functions of the body no longer operate (although some mental reactions to those functions may persist). On the other hand, the neocortex of the RE is essentially that which it possessed before death, and which evolved to deal with a three-dimensional world. The censor may no longer operate, but this does not automatically qualify the perception processes to deal with new kinds of sensory impression, and the individual will still see his surroundings in three-dimensional terms, but with disturbing and incomprehensible changes. This situation will persist until experience or deliberate training extends the programming of the brain to accommodate the new information. The major changes which can be understood and appreciated in a very short time are the elimination of illness and death (which in itself will introduce a new perception of time), a new sense of the value of the individual, and a vague feeling for the purpose and structure of society. Other than that, the daily routine does not seem to have changed much. One could say that 'in the midst of Death we are in Life'.

Again, the problem with such a scenario is that it seems too pat, too cosy to be believable. One has an irreverent mental picture of the dear departed, exact duplicates of their earthly bodies but cleaned up and sanitised (would Old Charlie really be recognisable as himself without the appalling odour of unwashed socks which used to surround him?), happily shopping for tins of astral sardines in a film set of Surbiton High Street. Surely wishful thinking must play a major part in such a concept. This argument is answered to some extent in later discussion, but meanwhile it is enough to emphasise that similar accounts have been received again and again in a wide variety of circumstances, and have convinced people who one would not expect to be easily persuaded.

Indeed, sceptics have argued that such consistency is only to be expected because of the powerful influence of Swedenborg's writings, a beautiful example of a 'Catch 22' argument.

Physical Mediumship And The Direct Voice

The subject of mediumship and messages received through mediums cannot be dismissed without mention of another aspect, the so-called 'physical medium', in whose presence phenomena may occur somewhat reminiscent of those in poltergeist infestations (in that they include noises, movement of objects, apports and so on). A major difference is that at well-run seances the effects are far more controlled, often occurring at the request of the medium or in answer to his questions (as in the well-known 'One rap for Yes; Two for No' syndrome). There is also a preponderance of events which obviously require a more deliberate control of movement and position, as in the playing of musical instruments (although the actual rendering of a recognisable melody seems rare!). If one accepts my previous suggestion explaining such movements – that an entity in a fourth dimension may move an object by applying a force to its extension into his own world – it would seem that such methods enable an RE to by-pass the censor barrier, in that they are evident to all present, irrespective of psychic ability. What is even more interesting, however, is the occurrence of physical phenomena apparently produced by organised groups of REs with the deliberate intention of facilitating communication with living people. A particular case has already been noted, the so-called 'Direct Voice'.

At some seances a voice, usually a distinct whisper, will be heard by all present (psychically gifted or otherwise) apparently originating from a well-defined point in space. I concluded in an earlier chapter that in such a case the sound wave itself was real enough, but postponed the question of how it could be generated. The spiritualists who believe in the complete astral body have no doubt on the matter, and the description by Findlay (as dictated to him from 'the Other Side') may be taken as typical:

> To obtain the Direct Voice we require, in conjunction with those in the etheric world, to make the necessary conditions . . . The group [of etheric helpers includes] one who gathers the substances from the medium and the sitters . . .
>
> First of all, we must accept their statement that the etheric body is in every way a duplicate of the physical body, both as regards all internal and external organs. In etheric life, communication takes place in the same way as in earth life. The vocal organs vibrate their atmosphere, the tongue moves . . . the only difference being that it is all taking place in a matter of much finer structure and at a much more rapid rate of vibration . . . The [astral] chemist, after mixing the substances he obtains from the medium and the sitters with his

own ingredients, takes the finished preparation and with it first materialises his hands and then forms a rough mask in the likeness of a mouth, throat and lungs . . . The etheric person wishing to speak then presses into this mask, slow in vibration, and with it clothes or covers his mouth, throat, tongue and lungs . . . The speaker then for the time being, has taken on the necessary conditions to make himself once more such as we are, as far as his capacity to form words which we can hear is concerned.[17]

Very simple, very explicit, very logical: I feel almost ashamed to admit that my first reaction is somewhat cynical. If the phrase 'Matter of a much finer structure and at a more rapid rate of vibration' is assumed to refer to atomic or subatomic movements such as the rotation of electrons around the nucleus, these are hardly 'vibrations' in any real sense, and even if they did occur at much higher velocities, this would not automatically render such matter immaterial and non-physical.

On the other hand, the description could be read as suggesting that astral entities communicate by high frequency (ultrasonic) sound waves in a rarefied atmosphere, in which case a partially successful attempt on the lines indicated could result in a falsetto voice! In fact, ultrasonic waves would have more difficulty in travelling through a less dense atmosphere, not less; and furthermore such waves would be easily detected electronically (being capable of giving false alarms on many security systems), and would leave our astral friends capable of being deafened by earthly steam jets and dog whistles. Similarly the idea of loading the astral organs with additional weight to reduce the frequency at which they vibrate is not acceptable. Many of the characteristics of the voice are governed more by the shape of the vocal tract than the material from which it is constructed.

This objection particularly applies to the whispered voice, which does not require any organ in the body to vibrate, and does not involve the larynx and vocal tract to any appreciable extent. (Feel the front of your throat lightly with your fingertips while speaking normally and again while whispering). Whispered sounds are formed mainly by the eddies of air around the teeth, tongue and lips, so the 'mask' would have no need to enter the throat, and certainly not the lungs. On the whole, it seems to me to be more than likely that such phrases as 'higher frequency' and 'finer structure' are derived subconsciously in the mind of the medium from the moral implications of such words as 'higher' and 'finer'; I can think of no rational basis for them.

On the other hand, I would not dismiss the Direct Voice phenomenon out of hand. It is too well attested. And who should know better how it is achieved than the mediums themselves and their informants, whoever they are? Furthermore, I must repeat that I cannot assume at this stage that an RE is any better informed on technical matters than his earthly predecessor, and the man in the street would make an awful hash of describing many quite elementary processes. So can I, while accepting at face value the basic description given by Findlay as to what the entity does, reinterpret the mechanics of the process?

Let me begin with the reasonable assumption that the fourth dimension of a molecule of air is similar to its other three. The RE is slightly more distant, and so is not in contact with our atmosphere, but he has astral organs capable of vibrating 'his own' atmosphere. What he needs is not so much a complete mask, as a kind of diaphragm which is light in weight but 'thick' in the fourth dimension (a kind of astral polystyrene?), so that when his voice moves his own side of the diaphragm, the movement is transmitted to the 'real' side of the material, and so to the 'real' air. It would be interesting to check whether such an object could be seen as the source of the sound at a seance where Direct Voice is experienced.

Ectoplasm

The substance involved, described as requiring material derived from the bodies of the medium and the sitters, and also from etheric sources, is identified elsewhere as 'ectoplasm', some kind of physical/astral modelling clay, which has been observed and photographed emerging from the mouths and other orifices of mediums. Michael Bentine discusses it (from his own and his father's observations):

> Apparently, when analysed by chemists, coarse types of ectoplasm, used for physical phenomena, have often proved to be mucosal in origin; an excretion of the mucous membrane tissues of the medium. The points of exudation were, at different times, the nostrils, the mouth, from the base of the throat and the solar plexus – and the sex organs . . . it manifests itself as a 'chill' form of energy . . . it appeared to generate as a rising spiral of force forming around our ankles and feet . . . An interesting side effect was the distinct smell of ozone, which was most apparent during physical phenomena . . .

The consensus of opinion on ectoplasm (as evidenced by Findlay, Bentine and many others) may be summarised as follows:

a) It emerges as a paste or foam, rather like toothpaste, from one of the bodily orifices of the medium;

b) The medium is in a trance condition during the whole of the time that the materialisation exists;

c) It is visible in subdued lighting and may be photographed by infra-red, but dissolves to nothing or is rapidly reabsorbed into the body of the medium when exposed to normal levels of light;

d) It is physical to the extent that it may be felt and handled, often feeling warm and soft, like human flesh;

e) It may be moulded into any shape, sometimes appearing in the form of 'pseudopods', crudely-shaped hands or feet emerging from the body of the medium and capable of basic movements (such as pinching one of the sitters!), sometimes as a two-dimensional shape in human form, and in extreme cases as a three-dimensional 'human' figure capable of being felt and heard!

f) It may be formed into 'rods', and in this form may be used to push, pull or lift objects.

Such phenomena are an open invitation to the fake medium, and the spate of exposures in the closing years of the 19th century brought the whole subject of physical materialisations into disrepute. However, it is plain from more recent reviews of the subject (such as the excellent one by Inglis in *The Hidden Power*) that cynicism can be overdone, and that there is at least a case to answer for the reality of ectoplasm. Findlay reports that his etheric informants were quite definite that ectoplasm was physical, and items made from it had weight, such weight being subtracted from that of the medium who supplied it (the loss being restored when the materialisation was over). Experiments confirming this were carried out by the engineer W.J. Crawford with the Goligher Circle of mediums during the First World War. Bentine's comment on the smell of ozone is interesting, and he (correctly) associates this with high-voltage electrical discharges.

In attempting to find an explanation for ectoplasm, it is first of all significant that, although Findlay's account refers to material obtained 'from the medium and the sitters', I can find no reference to ectoplasm materialising from anyone other than a medium in a trance. Under such conditions one may assume that the astral body of the medium, still resident 'within' the physical body, is in complete charge of the neocortex, and therefore of all bodily functions other than the autonomous ones. The orifices by which the ectoplasm normally leaves the body (such as the mouth, nose, sexual and excretory organs) are generous sources of mucus. It is possible that mucus is composed of substances which may be readily formed into the kind of material I referred to above, a kind of 'astral polystyrene' which is 'thick' in its fourth dimension. Then, although the DE itself may not materialise in this world, by forming a thick 'glove' on its hand it may be able to bridge that forbidden gap and so apply physical force directly to material objects (even those with small fourth dimensions), much as a man wearing an asbestos glove may handle hot metal. Similar principles would apply to 'boots' and other shapes made of material, and even, in the limit, a complete human 'body', which would by this theory be a DE coated in a 'suit of armour' of ectoplasm. Obviously, the concept has its weaknesses (Is there enough mucus in the human body? What about a 'clothed' materialisation? and so on) but it would seem to begin to address the problem of ectoplasm, a problem which must be solved eventually in physical terms if the study of the paranormal is to make any progress.

What About The 'Baddies'?

Despite the doubtful quality of much of the literature on the subject of deliberate mediumship, some of the books on the subject, such as those from which I have quoted, convince by their clarity and apparent honesty. However the difficulty one experiences in accepting, even in principle, the possibility of survival after death entitles one to be somewhat cynical, and after reading no more than a couple of them, nagging doubts creep into the mind. For instance, why is it that evil-intentioned or downright anti-social entities, although occasionally mentioned in passing in such accounts (particularly in association with unpleasant physical phenomena), seldom seem to figure largely in the communications themselves? Most of the people dealt with on the other side seem to be basically decent, kind, friendly and helpful: an atmosphere of white-European-Church-of-England-Bible-Class. But on second thoughts is this so surprising? Even in the cases where the author is not himself a medium, he will be sympathetic to mediumship and will tend to belong to a similar social group. Anyone with the intelligence, initiative and education to write this type of book must almost inevitably belong himself to the social classes reflected in the descriptions.

A similar comment would apply to the astral 'contacts'. Our earth alone is large enough to support a multitude of people of various races, originally separated by geographical barriers.

Given the ability to move in several infinite universes without the necessity to breathe or eat, there is obviously more than enough room for any number of different communities (without in any way implying any form of superiority or apartheid). It would seem inevitable that anyone in a state of shock and requiring to readjust to new surroundings would be drawn to (or would draw to him) friends, relatives or his social peers, who would be in the best position to understand his problems, so that each community would be likely to contain a majority of like-minded people. The situation would tend to be self-perpetuating, and indeed it may be a necessary factor in the peace and stability of society, particularly bearing in mind that many of its inhabitants may be just as prejudiced and bigoted as they were on earth. The same consideration would explain the relative absence of any mention of other nationalities and creeds. There seems to be no reason why there should not be dozens, hundreds or thousands of such communities, possibly working without direct knowledge of each other, and because of the 'multiple connectivity' characteristic, each would be potentially in direct contact with any place on earth. If this concept is anywhere near to the truth, the picture of the afterlife that we get from messages received from mediums must be heavily distorted, or at least incomplete.

Even so, the concept of 'like seeks like' may have far more important consequences than the bias it imparts to published material, in that it would operate in either direction. If one accepts that an RE 'passing over' will tend to be drawn to his peers in the next world, it seems equally logical that an RE seeking a source of psychic energy in this world, will again be attracted to his peers. It is not difficult to find evidence supporting this view. For instance, a major characteristic of poltergeist hauntings, commented on in almost every account, is that the effects are not random or accidental; there are definite indications of their being governed by an intelligent entity (in the sense of something capable of deliberate intention). One of the problems of investigation is that most of the phenomena occur when there is no-one present to observe them directly, sometimes (as described by Manning, for instance) when the room has only been empty for a moment or two. The effects are often noisy and disturbing, with loud bangs and crashes, objects thrown around, furniture overturned, and so on. Occasionally someone may feel a blow, but reports of anyone being seriously hurt by a poltergeist are rare. The whole picture is of someone trying to attract attention, to create alarm and concern, and to stir up mischief. Are these not exactly the characteristics one would expect from the spirit of a child, a teenager or someone mentally retarded? Imagine the average fourteen-year-old delinquent, brought up in a city slum, then dying and suddenly finding that he has the power to make himself a thundering nuisance to a quiet and respectable family, with no risk of detection or punishment. He would have a ball!

Like To Like

An equally accepted factor in poltergeist lore is that a haunting is centred on a young person in the house, and typically one passing through puberty. The focal person is not directly involved in the phenomena, but seems to provide the necessary energy. As typical examples, in the case of Hetty Wesley, sister of the evangelists John and Charles Wesley, she was observed to be asleep during the worst of the phenomena, but perspiring and restless, while in the case of Matthew Manning at school, poltergeist events happened in other dormitories, and once his connection with them was realised, the Matron would come to wake him to try to stop them. Putting these two undisputed facts together leads to an extension of the 'like-to-like' theory. It seems a very reasonable conclusion that poltergeist activity may be due to the RE of a young delinquent who has been drawn to the psychic energy of someone of about his own age.

Mischief and wrong-doing are not exclusively reserved to the young delinquent, so what about the more extreme baddies? How about the vicious, the mentally warped and the pervert, who must die like the rest of mankind? Each will be drawn to his peers, and although there may be well-meaning entities ready to help him (ex-Salvation Army?), his natural bad characteristics will be retained, at least through the adjustment period, heightened by confusion and fear, and encouraged by 'bad companions'. Some evidence of these less attractive characters may be found in many scattered references to accidental contacts with 'lower entities', 'retarded spirits' and so on, but these are usually mentioned in passing, with no detailed description. Humans who deliberately try to communicate with such entities will do so for dubious motives and the results are unlikely to be published.

Where psychic energy is deliberately offered for the wrong motives, such as greed, or lust for power, it is likely to attract equally selfish and destructive forces, and an unholy alliance between an unprincipled person and entities experienced in evil could have consequences considerably more serious than the minor mischief of the poltergeist. Examples of the Doctor Faustus mentality are well known. Aleister Crowley springs first to mind, and indeed the whole cult of black magic and black witchcraft is based firmly on liaison with, and control of, this type of entity. The belief that Adolf Hitler and the upper hierarchy of the Nazi party were very active in this field is not just journalistic invention, folktale or gossip, as Bentine establishes.

One would expect an entity with anti-social motives to maintain the same standards as it did in life, and to take full advantage of the young, the inexperienced and the weak-willed. I recall that when I found that my own children and their friends were 'playing at seances' and confided in my friend the Methodist minister, his first reaction was 'I hope they don't start something they can't stop.' There is plenty of evidence of students' pranks or light-hearted experiments getting out of hand with terrifying results, and Bentine describes in spine-chilling detail several such cases. The first concerns a young Divinity student at Cambridge in the early years of this century. Through his studies he became fascinated by ritual magic, and began to experiment alone. He eventually realised that the situation was dangerous and beyond his control, and he begged two undergraduate friends to help him. One of them was William Hope-Jones, Michael's 'Uncle Billy' (and later his tutor), who he describes as 'tall, immensely strong and gentle, a Rowing Blue, and a great all-round athlete and scholar':

They found him to be in a very bad way, his nerves shot to pieces, and absolutely terrified of the state into which the 'Dark Forces' of his mind had led him . . . The scene of the struggle for the possession of the Divinity student's mind was his room in college, a small study-cum-bedroom . . . At first everything seemed to go well. The young 'dabbler in magick' was comforted and encouraged to rest, stretched out on his bed . . . Bill Hope-Jones description of what follows was simple and dramatic. The room became depressingly cold and a sensation of unpleasant prickling started to affect the two watchers by the bed . . . The energy-sapping chill suddenly switched to a hot, stifling humidity . . . with the sour stench of decay . . . The gaslight had been lowered to facilitate the sleep of the Divinity student, who started to thrash around wildly in the foetid darkness . . . At this point, the hot stinging darkness seemed to solidify into a definite shape and, giving off a dreadful smell, it formed into a powerful, moving and gyrating spiral of force, like a dark, purple-coloured tornado . . . But now they were literally being physically attacked and thrown around the room by the mini-tornado, as though they were being set upon by a gang of toughs. Bill's principal memory, he told my father, was of being punched and pummelled while he fought desperately against that hot, stinking cloud of whirling shadows. During the struggle every stick of furniture in the room was caught up and smashed to pieces, while china and ornaments were shattered against the walls. The raging vortex of black force, which they were fighting with all their physical strength, seemed to have joined onto the threshing body of the Divinity student, as he tossed and writhed on the bed. By a tremendous effort of will, Bill managed to gasp out the words of prayer which seemed to be impressed on his mind, and by the sheer strength of their youth, the two of them forced their way out of the study.

A second case is simpler:

I cite the case of an acquaintance in Folkestone – a very earthy, rich and self-important character who, after a heavy drinking and eating session with some friends, thought he would have a bash at a table sitting . . . After bawling out a couple of rugger songs to parallel the pre-conditioning by music, and then upbraiding and insulting the stubbornly inanimate table, the small circle of 'experimenters' got the shock of their lives. They had generated ideal conditions for a demonstration of an elemental low type of intelligence and sheer brute force; the table became a living vicious manifestation of power without control and chased the terrified gathering around the darkened room, eventually pinning the originator of the experiment hard up against the corner where it physically hurt him.

A third case described by Bentine (unfortunately too long to quote here in detail) concerns the landlord of a pub in Dover who found that he could predict the winners of the races to be run the following day. Obsession took over until his wife asked for help, and at a 'Rescue Circle' session attended by Bentine's father, a friend and a priest, the 'possessing entity' was manifested in a revoltingly physical way. This cured the man for a time, but the pressure from his friends was too great, and he began his predictions again. He died, raving mad, in the padded cell of a Kent mental hospital.

The Dangers Of Amateurism

These three cases can be taken to illustrate some general conclusions. The most obvious point is that in each case the source of the psychic energy on 'this side' was unskilled and inexperienced and (if one makes some reasonably safe assumptions as to the motives of the Divinity student), was using his ability for selfish or stupid purposes. One does not need to push the concept of 'like-to-like' too far to appreciate that this could well attract the attention of an RE with similar intentions, but the principle seems to go much further than that. The character of the student is not defined, but one could assume, from his chosen profession, that he was not by nature a violent man. Given the number of potentially dangerous weapons available in his room (in the way of table lamps, broken chair-legs, etc.) and men who could not see a blow coming, the conditions were obviously there for the infliction of serious injuries, and yet the whirling vortex of energy which they fought, and which smashed china ornaments against the walls, left them 'punched and pummelled' and 'bruised and bleeding profusely', but with no major injuries. On the other hand, at the booze-up, the energy source was by inference a very physical man and the entity he raised used the table itself as a weapon with which to inflict injury. Can it be that the principle of the attraction of like natures goes as far as this, the RE being attracted to an energy source reflecting its own physical character also?

There may also be an indirect pointer to an interesting variation of the 'like-to-like' theory in the smells associated with the first and last case. If one accepts such evidence as the soaking-wet apparition of John the pilot and the reality of apports, there seems no particular obstacle to the transference of small objects from one world to another, and this would include dust particles or molecules of vapour required to generate a quite real and physical smell, so one should not be surprised to find these accompanying an entity who had been surrounded by them 'on the other side'. In the case of the pub landlord, the manifestation of the entity included a revolting stench of stale beer, while that of the Divinity student included 'the sour stench of decay'. Could it just be possible that he had been experimenting with necromancy (calling up the newly-dead)?

This idea finds support in some surprising places. Pullar, discussing the Sahaja Yogic doctrines, writes:

> The atmosphere around us is, according to Sahaja Yoga, a bank of spirits . . . Through occult practices the sorcerers have acquired the means to overpower and control all these . . . depraved and otherwise, and inoculate them into the psyches of their victims, always matching a corresponding spirit to its subject, the weak receiving the weak, the imperious entertaining the spirit of some general perhaps, some dictating executive, so that the imbalance may be further exaggerated.[71]

One aspect of the case of the Divinity student refers back to the discussions on psychic and physical energy. The two undergraduates fought nothing tangible, just concentrated physical energy. To a physicist this is unimaginable, but just think of two little water-bugs caught up in the whirlpool caused by a little boy thrashing about in the pond with the end of a stick. Expressed in such terms the idea of energy from another dimension becomes very real. Similarly, one could not reasonably conceive of one young man providing the energy to throw around the room two strapping young rugby-playing undergraduates. The student may have been a necessary focus of energy, the catalyst without which the event could not have happened, but the majority of the physical energy must have been provided from the other side of the dimensional barrier.

Summary

This chapter began with a stupendous supposition: I assumed that some part of the human personality could survive physical death and therefore it may, in principle, be possible to communicate with a 'dead' person. Even if that vast and awesome assumption were proved true, it is evident that the investigation of such communication would be fraught with problems, not least those inherent in the characteristics of living man, notably:

a) The massive potential of the human character for wishful thinking and self-delusion;
b) The tremendous capacity of the human brain for self-censorship and over-rationalisation;
c) The greed and pride of man, generating enormous temptation to fraud for monetary gain, as an ego-boost, or as a substitute for failing powers.

Such difficulties, superimposed on the enormous demands on the credulity imposed by the initial assumption, make it no wonder that the authenticity of apparent communication with the dead is still one of the most contentious of subjects, even among the few who are prepared to accept the fundamental possibility. Having once accepted that possibility, however, and having accepted that the major evidence to be considered must lie in published versions of such communications, a remarkably consistent picture seems to emerge, and one which appears to support my earlier conclusions on the nature of the fourth dimension.

Expressing that picture in my terms of suspended disbelief and surrealist logic (and continuing the list at the end of the previous chapter), the scenario is something like this:

1) Although much of the material claimed to be 'messages from the dead' must be treated with suspicion, there is sufficient consensus among apparently level-headed and intelligent writers to make tentative general assumptions about the 'life after death';

2) The general picture is of a communal life superficially similar to that on earth, but with strong emphasis on mutual help and support;

3) Communication with living people through the minds of psychically gifted people is achievable, but with considerable difficulty;

4) A 'newly-dead' RE will usually be taught by his new friends the skills required to communicate, should he so wish, and concerted action by organised groups may result in advanced physical phenomena, such as the use of ectoplasm;

5) There is a strong tendency for an RE to be drawn to his peers in the other world, and to use psychic energy drawn from his living peers;

6) The tendency of 'like going to like' may allow mischievous or evil entities to operate in this world via the minds of young, weak-willed, inexperienced or ill-intentioned people, to the extent of the emergence of 'demonic possession'.

CHAPTER 14

THE HOLY PART – OR A PILGRIM'S PROGRESS

'It would not surprise me if the roots of religion went much deeper down into biological history than is generally conceded, and that it is part of the very nature of the living stream.'
Sir Alister Hardy

Contrary to first appearances, the conclusions at the end of the previous chapter do not represent a complete flight from popular opinion. On the contrary, my mental wanderings have brought me to an area of human thought which is flattened and worn in all directions by the feet of multitudes, all in an earnest and instinctive search for some real indication of the relationship between man and the universe he inhabits. My problem is not that there is no path to follow, but that there are far too many, each with its insistent devotees who are confident that theirs is the only way to 'The Truth'. However, my immediate task is simplified, in that, as far as my present subject, life after death, is concerned, there is a remarkable degree of consistency. The vast majority of the religions of mankind (with the possible exception of the early 'purer' forms of Buddhism), accept in some form the survival after death of some aspect of the individual human being.

In most branches of Christianity, however, this belief is one side of a most peculiar contradiction. The formal doctrines include firm commitment to the concepts of Heaven and Hell, and the Judgment of the individual, and yet all forms of spiritism and Spiritualism, which one would have expected to be welcomed as possibly providing support for those doctrines, have been feared and reviled throughout the ages, and dismissed as superstition and charlatanism. This attitude is extremely persistent, particularly among the theologians and the upper hierarchy,* despite the fact that learned committees set up by them to study the problem have reported cautiously in favour of the reality of communication with the dead. As The Revd Kennedy points out:

'The Committee on Supernatural Psychic Phenomena' [appointed by the Church of Scotland] consisting of eight Professors, one Law Lord, seventeen Ministers and two Medical Specialists had reported:
  '1) The Church cannot dismiss these phenomena with indifference.
  2) Ministers may even encounter genuine phenomena in the course of their duties.
  3) There is room in the larger life of the church for Christian Spiritualists whose special experiences have been sufficient to convince them.'[45]

Similarly, he quotes the majority report of the Church of England's Committee of Enquiry which stated:

'We think that it is probable that the hypothesis that they [i.e., messages received by mediums] proceed in some cases from discarnate spirits, is the true one.'

It is significant that the latter report, although commissioned by the Archbishop of Canterbury and taking three years to compile, was 'pigeon-holed' for thirty years before being published unofficially (Sic!).

The reasons for this prevarication and – dare one say it – hypocrisy, are fit studies for sociologists and psychologists, but I cannot avoid the nasty suspicion that one of the primary reasons why the priesthood discourage spiritism, is that it tends to undermine their monopoly in matters spiritual. There is also a more subtle and possibly more damaging explanation. Putting it bluntly, as far as I can judge in such material as is available to me, *there seems to be nothing in the messages received 'from the other side' to support convincingly the doctrines of any of the world's major religions, Christian or otherwise.*

After all, if the after-life as experienced by the RE of a person who has recently died bore any resemblance to that which he had been led to expect, one would take it for granted that this would be specifically commented on, and even emphasised. A strong and specific bias is particularly to be expected in the many cases where the dead person, the medium and the recipient of the message, all

---

* There are notable exceptions. 'The Churches Fellowship for Psychical and Spiritual Studies' does important and sterling work, which too frequently escapes notice.

shared a common strongly-held conviction, but in well-controlled seances with reputable mediums this does not seem to occur.*
Take as an extreme example the communications to Bishop Pike[35] (a Bishop in the American Episcopalian Church) via the medium Arthur Ford (an ordained minister in the Christian Church – Disciples of Christ) from his son Jim (a 'drop-out' and drug addict, who had committed suicide), and from Mrs Marian Bergrud, a very devout churchwoman who was for many years the Bishop's secretary, and who had committed suicide in the belief that she had cancer. Some five weeks after his death 'Jim' says specifically, '. . . there is nothing over here to make me any more inclined to believe in God.'

And six weeks later:

Now I feel that there is *something*. It's beginning to make sense to assume that Someone is making things hang together and develop, but since I've been here I haven't heard *anything* about a Jesus.

– while the following exchange takes place with Mrs Bergrud:

M.B. I firmly believe I am going to see Jesus one day.
B.P. Do you really? Do you hear about him?
M.B. No, He's just another person, been here longer, but I have been told that the people who have been here long enough to advance to a high plane or a high dimension can always come down to a low plane to help us. But we who are just here have to earn the right to go up . . . I know one thing – Jim and I are in what we call the etheric body in the etheric plane . . . And we will generally stay here, I am told, until the people we care about on the earth plane have come here or somehow we are no longer concerned about them.

This account, and many similar, highlights the paradox. It is clear that the motivation and personal beliefs of a medium can have a profound effect on the type of entity he contacts and the outcome of the contact, and it is evident from the most cursory study of the literature that most of the leading and most successful mediums are, in one sense or another, religious people, and yet the best and most consistent of the accounts of life after death seldom refer to anything supporting a specific religious doctrine.

Supporting this statement, and running parallel to it, is the fact that no religion has the monopoly of psychic support. There are, and always have been saints, mystics, healers and evangelists in

---

* One would also expect the same characteristic to appear if the messages were telepathically received from the minds of those present at the seance, by the process of 'wishful thinking' previously discussed.

any major branch of philosophy or religion. Many of these, by their very nature, will be psychically gifted, seeing visions and performing 'miracles'. Although my reading is heavily biased towards Western literature, there is plenty of evidence that Buddhist, Islamic and Hindu traditions could at least match the Christian in paranormal content. There is therefore no justification whatever for arguing that the undoubted existence of paranormal abilities in followers (or leaders) of a particular religion is itself evidence of the truth of that religion. So, on both counts, unless there is stronger evidence in non-Christian writings not available to me, I must assume that no religion can claim firm support for its teachings from psychic phenomena.

The Problem Of Visions

I must confess that even if such 'proof' were offered, I would be forced to treat much of it with some suspicion for the following reason. A common event in the literature of most religions is the ecstatic vision of some central figure of that religion, usually as an accompaniment to a divine revelation. Now let me refer back to the discussion in Chapter 7 of the reaction of the brain to a simple emotional stimulus, and let me assume that such an impulse, conveying 'maternal tenderness and protectiveness' was introduced into the right-hand brain of devoted adherents to different religions. There can be little doubt that the Roman Catholic would 'see' a vision of the Virgin Mary, a Hindu would see Lakshmi or Parvati, the Chinese Buddhist would see Kuan Yin, and an atheist his own mother, wife or childhood nurse. In each case the ardour of the experient, acting through his subconscious, would provide more than enough associated characteristics to ensure absolute proof (to him) of the identity of the ethereal visitor.

As with the simple case, so with the more complex examples. The ability of the human brain not only to colour an impression, but to fabricate a complete experience from a single stimulus, must cast considerable doubt on the reliability of any ecstatic or strongly visionary episode and much of the religious evidence is of this type. If a psychic Quaker received a message from the Virgin Mary, or a Jesuit priest claimed inspiration from Guatama Buddha, one would be forced to give some credence to the event, but as it is, the ecstatic pronouncements of the various devotees cancel out, and leave – for me – no conviction. This does not mean that I doubt the reality of the event to the experient, or the existence of the impulse that initiated it, but only that I cannot see how the actual content of the experience can be held to provide evidence as to the truth or otherwise of a particular doctrine.

The Broader View

Nevertheless, it cannot be denied that many phenomena take place in a religious context and show a sensitivity to religious beliefs. For instance, there is a notable response to religious sites, buildings, rituals and symbols of all creeds and denominations. Many people who would not claim to be particularly religious will nonetheless feel a sense of awe and reverence in one of the great cathedrals, but psychic sensitivity seems to go much deeper. Michael Bentine writes:

> I had always felt strong bodily reactions, mainly in my spinal column, which seemed to be caused by specific places and buildings such as earth-temples, ancient fortifications and cathedrals. Certain houses, or even rooms in houses, can affect me emotionally, and sometimes I find it very difficult, or even impossible, to remain in such a place for any length of time.
>
> In most churches, cathedrals, temples and other places of worship, no matter how primitive, I find a wonderful sensation of peace and contentment and a fulfilment of spirit, but in others I have been so uneasy that I have had to leave them.[3]

It could be argued that this is no more than an emotional reaction to grandeur, or known history, but there are many cases in which such explanations cannot be applied, in which the source has been invisible or unsuspected. Two such cases are described by Mrs Rosalind Heywood who, despite an absolutely typical upper-class Church of England upbringing, claims to have an 'agnostic outlook' and to have 'flung away from the Church in adolescence and never returned'. She also has a horror of what she calls 'Holy Crankhood' and of Cults and Sects of all varieties. This does not prevent her from showing a deep sense of religious feeling (in the widest interpretation of the phrase) and a fundamental respect for the symbols embodying that feeling. Consider her discussion[35] of 'The Singing' (see page 92), a variety of non-vocal sounds she sometimes 'hears' as a reaction to spiritually or emotionally stimulating surroundings or atmospheres. She says:

> I listened for the Christian note in several quiet empty churches and found that in some it would pass over into a more intense experience, as if – I repeat as if – an inner force were streaming from the altar. This impression seemed more marked in churches where the

Sacrament was reserved*, and I tested it in some Anglican churches before looking to see whether or not the light indicating its presence was burning before the altar . . . When living in Budapest in the nineteen-thirties I had a chance to check this type of experience. Although I was an unbeliever, the Archbishop kindly invited me to hear the famous Easter Saturday music in the *Matthias Kirche* . . . I found that a seat had been reserved for me in the choir itself, and from it I could see the lamp burning quite near above the altar.

[She received no reaction, and despite the evidence of the lamp, was convinced that the Host was not in the Church.]

. . . Shortly afterwards the service began and during its course a procession came in from the vestry bearing aloft the Host. On enquiry afterwards I learned that it is always removed from a Church on Good Friday and returned on Easter eve.

On another occasion she visited an elderly invalid, and was totally nonplussed by 'a blast of the Christian note so strong that it knocked out my power to talk'. The influence was traced to the old lady's ring, which had been blessed by a Christian bishop. It would not be difficult to find examples of the inverse of this kind of event, when, for instance, a totem or idol from a primitive religion such as Voodoo has 'radiated' a sense of fear and horror to a sensitive person, even from its innocuous position in a museum showcase.

What are we to make of a situation in which an inanimate object, a mere symbol, can communicate with a subconscious mind even if its significance or its very presence is unsuspected? There seem to be two primary possibilities. Either it is possible for inanimate matter to have a 'soul' (the animist theory), or else some strongly emotional episode in which the object was involved may in some way cling to it, so that it is able to trigger off in a sensitive person an extra-dimensional telepathic communication with the event. The details of the event may then be blocked by the censor, leaving only the strong emotion itself, which may be rationalised in any of the ways discussed in Chapter 7. A similar suggestion has already been offered to account for clairvoyance and the sceptic effect operating over a time lag (see page 131). It could also provide a basis for psychometry, the ability of a psychic person to tell something of the history or association of an object simply by holding it, so there would seem to be a considerable body of support for the concept, in a variety of contexts. It is a fascinating idea, which could be pursued in depth by suggesting that the

---

* Some of the consecrated elements of the Eucharist were kept in the Church.

emotional 'history' of an object may in some way be recorded on its extension into the fourth dimension. Unfortunately, not only would such discussion be even more speculative than much of the other contents of this book, but it would not be relevant to my immediate problem.

As I argued above, the fact that such powers do not seem to be limited to symbols from one particular doctrine, and can convey either good or evil, and affect people who do not believe in (or may be ignorant of) the teachings underlying the original event, all suggest that the existence of such phenomena does not support any particular doctrine. It seems far more likely that such powers (however they may manifest themselves), are generated more by *the strength and quality of the human emotions and motives* associated with some climactic occasion, and not on the truth or otherwise of the beliefs underlying those emotions.

The Origins Of Religious Sects

Having concluded that paranormal phenomena do not support any particular major religious doctrine, it may seem illogical to look at those beliefs themselves for clues as to the nature of the paranormal, but in fact it makes sense to do so. If one accepts that no one religion is supported, then all religions may be considered equally valid, or equally false in this respect. Furthermore, although theologians may recognise fundamentally different philosophies in the religions, if one studies the various sects and offshoots of the great religions introduced over the centuries, one is struck not so much by the variety of thought, as by the similarity. Each primary source has produced its authoritarian and hieratic branch (obsessed with tradition and rigid dogma), its free-thinking, pragmatic and outward-looking branch, its violently militant branch, its pacifist branch, its mystical branch, its evangelical branch, and so on. Whatever the teachings of the founder, whether expressed in writings or orally, these have been selected, distorted and manipulated as required to justify each of these different attitudes, and each resulting variation claims with passionate conviction to embody 'The Truth'. Hans-Joachim Schoeps, discussing mysticism, points out:

> Similar phenomena can be observed in all religions. Rudolph Otto has carefully compared the Hindu mystic Shankara and the German mystic Meister Eckart and shown how much they have in common, although their mysticism is rooted in an entirely different history

and cosmology. Even Islam has produced mysticism. The nature of the religion would seem to obviate this.[74]

One begins to suspect that religious doctrines are man-made, and that each individual carries within himself his own instinctive view of his relationship with the universe, so that atheists, ascetics, evangelical preachers, missionaries, hermits and martyrs are born to be such, and not made by philosophic discussion or inspiration from a particular source, human or divine. The implication is that, given a complete freedom of choice and a knowledge of all available doctrines, a man would adopt a specific philosophy *because it fulfilled his own inner needs* rather than because he was convinced by rational argument of its fundamental truth. In practice, most of those who seek imposed moral standards, and social and spiritual support, can find them adequately in one or the other of the orthodox denominations. Many who cannot come to terms with any of the alternatives on offer take the easy way out and 'opt out' altogether. A few have the courage and the drive (or the obstinacy and the egotism, according to one's point of view) to refuse to accept the situation, and will either try to change the doctrines of an existing church (often by joining its priesthood) or will set up yet another sect. In every case, the urge is to find or formulate a doctrine which satisfies one's own instinctive requirements. As Voltaire put it, 'If God made us in His own image, we have certainly returned the compliment.'

This leads ultimately to the situation summarised by Stan Gooch, who writes:

> All faiths are equally valid – or equally invalid, if an individual chooses to disagree. Not only is every religion as good as any other, but the personal religion which Joe Bloggs invents for himself is automatically better than *any* other – for him, as long as he thinks so . . .
>
> . . . The very most that religion can do is to provide a path for each of us personally to explore his or her own being and the nature of being . . . It is one part of the process by which the unconscious mind attempts to communicate with consciousness.[24]

Clues In Beliefs

Accepting this line of argument, it seems eminently reasonable to suggest that the *common factors* between the world religions may indicate the subconscious yearnings of all humanity, and the instinctive knowledge of countless generations, and so reflect some underlying truths. This idea is indeed a fit study for psychologists, anthropologists and sociologists, but for my present purposes I propose to concentrate on one particular aspect of it. I propose to look at paranormal phenomena, and particularly spiritist and Spiritualist communications, and see to what extent these may be supported by (or may contradict) the 'common grounds' I referred to.

I shall begin by considering what was probably the earliest interaction between religious thought and paranormal phenomena: ancestor worship. I have already discussed (see page 133) the theory advanced by Sir Alister Hardy and others that the phenomenally rapid growth of the neocortex of man during the last few hundred thousand years may have suppressed psychic sensitivity, and it is a reasonable assumption that primitive man was far more psychically active than are his descendants, an opinion frequently expressed in the literature. The sculptor John Skeaping spent a considerable time with the natives of Oaxaca, on the southern coast of Mexico. In his autobiography he writes:

> There are things about these primitive people I can never hope to understand. On the one hand, the intelligence of the average adult is that of a seven-year-old child, on the other, they are capable of thinking in the fourth dimension – they have an extra-ordinary power of extra-sensory perception and a sense of direction as acute as a homing pigeon. It is on these gifts they rely for their guidance, and even survival.

I have also pointed out that the refusal to accept the possibility of communication with the dead is a relatively recent development, so that in primitive man such communication would have been completely accepted on a routine basis, as Mrs Heywood indicates (see page 172). This situation persists, particularly in the East. Schoeps, discussing Shintoism, the 'state religion' of Japan, writes:

> In the Shinto of the second period [6th-19th centuries] every deceased person would become a *kami* (supernatural being), that is, the embodiment of the family's vital force and as such eternally present. This idea is the root of the ancestor cult so characteristic of Japan and China. The kami is worshipped on certain memorial days, prayers and sacrifices being offered to it. The members of the family stand before the ancestor tablet and say: 'I speak to you, exalted soul of our father who has become a god . . . '
>
> The Japanese ancestor cult leaves no room for individual freedom. The dead become tyrants over the living. Every day they are appealed to; every day they must be thanked: 'For help given by day

and night receive, you exalted ones, our respectful gratitude.' Daily, they are permitted to participate as living, present beings in all family events; they are informed of the birth of children and of all other important happenings, and in periods of distress they are asked for aid.

From The Very Beginning

If in the prehistoric era contact with the dead were on such a regular basis and so wide-spread as I suggest, and to recently-dead persons, could it really be called 'worship' and the higher entities 'gods'? Any source which could use its extra-dimensional knowledge of events at a distance, in the past, and possibly in the future, so as to give advance warning of a flood, or pass on the plans of an attacking tribe, would certainly warrant the utmost respect but, if my picture of the continuity of character after death is correct, the sources may be no more reliable than their originating humans. Liars, cheats, traitors and the weak minded would still be capable of deliberately or accidentally misleading or betraying. Some form of selection would be inevitable.

A tribal chief would be selected initially for his virility and fertility (and during his lifetime would be required to provide continuous evidence of both), so that after his death he would be approached as ancestor-in-common by a large number of the tribe. If his other exploits were noteworthy and his post-decease advice proved reliable, he would soon be promoted to the status of a folk-hero and a deity. As such, social pressures would ensure that contact with his entity would be reserved for his successor as head of the tribe, or by the head priest (and it is relevant that in many primitive religions these two functions are closely allied). When these in their turn came to die, and so acquire spirit-hood, they would inevitably be regarded as 'contact-men', as go-betweens to carry important questions from the tribe as a whole to the higher divinity, and the answers in the other direction. The steps from this situation to the complex pantheons of Hinduism and Greek mythology, and then to the involved hagiology of the Roman Catholic Church are largely a matter of time.

Prayer And 'Guardian Angels'

The ability to ask for help from a former leader would lead naturally and inevitably (particularly as psychic ability decayed) to one of the most fundamental and widespread of religious concepts, a belief in the efficacy of prayer. In most faiths this is seen as a method by which a man may communicate with a deity, either directly, or through the deity's earthly or heavenly servants. The conditions usually accepted as conducive to effective prayer are either religious ecstacy, tranquil meditation, or strong personal emotion, and it is noteworthy that these are exactly the circumstances which tend to weaken the control of the censor in the brain. If one assumes that such censorship would normally be exercised on messages passing both into and out of the neocortex, it seems logical that a sincere prayer may be 'broadcast' into the fourth dimension, and so could be 'picked up' by an interested and sympathetic entity. This leads naturally to another universal religious concept; Jung would refer to it as an 'archetype'.

Almost all religions include the idea of a person having a 'guardian angel', an ethereal entity with a specific responsibility for looking after his interests. The Roman Catholic has his patron saint, the Buddhist a Boddhisatva, in the Shinto religion one's ancestors carry out the function, and so on. This is fully supported in spiritualist tradition, in that there are frequent references to individuals being 'looked after' by a friend or relative on the other side (as the rabbi was taking care of Neville, or as Myers tried to help Lodge). It seems reasonable to assume that such a guardian would have some access to the mental processes of his charge, within the limits allowed by the censor, and that one of his functions would be to 'listen out' for prayers. However, as suggested above, it is probable that the achievement of a mental condition which will weaken the control of the censor is more important than a deliberate intention to pray in the formal or religious sense. Apart from such requests, it is reasonable to assume that the guardian may himself observe the difficulties facing his charge, and there are also strong implications that he is capable of foreseeing problems, or ill-fortune in the near future, and may take independent action to avert them or reduce their impact.

Just what powers are open to the guardian to help his charge or to affect events on earth is not clear. The occurrence of major physical paranormal phenomena in response to prayer seems very rare, but there is considerable evidence for the occurrence of the kind of 'Orders' described by Mrs Heywood and The Revd Wilkerson (see pages 94 and 117). These consist of positive instructions, impressions or suggestions introduced into the mind of the person praying, or a third party. From earlier discussion, I would suggest that the implantation of a simple Order is one of the most fundamental and probably the simplest of psychic exercises, and the sheer quantity of recorded cases in which a catastrophe has been averted by a sudden warning 'voice in the head' fully supports the concept. It would seem that even if the power of the guardian were limited entirely to this function, its power for good* is still enormous.

The ability to generate such Orders could be used in a number of ways, other than those illustrated by the quoted episodes. The recognition by modern medicine of the powerful influence of the subconscious mind on the physical health of an individual[5] suggests a very important one. Watson[83] describes the cure by hypnotic suggestion of a severe skin condition previously believed to be genetically transmitted and incurable, while the influence of the mental attitude of the patient on the possible remission of cancer is only recently beginning to be fully appreciated. There is obviously a tremendous potential for the cure or alleviation of many physical ailments by the implantation of a psychically induced 'suggestion' into the subconscious mind of the sick person, who would not necessarily be aware that it was present. Such potential would be capable of enormous reinforcement by the use of a psychically-gifted healer as an intermediary, who would provide a local source of additional psychic energy, and may be able to reduce the blocking effect of the censor.

More advanced powers could be made available to the guardian by consultation or cooperation with more experienced entities, as described for the Direct Voice effect, while if necessary, the ultimate aim of prayer, access to the Deity itself, could be achieved by 'passing on' the message. It is interesting that the concept of such contact via a lower-level intermediary occurs in religions as diverse as Catholicism and Buddhism. If my basic premise is accepted (that common factors between religious doctrines reflect instinctive subconscious knowledge of the truth), then there seems adequate justification for suggesting that the universal beliefs in prayer and etheric guardians give strong support for the reality of life in extra dimensions.

---

* – or evil, possibly accounting for many of the troubles of the world.

CHAPTER 15

CLIMBING UP THE GOLDEN STAIRS

'Ah, but a man's reach should exceed his grasp
Or what's a Heaven for?'
Robert Browning

Mention of 'consultation' and 'passing on a message' introduces another almost ubiquitous theme, the idea that the society of the after-life is divided into strata in much the same way as those on earth. At first sight there are two major systems of division. Firstly, there is the separation between the 'Goodies' and the 'Baddies' – very few religions do not include some concept roughly equivalent to the Christian ideas of Heaven and Hell. Secondly, there is a very strong tradition that the 'Goodies' themselves are arranged in some kind of vertical social structure, an idea to be examined later.

'Heaven' and 'Hell' appear in different doctrines under a variety of names, but in general the former is an 'abode of the blessed' conveying certain rewards. These vary somewhat: Islam tending to emphasise the physical and sensual pleasures in store, while Christianity concentrates more on spiritual delights and the satisfaction derived from the recognition of one's virtues, but the principle is common. Descriptions of the after-life by 'Raymond' and others certainly support the idea of a pleasant existence, many being quite explicit that any things desired by a newly-arrived soul are manufactured to order, whether they be houses, jewellery, clothing, tasty food or cigars. Sex is still enjoyable, as is the thrill of making money or other achievements. However, there is a major discrepancy between such accounts and the doctrines of all religions, in that the latter insist that Heaven is a reward for holding to the faith and complying with stipulated rituals. In contrast, the spiritualist accounts make no mention of the importance of any religious ritual. Baptism, circumcision, moral purity, religious Haj, Oaths and Covenants, Last rites, attendances at Masses, all seem to be totally ignored and convey no extra benefits. On the contrary, it is asserted that the delights are provided only insofar as they are necessary to the entity while he adjusts to his new life, and that as he matures he will find them less satisfying and no longer required. If the universality of the Guardian Angel concept is evidence of the existence of an after-life, then the total absence in such communications of any mention of ritual requirements is equally strong evidence of the extent to which religions have been moulded by the egotism and the political and social ambitions of men.

Similarly, although there are implications of a kind of Hell as suffering for previous misdeeds, these do not seem to include sins against religious dogma, the omission of some religious duty, or the non-acceptance of certain beliefs, nor does the punishment involve toasting on gridirons or torture by fiendish devils. Instead, there is an extremely effective Hell of ones own making, and one which may be seen as directly consequent on the characteristics I have attributed to the RE.

I suggested that at death the entity passing over retains all the long-term memories of his earthly life, but that the censor no longer operates. It follows that all events in his previous life are directly accessible to the conscious mind, and there can be no repression into the subconscious of trauma or feelings of guilt. Furthermore, his colleagues and companions, being blessed with the power of telepathy, will have equal access to his mental processes. He can hide nothing in his past from them or from himself. Surely, the inability to avoid public recognition of one's misdeeds, and the taking of direct responsibility for all the consequences of them, cannot help but be a most effective Hell, as all who have experienced remorse will confirm. Such a concept is aesthetically and morally satisfying, implying a degree of suffering proportional to the evil in the original crime *as judged by a superior and totally-informed standard*, and it also carries with it the possibility of expiation of that sin by public recognition of it and the acceptance by one's friends that one has made amends.

Colin Wilson describes the teaching of Rudolf Steiner, one of the major prophets of Theosophy:

> After death, the astral body and ego leave behind the physical body . . . Then it enters a realm called *kamaloca*, which corresponds roughly to the purgatory of Christian doctrine. The past life is relived and examined. Since the astral body is still capable of feeling, it will suffer from its unsatisfied desires and lusts. When purified by suffering, it can finally dissolve. In kamaloca, the astral

body also experiences all the suffering it has inflicted upon others from its own point of view.[89]

Typical of the messages supporting this idea are those received by the medium Eileen Garrett from Captain W.G.R. Hinchcliffe, who died in March 1928 while attempting the first East-West crossing of the Atlantic by air. These include the following:

> I cannot understand why humans say that after death all is happiness, all joy, all rest, all cheerfulness, all brightness. Surely they should be brought to the realisation that as they have lived on Earth, and worked, and done the right thing, so shall their reward be in the hereafter. For though here physical suffering is not, mental suffering is much more severe than it can ever be on earth.
>
> People will say: Why? Because here you are more awake, more able to perceive things by virtue of possessing a much freer mind, housed in a much finer body, which does not bind you as much. Altogether you are in a refining process, and not until you have passed through every scrap of refining process there is in every state of life here, are you permitted into the brighter state . . .
>
> I have not found any evil here. I have found many people, I assure you, who are ignorant of any law, but that does not constitute evil. I have nothing to say about the man who is an atheist. So long as he truly believes what he professes, he stands as great a chance as the man who is bound up in his religion . . .[20]

The first paragraph may be interpreted as supporting the Christian idea of Judgment, but does not suggest any standard on which that judgment is based, or any higher authority imposing that judgment. It is much closer to the Buddhist concept of *Kharma* (or *Kamma*), the fundamental law of the inevitability of cause-and-effect. Schumann writes:

> It is a peculiarity of Theravada Buddhism [the earliest Buddhist teaching] that everyone has to obtain liberation through his own efforts and that the possibility of assistance from without is denied except for instruction about the Way. Neither prayer nor the belief in heavenly beings can hasten delivery from suffering, for the natural law of *Kamma* is incorruptible.

The same theme is emphasised throughout spiritualist literature, that each individual is directly responsible for his own actions. As the devil told Tomlinson in Kipling's poem: 'For the sins that ye do by two and two ye must pay for one by one.'

All Things Change

Two points mentioned above are recurrent themes in spiritualism: that neither the enjoyment of a physical Heaven nor the suffering of a mental Hell is eternal or irrevocable. In the former case the entity (inevitably?) matures in his self-knowledge and under-standing until he is ready to move on to higher things and has no need for such diversions, while in the latter case he comes to terms with his own limitations and expiates his guilt by working for the good of others. In either case, the emphasis is very much on the 'expanding level of consciousness', the assertion that 'the evolutionary thrust towards expanding awareness is cosmic and eternal and does not stop at death.'

There is another contradiction here between the spiritualist version of the after-life, and the views of the Christian Church (to which so many spiritualists belong). Heaven and Hell, far from being the separate and selective places described in Christian literature, are states of mind of entities *who may well intermingle*. Insofar as the 'Good' and the 'Bad' may avoid each other's company, it is by choice rather than through physical separation. This makes sense, as part of the agony of contrition must surely lie in seeing the peace of mind of those who have come to terms with their own weaknesses and have been accepted as such by their peers, and in being shunned by those one respects; and similarly some of the pleasure of learning is in the satisfaction (smug but very human) of being able to pass on that knowledge to help others.

THE PLANES OF EXISTENCE

So I come to the second system of social division in the hereafter: the hierarchical structure in the levels of power. If there is a single archetypal idea common to virtually all concepts of ethereal life, from the journeys of Orpheus, Gilgamesh and Dante, to the Nordic Valhalla and the Catholic and Hindu pantheons, it is that of an ascending scale of achievement and power. Surely, it is relevant that when Christ said 'In my Father's house are many mansions', the word He used is related to the Latin *mansio*, meaning I stay or remain, implying a step or a temporary resting-place, rather than the modern English meaning of a large house. This concept is particularly evident in spiritist communications, in the form of references to 'Planes of Existence'. The descriptions in the Myers messages (as discussed by Arthur Ford[18]) are particularly explicit. Myers describes Seven Planes, ranging from the First Plane, life on earth, to '. . . the Seventh and final plane – in which the soul reaches the final partnership with God.' Some of these planes have already been discussed in more-or-less explicit terms, which I will summarise here, but in addition I will attempt to relate Myers account to the extra-dimensional concepts developed in this book.

The First Plane

The First Plane is simple enough: life on Earth, in which the physical body is constrained to move in a single three-dimensional universe, and is subject to physical damage and decay. All knowledge of other dimensions is normally suppressed by the censor mechanism, but this, like all other parts of the body, is fallible under stress and can be weakened or partially disabled by damage, disease or possibly genetic factors. At death the physical body remains in this world, but the rest of the individual, now free of physical limitations and the restrictions of the censor, moves into the Second Plane.

The Second Plane

This is described as a dream-like condition of rest and readjustment, (inviting comparison with the concept of 'Limbo'), and I have suggested that such readjustment must include:

a) Coming to terms with the fact that he is dead;
b) Beginning to understand some of the more elementary consequences of his new status;
c) Being accepted into, and accepting the help of, a community of like-minded REs.

It seems that this plane may provide a more permanent home for such spirits as cannot or will not meet these requirements, and these will include retarded or delinquent entities who may be responsible for most of the mischievous or evil-intentioned paranormal phenomena on earth, and it is such entities that are most likely to be contacted by amateurish, ill-intentioned or accidental mediumship. For the normal entity, movement into the Third Plane seems automatic in a matter of a few days or weeks after death (the first contacts with Ann Kennedy, Jim Pike and Raymond Lodge all occured about 14-20 days after death).

The Third Plane

Most of the more coherent communications through skilled and experienced mediums is with inhabitants of the Third Plane, and so most of the information we have acquired, from Swedenborg onwards, applies to it. The many sources show a remarkable degree of agreement. The surroundings are at least outwardly similar to earth, as are the houses, the bodies of the occupants, clothing and so on. As regards society, while there are obviously leaders and followers, helpers and helped, weak and strong, there seems little evidence of a ruling class, a law-making process or a fixed code of conduct. The emphasis is on a fluid community with direct inter-personal affection, and mutual help and respect. New arrivals are welcomed and comforted, and then helped to adjust to their change of circumstances, while for the more experienced entity, there is continual group activity of one form or another. Ford, quoting information received from Myers, writes:

> The grouping urge, instead of being a family structure, may be a special interest, a religion, a profession, a trade, an art or almost anything that would join people in a joint exercise of their imaginations. Since communication is by direct-image telepathy, there are no language barriers. And since enthusiasms are no respecters of centuries, time is of little account. So it is perfectly possible for a soul to find itself part of a group from other nations and other centuries.

More prosaically, David Kennedy comments:

> If eternal life means progress and challenge and new discoveries in an ascending pilgrimage of closer proximity to the living creative force we call God, then our loved ones have things to learn and work to do.[45]

Communication into the minds of mediums on the First Plane seems to be well organised on a group basis, with experienced entities acting as coordinators and middlemen. One cannot avoid the conclusion that the major, possibly the only, obstacle to free communication between the two planes is in the censor mechanism in the minds of the living.

There are two more important differences to be noted here between the spiritualist teaching and the Christian doctrines. Firstly, whereas the Christian Heaven contains the Blessed of all 'ranks', from the newly-passed soul to Christ Himself, the Planes described by Myers and others are specifically referred to as separate places (possibly in other dimensions), to which one may journey, if qualified, and from which one may return. The second point is more fundamental in concept. In Christian doctrines, there is a somewhat confused description of a heavenly hierarchy of Saints, Angels, Archangels and so on, but insofar as can be determined, the former hold their office by virtue (literally) of the life they led on earth, while both of the latter are of 'different species', not necessarily originating from, or organically related to, humanity. On the other hand, the spiritualist descriptions suggest a world populated entirely (or primarily) by the souls of deceased humans, in which each of these souls has the ability to progress to higher things (through the Planes) *by its efforts after death*.

What may be thought surprising is that many of the activities described on the Third Plane have no particular moral or spiritual content, but read almost like the syllabus of local Adult Education Classes. The inference is that any activity which encourages an entity to expand his understanding and share his knowledge with others is in itself worthy. But does this imply that all knowledge is equally valuable? Do we have a continuation of the attitude of Science that the mere acquisition of facts constitutes 'progress', and requires no justification? I can find no evidence of a major scientific advance initiated by information received at a seance, despite the obvious advantages of four-dimensional powers. One cannot avoid the thought that, from the standpoint of a four-dimensional entity to which the stupidity and pettiness of mankind is evident, the temperature of the atmosphere of Jupiter is not of any particular interest, nor does it justify any great effort to discover it. Pure Science must be seen in its true colours, as the idle curiosity of a minority, undertaken for a purely selfish motive – self-satisfaction. It certainly cannot be claimed to have engendered any evident improvement in the warmth, humanity or happiness of those involved in it, any more than a career in banking or farming. That kind of activity may have its uses in the early stages of development of an entity, but it remains arid, and ultimately unsatisfactory. It is highly likely that an entity will progress towards those activities which are more directly helpful to others when the interest in mere fact-finding has palled and when he feels the need to justify his own existence.

The qualifications for promotion to a higher plane, although not specified, seem to bear out this idea, being expressed in such terms as 'spiritual development', 'expansion of consciousness' and so on. It seems that one must arrive at a certain state of self-knowledge, understanding, and emotional and spiritual maturity, so that one feels the need for, and is capable of using, the higher standards and increased powers. There is also a factor (mentioned by Marion Bergrud – page 210 – and many others) that entities who retain an interest in people and events on the First Plane will tend to remain in the Third, and one must forgo such interest if one is to progress.

There are some references to the possibility of reincarnation to the First Plane, either as a standard procedure, or (more likely) voluntarily to 'acquire merit' in the Buddhist sense, but these seem insufficiently specific to provide reliable evidence for reincarnation as such, and I will not elaborate on them here. While entities from higher planes are referred to with respect, and described as being able to return to help the progress of others, there seems no pressure or persuasion to acquire some standard or token of 'goodness'. Nonetheless, although an entity may remain in the Third Plane almost indefinitely, many of them seem to develop an ambition to move on to the Fourth.

The Fourth Plane

At the time of the Myers communications, his experience of the Fourth Plane was limited to a single 'journey', and he confesses to increasing difficulty in finding words understandable to us in order to describe it adequately. He says:

> A human being cannot imagine a new sound, a new colour or feeling entirely outside the range of his previous experience. It is impossible for him to conceive the infinite variety of new sounds, colours and feelings experienced by us on the Fourth Plane.

There is a strong resemblance here with the descriptions of the effects on the living mind of psychedelic drugs such as LSD (see page 110) and ecstatic experiences, so that it seems completely logical to suggest that the move from the Third to the Fourth plane involves an expansion of dimensional capabilities – probably an improvement in the processes of perception to enable them to handle all the information received from four dimensions. This includes direct and deliberate telepathy and 'bodily' projection through four-dimensional space. There is some suggestion of actual travel in time.

The Fifth And Sixth Planes

Myers experience of higher planes than the Fourth was based on hearsay only, and the difficulty of finding an adequate vocabulary is correspondingly increased. He says that to enter the Fifth Plane requires an experience similar to death and rebirth, and endows the entity with complete freedom of movement and thought within the 'stellar universe' (Sic!). On the Sixth Plane:

> . . . Individuals . . . are matured spirits, having lived through, with conscious comprehension, all the aspects of the created universe. They are capable of living now without form, of existing as white light [Sic! – e.m.r.?? – see page 75] in the pure thought of their creator.

Probably the nearest I can get to such a situation is to suggest that the Fifth Plane includes true time travel, possibly with an ability to communicate across a fifth dimension. The Sixth I will not attempt.

The Seventh Plane

On the Seventh Plane:

> . . . The soul enters full partnership with God . . . It baffles description; it is heartbreaking even to attempt to write of it.

Inevitably, I must remain equally baffled, but there are questions to be asked, even at this stage – see below.

The Philosophical Aspects

As a rational approach to the Seven Planes in terms of multi-dimensional capabilities, the description above holds together reasonably well, but I cannot leave it at that. The moral, spiritual and philosophical implications are so overwhelming that they must be explored, even though such exploration must inevitably be completely subjective.

The most basic concept is that of the upward progression of the individual through the planes *as a result of its own efforts*. What is surprising (to me) is the point already made: that there seem to be no specifically moral standards to be attained. The emphasis is always on the expansion of knowledge and awareness of the entity to the point at which it can accept a quantum leap in its powers. On consideration, I find this principle to be aesthetically and logically satisfying. The urge to understand more, to experience more deeply, to widen one's mental and spiritual horizons, seems instinctive, and indeed, if one accepts some modern thinking, such an urge is the driving force behind evolution itself. Nothing could be simpler and more fundamental than the assumption that this urge, acting on earth over aeons of time and in terms of species and genera, should continue after death on a more personal and individual basis.

Applied to earthly religions, the principle strongly favours freethinking and introspective doctrines which emphasise individuality, rather than those which demand the unthinking acceptance of rigid dogma. The doctrinal and ritual details of one's religious practice are totally irrelevant; it is the influence of one's belief on one's understanding and spiritual maturity (and therefore one's attitude to others) that matters.

A Worrying Aspect

There is a disturbing facet of this argument. If progress is not on a moral basis, then surely evil may flourish, the bad obtaining more power along with the good. It may be suggested that the answer is that the basic cause of evil is ignorance, so that any increase in knowledge, and the ability to understand the situation of others, will automatically imply an improvement in spiritual standards. This is temptingly simple, but is it necessarily true? Allied with this is a second major question: One tends to associate 'goodness' with conformity, and hence with uniformity, while 'badness' is basically a refusal to conform, and so a characteristic of individuality. Would the attainment of higher levels of understanding *inevitably* lead to a loss of the individuality which distinguishes 'Me' from the rest of mankind? Is it reasonable to expect me to strive for greater knowledge, understanding and spiritual insight if it may result in my eventual emergence as a mass-produced, anonymous, dessicated, whitewashed, saccharinised 'soul'? And if I am not allowed my own freedom of judgment on important matters, this fate seems inevitable. Myers is comforting on this point; he says of the Fourth Plane:

> . . . Not only love, truth and beauty are present but also hostility, hate and anger . . . If on earth some other man or woman was your enemy and you hated one another the old emotional memory will awaken when you meet. Love and hate draw you together in the pattern of your particular designs.

So despite some echoes of Buddhist philosophy, the Buddhist

ideals of total unemotional detachment and withdrawal from a world of illusion do not seem to be supported in any way. On the other hand, if moral standards are not involved at all, then one can achieve the tremendous potential powers over the human world implicit in the occupation of a higher plane, without any commitment not to misuse those powers; in effect, I can play Faust without a binding contract. Could the phrase 'a clever devil' be more than a flippant acknowledgement of grudging admiration?

Fundamentally, such questions revolve around a single vital point. Of all the characteristics of mankind which we label 'Bad' or 'Wrong', some are no more than the products of want, fear, pettiness and mental immaturity, and as such will be weakened or eliminated by knowledge, security and further progress. Others are fundamental features of the character of an individual which will survive as long as 'I' am 'Me'. I could no doubt make some attempt to list the two categories, but would inevitably end up hopelessly bogged down in a swamp of speculative philosophy. The point would still remain; if all the shortcomings originating from ignorance, immaturity and other temporary causes are eliminated, will the rest – those fundamental to the personality – include any 'Evil'? I suppose that I could dodge the issue, pointing out that while on Myers' evidence the personality survives at least to the Fourth Plane, further promotion may involve 'a voluntary dissolution of Self into the Life Force' (or some other impressive and equally meaningless phrase). Since there is no firm evidence to refer to, and at this stage the inadequacy of our language is complete, such arguments would again be pointless speculation.

So the bafflement concerning the Seventh Plane conceals more than just an ignorance of the physical nature of the Ultimate Deity, it includes an equal ignorance of its moral status; whatever it is, is it 'Good' or is it 'Bad'? While there is endless discussion of the nature of God, both in religious writings and in psychic communications, most of the former beg the question, while the latter consist (understandably enough) of metaphysical and philosophical superlatives which get me no further. An outstanding characteristic of the latter, however, has already been referred to, the 'negative element', by which I mean that in the descriptions of the after-life, the established and recognised Deities of the world are conspicuously absent. There are no consistent references to the vengeful and nationalistic Yahweh, or the dogmatic and equally partisan Allah, or the paternal and merciful Christ-God of the Christians (in any of His three forms). The original concept of Brahman as the eternal soul which penetrates the whole universe may have some elements in common with what Myers describes as 'The Creator Himself . . . conceived as pure creative thought-energies source – "The Great Imagination",' but the earliest Buddhist concept of nothing but an absolute and axiomatic law of Kharma, while supported to some extent, does not begin to approach that vision. Putting it bluntly, if Myers and the others who paint the same picture are right, then all of the major religions in the world are completely and utterly wrong in their concepts of God.

This is not blasphemy. There can only be one Truth, and the fact that only a tiny minority of the world population can agree on any single doctrine suggests that there is no Church (in any sense), no Book, indeed no single source available to man, that contains it all. Even the parts that may be contained in any one source are usually seen only vaguely and distorted under a mountain of obscuring and polluting 'religion', mostly added by human intervention, and for purely secular purposes.

So again I draw a blank. I suppose the logical way out is to assume that since there is no positive evidence either way, I should assume that the Deity is neutral, neither good nor bad, or that the good and evil forces of the universe are balanced (the mediaeval heresy of Manicheism). I find that I just cannot accept this philosophy of indecision; it is too much of an admission of ignorance and defeat. Since all else has failed, I can only fall back on the ultimate arbiter in such matters, my own instinct (including in the term all factors hereditary, environmental and educational, in fact everything that defines 'Me'). In doing so, of course, I recognise that I am doing consciously exactly what I have suggested that all people will try to do consciously or subconsciously: making my own religion to suit myself.

My gut reaction (or gumption, call it what you will) focuses on two basic observations. Firstly, that the recognisable evil in this world originates from a small minority of individuals. Most people, if freed from the pressures of want and political or religious dogma, would be at worst petty, mildly selfish, self-important and apathetic. At best they are wonderfully tolerant, loving and unselfish. The second half of this book develops a picture of mankind as *organically capable* of freely communicating, if not actually blending together, in the Fourth Dimension. If there is any reality at all in this concept, this 'collective unconscious' of Jung's, then the pressure of progress must be upwards towards goodness. Secondly, the idea of a scale of expanding knowledge and awareness seems absolutely fundamental to the whole organisation of living things in the universe. Knowledge brings Power; Power gives Freedom; and Freedom involves Responsibility. The hallmark of evil is that it is irresponsible; it deliberately causes suffering, and then either ignores or delights in that suffering. Ignorance or apathy is not a characteristic one can associate with the Ultimate, and to understand and yet delight in the suffering of others must be unnatural, on any plane of existence.

Undoubtedly, God is Good.

CHAPTER 16

SO WHERE DO WE GO FROM HERE?

'One day, perhaps, ESP will get its own Einstein who with some inspired generalisations will make this jumble of apparently irrational phenomena fall into a meaningful pattern.'
Rosalind Heywood

So I have come to the end of my exploration. I began with children's games and imaginary water-bugs and ended with contemplation of the nature of the Ultimate Being (surely a literal case of 'from the ridiculous to the sublime'). To explore further, even if that were possible, could lay myself open to charges of *lèse-majesté* of the worst kind. It only remains to consider the implications of my ideas, and their possible consequences.

The basic concepts that I have studied are extremely simple, reducible to no more than half a dozen suppositions, each expressible in barely fifty words, and each having a logical consistency with the others. To give support to those suppositions, one can draw on the evidence and opinions from a remarkably wide spectrum of disciplines and philosophies. Scientific fact ties up with mythology, mystical mutterings support laboratory observations, abstract mathematics buttresses findings in neurology; the whole is interlaced with tie-rods of traditional beliefs and honestly-given evidence. One wonders, if the whole concept is apparently so obviously irrefutable, why on earth should it still remain unaccepted and ridiculed?

The first reason is somewhat complex. In the 18th century, the scientists and philosophers of the Western world accepted the dualism of Descartes, concluding that the universe was divisible into two separate parts: the physical world of material objects, which was real, reliable, predictable and obedient to natural laws;

and the minor world of sensory experience, thought and imagination, which was unreal, unreliable and not obedient to any rational laws. The major, possibly the only function of the latter, was to observe, understand and enjoy the former. If there is anything of substance in this book, then that conclusion was the greatest blunder ever committed by thinking men.

One could suggest that the fourth dimension offers the possibility of a Third World (not in a political or geographical sense) which bridges the other two, but this is far too inadequate a concept. There is no reason for suggesting that the extra-dimensional world is not just as physical as our own, in that objects in it obey rigid laws of cause-and-effect, of which our own 'Laws of Nature' are minor extracts. It is also 'mental' in that it is perpetually alive with the conscious and subconscious communications between all minds, human and animal; such communications extending over all space and time and between all levels of evolution. The Third World does not so much bridge the first two, as absorb them into itself. It has been swept under the carpet for over two hundred years because the two-world theory satisfies men's craving for new discoveries and technological toys, and also because it feeds his ego in his role as self-appointed Lord of Creation. He is not only ignorant of the Third World, he is afraid of it.

The Key-stone

The second reason why this scenario is not accepted is much simpler, and explainable by a simple (and final!) analogy. I sometimes recall, and never without an inward chuckle of appreciation, a cartoon which appeared many years ago in *Punch*. In the foreground of the sketch (which had no caption), two men stand on a hillock overlooking what is obviously the stony plain of Egypt. One of them is the Pharaoh Cheops, and the other his Chief Architect, or Clerk of the Works. They are gazing across the desert to where the Great Pyramid is nearing completion, and on the face of each man is an expression, not of pride and achievement, but of horror, incredulity and despair. They are evidently just becoming aware that at some time in the early stages of their project a slight error has crept in, and the whole magnificent edifice has been built *upside down!*

In the later stages of writing and editing this book, I have sometimes experienced a fellow feeling for those men. I too have constructed a massive and imposing structure, albeit mental rather than physical. My structure is, as I suggested above, so simple, consistent and logical that it seems self-evident. Then realisation dawns, as it did on Cheops, that the whole of this structure is balanced, like the inverted pyramid, on a single keystone assumption, that a Fourth Dimension physically exists. Prove that true, and all the ideas become, if not self-evident, at least feasible and worth studying. Prove it false and the whole structure crumbles back to the present-day untidy and intolerable situation in which science is seen to be inconsistent within itself, forcing unacceptable paradoxes to be accepted; honest people are accused of lying simply because their evidence is inexplicable; intelligent men are afraid to tell the truth as they see it because to do so would damage their careers; and society as a whole pays lip service to ideas and concepts which the majority of individuals believe to be false.

A Dream Of Unity

Such a situation applies primarily in Western societies; east of Suez they have more sense, once one has stripped away the thin veneer of pseudo-civilisation that has been acquired along with the TV set and modern armaments. Common paranormal phenomena such as poltergeists, telepathy, clairvoyance and communication with the dead are quietly taken for granted by the majority as simple facts of life, requiring no formal proof any more than one seeks to prove that a man must breathe to live.

Now just suppose that those two contrasting attitudes could be combined, and the connection that I have suggested between scientific thought on one hand, and paranormal events on the other could be confirmed, supported, strengthened and eventually welded into an indisputable chain of logic backed by experimental evidence *available to all*. As practical examples, suppose that a TV documentary film could be made which incontrovertibly proved (to any reasonable person) the reality of communication with the dead, or a drug could be marketed which safely and reliably modified the action of the brain censor, so allowing repeatable experiments to be carried out in OBE and deliberate extra-dimensional communication. What would be the result?

The effects on many of the Eastern races would probably not be particularly drastic. The reaction of the Indian sub-continent and the surrounding countries would be a slightly sardonic 'So what? Have you only just found out?' Such countries as Japan, which have flung themselves headlong into Western culture, would probably get more excited, developing a more cynical attitude to Western philosophies and returning to their own mystical religions.

Undoubtedly it is the American and European peoples who would suffer the worst trauma. The reaction of the Victorians to Darwin's Theory of Evolution, which suggested that man was not the deliberate and individual creation of an all-powerful God who made him in His own image to dominate the universe, but the latest product in a long chain of random natural processes, was one of shock and horror. Think, then, of the reception which would be given to the proposal that man's universe, which he tries so desperately to understand (and largely fails) is but one of many, and others exist which are beyond his knowledge and understanding. Think of the suggestion that Man, with his much-vaunted intelligence and capacity for learning, is no more than the least-gifted first stage on a ladder of mental and spiritual evolution. Think of the shattering of the edifice of 'scientific knowledge', so laboriously built up over the years; a return to square one and a revision of every fundamental concept. Even more catastrophically, think of the shattering of the self-confidence of the scientific fraternity who are so convinced of the infallibility of their own attitudes and procedures that they defend them with all the irrationality they presume to despise in others.

A Dream Indeed!

Lastly, think of the effects on the man in the street, to *know* (not think, not hope, not believe, but to *know* in the literal meaning of the word) that death is not the end, but rebirth to a new life, with a chance for him to go forward, to make amends, or to do better next time. Any change which robs the religious and political organisations of the world of their power to brainwash, bully, bribe or blackmail a man into carrying out such distasteful and unnatural activities as torture and murder, must result in a better life for all. Prove to a man that his private life is subject to continual supervision and judgment by his forebears and others, convince him that he must stand or fall by his own actions with no alibi or protection from his leaders or priests, show him his own existence in proportion to the life of all mankind, all living things in all time, and finally take away his fear of death, and you are likely to change his outlook rather drastically. Many who have experienced the cleansing and exhilarating effect of enlightenment or religious conversion can confirm the power of new beliefs to give a massive renewal of inner strength to defy social pressures. The difference between this situation and the scenario I envisage is that this 'conversion' would not be of individuals, or a few hundred people, but a mass effect on whole countries and societies at a time, persuaded not by the charisma of one man or one message, but by solid and incontrovertible evidence demonstrated through the mass media, and reproducible at local community level.

The Grim Reality

Obviously, such changes could not take place overnight, nor could they occur without the bitterest of wrangling and bloodshed – and it is evident that the underlying cause of most of this would be the loss of face in the eyes of the world of those political and religious leaders who have been most dogmatic in their assertions of the infallibility of their own beliefs, and the scientists whose materialist philosophies have so dominated the last couple of centuries. Given the kind of factual evidence that I have supposed, even the most pig-headed of scientists, if he makes any pretence of possessing a logical mind, must eventually accept it, but politicians and the leaders of the world religions (it is difficult to differentiate between them) are not subject to the same constraints, and are perfectly capable of denying the obvious and trumpeting the patently untrue for an indefinite period.

There would, of course, be attempts by many religions to adapt their doctrines to the new discoveries, much as the Victorian Churches desperately sought an interpretation of the Book of Genesis compatible with the concept of evolution – and probably just as successful; and no doubt there would be no shortage of head-in-the-sand last-ditch martyrs in all religions, prepared to die for their discredited beliefs (and thereby, ironically enough, to discover their errors before they needed to).

It is also ironic that total disaster may possibly be averted by the same delaying tactics, which would ensure piecemeal and gradual acceptance of the new knowledge. Even so, the prevention of major conflict initiated by the more obdurable sects and individuals, and those who can never miss an opportunity for personal profit and advancement, would require inspired leadership and international statesmanship of a standard woefully and obviously lacking in today's unclean, self-centred and totally irrational dogfight between the nations.

The Way Ahead

Having painted a glum and possibly cynical picture of what may happen *if* such discoveries were to be made, it is not unreasonable to consider *how* they may come about. Old Moore and Nostradamus do not seem to offer such predictions,* so I must consult my own crystal ball.

Since all of my scenario is based on the reality of a Fourth Dimension, one would like to imagine the situation envisaged above – a single convincing demonstration which would settle the matter once and for all, just as the shift in the apparent position of stars caused by the gravitational field of the sun convincingly clinched Einstein's case for the General Theory of Relativity. However, it seems unlikely that the single-experiment proof will be achieved in the foreseeable future. Philosophical arguments advanced by Sir Karl Popper suggest that it is impossible *even in principle* to prove that a Fourth Dimension cannot exist, and the intransigence of scientism (discussed in Chapter 2) virtually guarantees that the alternative – to prove by a single experiment or observation that it does exist – is almost as impossible. In the absence of such proof, the best alternative would be a well-founded, concerted and organised effort to study, as a single subject, the whole sweep of all the relevant sciences, concentrating wherever possible on identifying and confirming the kind of hitherto unsuspected relationships which I have tried to indicate. By this means it may be possible to accumulate such a mass of diverse evidence as to overwhelm the objections of those who insist that the evidence of many straws cannot be used to deduce the direction of a single wind.

Unfortunately, that again is a most unlikely prospect, in that it would require a subordination of identity and a cooperation between opposing philosophies totally unprecedented in this world, and certainly anathema to the average professional scientist. Inevitably, then, the first steps must occur in the form of isolated discoveries in unrelated disciplines.

Physics And Medicine

Possible lines of approach in the important fields of quantum physics and cosmology are hesitantly offered in Appendices 3, 4 and 5, but there is a dangerous possibility of 'going overboard' and

---

* . . . or do they? Does not the year AD 2000 loom large in the predictions of the latter?

seeing these sciences as providing the whole answer, as discussed in Chapter 2.

In the field of medicine (using the term in its widest sense), there are a number of possibilities. Even the shallow and elementary discussion in this book has been enough to indicate that the key to many paranormal events lies in the processes of perception, and the action of the censor mechanism in the brain. Insofar as the action of both is modified by hallucinogenic drugs, the study of the effects of these is all-important. Before the abuse of LSD led to its being virtually prohibited, there were signs of considerable progress in investigation of hallucinatory states. For instance, it has been shown that there are some similarities in the sensations experienced under LSD, under carbon dioxide poisoning (partial suffocation) and in the preliminary stages of the process of dying.[60] The similarities in the EEG traces produced by LSD and those during deliberate efforts to exercise psychic powers have already been mentioned (see page 112). Ideally, one would like to have available several LSD-type drugs which had no harmful side-effects, which were not addictive, and which could be directed specifically at known areas or functions of the brain.

Allied to this would be a considerable refinement of present-day techniques of EEG recording. The technique of studying neural activity by voltages detected on electrodes external to the skull is very limited. I have suggested elsewhere[72] that it may be possible to detect direct radiation of infra-red from the neural system, and if this should prove true it will allow a far greater degree of accuracy in obtaining a three-dimensional picture of brain activity. It is possible that such a model, if studied by the methods of bulk signal analysis developed in the fields of communications, radar and sonar, could be used to trace the paths of individual mental processes deep in the brain.

As an alternative to drugs, it may prove possible to employ focused infra-red, radio or ultrasonic waves to modify temporarily the operation of a small area of the brain. Such methods may be hazardous to begin with, involving the risk of permanent damage, but they would have the advantage of remaining in the hands of skilled users, with no chance of their being abused by young people seeking a 'kick'.

Psychic Research – A Warning

Fascinating and valuable as evidence from the fields of Physics and Medicine will be, one must ultimately look to psychic research itself to provide the bulk of the evidence, and since such research covers a very wide field, and presents peculiar problems, a short review of its history may provide useful pointers and warnings.

During the latter half of the 19th century, and particularly in the early years of the Society for Psychical Research, tremendous effort was put into the serious investigation of the physical effects which accompany spiritualist seances, such as bell ringing, gusts of wind, temperature changes, table tilting, and levitation of the medium himself. Quite simple measurements, such as apparent changes in the weight of a table being levitated, and the physical reactions of the body of the medium, gave significant and often startling results. Sir William Crookes and others reported that a medium sitting on a weighing machine was capable of reducing his indicated weight by at least 20 per cent with no evident physical explanation. Crookes, reporting his investigation of D.D. Home, recorded that under strictly-controlled conditions an 8 lb (3.6 kg) weight on a weighing machine registered a weight varying between 23 and 48 lb while Home was two or three feet away from it.

Unfortunately, all such work was fogged and stultified by charges and counter-charges of fraud, charlatanry, and blind prejudice (both for and against), and rendered totally worthless by the determination of journalists, confidence tricksters and stage illusionists to cash in on the tremendous public interest. Most of the effort applied to the work was expended in attempts to make the experiments so fraud-proof that they would satisfy the ultra-cynical – and of course they failed to achieve this. An even less attractive aspect was the determined and vicious character-assassination practised by those professional men who saw their whole philosophy of life (not to mention their incomes!) as being under attack.

This situation brought the study of physical mediumship into disrepute, and led to conditions in which the best and most dedicated of investigators hesitated to publish even the most striking and significant findings. This demise of the study of physical effects was followed, in the early years of this century, by intensive investigation into the process of spiritualism itself, involving the verbatim recording (in manuscript, of course, since audio recording was not yet available) of lengthy seances, and the detailed analysis of reams of automatic writing. A great body of this type of work was carried out under carefully controlled conditions by the SPR in this country and their overseas equivalents, and reached its zenith in the twenty-year series of cross-correspondence communication with the dead Myers and others to which reference has been made, and the intensive study of the mediumship of Mrs Leonard and others. I would venture the opinion that anyone who is excessively cynical about this work, and who suggests that those involved in it were all either dishonest or gullible, should be referred to one of several books analysing the subject (such as Mrs Heywood's *The Sixth Sense*), and politely told that his opinion is worthless until he has read it. (As a general rule, the more obdurate and vociferous the sceptic, the more ill-informed he seems to be!)

The view expressed by Sir Alister Hardy that the Myers cross-correspondences represent the strongest evidence for survival after death that we have, is far more realistic. However, those who took part in these investigations (both human and entity) seem to have ended up disappointed and disillusioned, having accumulated a huge mass of evidence apparently supporting the concept of life after death, but containing no rigid proof which would stand up to ultra-cynical criticism. There, it seems, the subject has rested, and it is unlikely that repetition or confirmation of similar material will make it any more convincing: the ability, dedication and intelligence of those involved on both sides was such as to make it most unlikely that others could succeed where they failed.

However, there are minor facets of such work which could yield interesting results. For instance, comparisons have been made on a large scale between characteristics of Near-Death Visions (see page 153) as reported in America, and similar events in India,[89] and a considerable degree of correlation was found. Such a comparison largely eliminates the bias caused by the 'like-to-like' principle, and an extension of such work to investigation of phenomena at spiritualist seances, and particularly to the content of the messages received at them, could prove invaluable.

Laboratory Investigation

It may have been the failure to convince of the Myers correspondences that caused a major change of direction in research into the paranormal in the 1930s, turning to attempts to prove the reality of telepathy and psychokinesis. The pilot investigations were by Dr Rhine at Duke University, USA, and consisted mainly of large-scale experiments in card-identification, dice-throwing and (later) sophisticated electronic equivalents. In such experiments, attempts by a large number of people to exercise telepathy (for example) under controlled conditions are compared mathematically with the results to be expected if their 'guesses' were determined by chance alone. Positive results in Rhine's early experiments, which apparently proved the existence of telepathy, were first attacked by questioning the mathematical techniques, and the capabilities of those applying them. When this argument was satisfactorily answered, the next stage was to question the honesty of the experimenters, postulating large-scale collusion and mass perjury among university staff and students, most of whom had nothing to do with the experiments. The latest ploy, on which the situation seems to have stabilised, is to advance the theory that chance itself may not result in purely (i.e., mathematically) random results: there may be a fundamental guiding principle which 'deliberately' causes coincidences to happen!

The present situation is that most research into the paranormal is carried out almost coincidentally as part of the general research into normal and abnormal psychology and psychiatry, and as such has attained a measure of respectability. Any attempt to extend that work into physical considerations, or to deal with phenomena in material terms, is met with hostility and ridicule, or at best a head-in-the-sand apathy.

Once More Into The Breach

In view of the considerable advances in the last few decades in techniques of the measurement and recording of physical quantities, I would suggest that a renewed attack on physical effects is well overdue. Modern techniques of infra-red and ultra-violet photography, the application of waveform and signal analysis to sound and video recording, electronic methods of continuous measurement and recording of physical quantities such as weight, temperature, air pressure and so on are all ideally suited to studies of auras, ectoplasm, levitation and poltergeist-type phenomena with a high level of protection against fraud.* The same techniques can also be applied to such phenomena as Kirlian photography and the so-called Raudive effect (the recording of 'spirit messages'

---

* I refer here to fraud by the psychics under investigation, deceiving the experimenters. Over-optimism, carelessness, data 'laundering' and fraudulent claims by the experimenters to deceive other researchers and the public can only be countered by repetition of similar experiments elsewhere (not always a practicable process!) but this is a lesser problem, and one by no means peculiar to this field.

on tape recorders). Bentine's description of the blue glow (presumably corona) around the hair of the sitters at a seance, and the smell of ozone, certainly indicate the presence of high electrostatic voltages, which could be measured and the source traced. In view of the discussion in this book on the nature of the sixth sense, and the repeated emphasis on the extra-dimensional nature of e.m.r., detailed and thorough monitoring of all frequencies up to visible light should be as routine as EEG recordings. However, such monitoring must include facilities for not only detecting the presence of a signal, but also for analysing its structure.

Such techniques, in conjunction with the psychological approach to 'artificial mediumship' of Bacheldor and others (see page 166) could probably give significant results in a relatively short period. A single fully attested, recorded and incontrovertible apport, for instance, would puncture the stone-wall defence of orthodox science sufficiently to demand serious attention.

To declare that paranormal effects are 'all in the mind', and so beyond the reach of physical measurements, may prove to be no more than an error of judgment; but to dismiss all reports of physical effects on philosophical grounds alone, and without having first applied to them all the power of modern science and technology, is manifest folly. Even a cursory examination of the literature on such matters suggests that those involved in research into physical paranormal effects are all too frequently badly advised on technical and engineering matters, rendering much of their effort open to criticism on practical grounds (Raudive, mentioned above, is a particular case in point).

The Vital Requirement

One of the major problems in any such investigation must be the acute shortage of suitable subjects capable of producing physical phenomena with reasonable reliability. Powerful psychics of the calibre of D.D. Home, Matthew Manning and Uri Geller who are prepared to undergo intensive investigation are few and far between.

Manning's experience is cautionary.[52] After close cooperation with virtually any qualified authority who offered to investigate his powers, he has finally declined to take part in any more such experiments. He complains that, despite the success of investigation after investigation, no major body of any professional significance is prepared to endorse publicly his claims. Each new team insisted on totally ignoring all previous work and repeating the same monotonous, repetitive and unimaginative experiments for themselves. Having once convinced themselves of the absence of fraud, but being unable to find any convincing explanation of his powers (acceptable to their own theories), they went away and nothing more was said, nor were their findings made public. One cannot blame him for deciding that such a process is a waste of time, and that it is infinitely more satisfying to himself, and beneficial to others, for him to develop the Healing aspects of his gifts. Equally, one cannot blame those psychics who, like Geller, use their powers to earn themselves a higher standard of living; nor does this attitude automatically imply fraud, as some would claim.

One cannot break the impasse without facing up to the fact that such opposition, which claims to be based on scientific grounds, is the exact opposite, being rooted in prejudice and preconceptions. I would maintain that no more time and effort should be wasted on arguments with the hysterical rearguard of orthodoxy, until the breakthrough to self-consistent and verifiable explanations has been achieved. If Columbus had waited until the academia of his day had all agreed that the world is round, Red Indians would still be chasing buffalo across the plains of North America.

More Dreaming

So let me assume (extremely optimistically) great progress on all four fronts (mathematical, physical, medical and psychic). I envisage the establishment of the following conditions:

a) Most reasonable-minded physicists, cosmologists and mathematicians accept that the *assumption* of extra dimensions allows them to construct completely self-consistent and experimentally-verifiable mathematical and conceptual models of the nature of matter and the construction and history of the universe;

b) Neurologists, physiologists and psychologists have identified the location and nature of the censor mechanism in the brain, have studied its action, and achieved some degree of reproducible control over it. This is probably equivalent to saying that the factors which generate or encourage psychic sensitivity have been identified, and we are able to induce it artificially in a non-sensitive person;

c) Psychic and quasi-medical researchers have identified the mental conditions which encourage or discourage physical paranormal effects and with the help of engineers and physicists have studied the physical and physiological conditions involved;

d) Physicists and engineers have studied the force and energy relationships involved in paranormal physical phenomena, and can offer suggestions as to the sources of the energy involved, and the natural laws controlling them;

e) Similarly, phenomena involving the 'sixth sense' (including telepathy, clairvoyance, divining and communication with the dead), have been studied from an engineering standpoint to establish the mode of communication used;

f) Application of the knowledge derived in (b) and (e) has enabled us to achieve more reliable communication with the dead, and a central library of such communications has been set up including material from all cultures and ethnic groups.

Breath-taking as each of these advances in itself may be, they are not enough. At some time they must be pulled together and inter-related. The physicist's 'hypothetical' fourth dimension must be shown to provide the mechanism whereby physical paranormal events are generated. The communication channels between living brains, between present, past and future, and between living and dead must be shown to be one and the same. Lastly, the continued existence of the dead must be explained in terms of the same fourth dimension.

To achieve this degree of unification and rationalisation of work in such widely disparate disciplines will require a colossal overview of man's knowledge unparalleled since the days of Descartes, and a magnificent exercise of Koestler's Principle in tracing, through the tangled web of mathematical theory, observed facts and mystic's visions, the threads that hold the universe together. The comment of Rosalind Heywood's quoted at the beginning of this chapter can be repeated here to sum it up:

> One day, perhaps, ESP will get its own Einstein who with some inspired generalisations will make this jumble of apparently irrational phenomena fall into a meaningful pattern.

Over to You, Einstein Minor!

APPENDICES

THE EVEN MORE EGG-HEADED PART

'The quick harvest of applied science is the usable process, the medicine, the machine. The shy fruit of applied science is Understanding.'
Lincoln Barnett

Most of the deeper discussions of a mathematical, scientific or technical nature have been omitted from the main text of this book, and are given here under separate headings, allowing the reader a degree of flexibility to pursue them to the limit of his knowledge or his interest. These matters fall principally into three categories:

a) A technical discussion of radio communication, in the context of suggestions that radio may be used in Telepathy. I believe that I am qualified to discuss this in some detail;

b) Subjects which may be of interest to a reader with some technical or scientific knowledge, giving a sketchy outline of key facts and opinions, with guidance to references enabling him to follow up the subject in more detail;

c) Some vague and tentative ideas in more esoteric subjects, hesitantly 'floated' in the hope that a specialist may find some food for thought in them.

1. Radio Communication[3,77] (See page 60)

This section discusses the technical reasons why I reject the possibility – discussed by Professor Taylor – that the communication medium for telepathy or other 'sixth sense' functions may be a *'normal'* radio link. (I reject even more vehemently his suggestion that the physical force used in psychokinesis is transferred by this means, and I do not propose to pursue this particular aspect further.)

The fantastically wide range of wavelengths of e.m.r. has already been described, but it may not be appreciated that a difference in wavelength will in itself cause differences in the behaviour of a wave and the techniques appropriate to it, so that many statements are only applicable to a relatively narrow band of frequencies. To ignore this fact can lead to very misleading conclusions, as when Taylor takes the weakest signal detectable by a wide-aperture radio telescope at high frequencies, and attempts to compare that with the hypothetical signal level detectable on the other side of the world from a human 'brain wave' at 5 Hz.*

To try to avoid such errors, let me first outline some fundamental factors applicable (in principle) to all frequencies:

a) *Aerial Size.* To be at all efficient in radiating or receiving a radio wave, an aerial (used here as a convenient shorthand for any known radiating or receiving structure – and there are many) must have at least one overall dimension comparable to or greater than the wavelength at which it is expected to operate. An aerial system which is much smaller than a wavelength is not only insensitive but it has poor directional properties** (i.e., it cannot 'focus' energy in one direction when transmitting or concentrate its sensitivity in one direction when receiving).

b) *Bandwidth.* One cannot transmit information by means of a signal which does not change. In particular, a sine wave (see page 75) must have some characteristic (such as amplitude or frequency) varied by the information to be carried. This process 'smears' the signal over a range of frequencies, depending on the rate at which information is flowing. For example, the techniques used in Medium Wave broadcasting (AM/DSB) can carry a speech signal in a 'bandwidth' (i.e., the range of frequencies occupied) of about 6000 Hz. Better techniques (SSB) can halve this, and very

---

*

Nomenclature and Frequency/Wavelength relationship:
1 Hz = 1 cycle per second;
1 kHz (kiloherz) = 1000 cycles per second;
1 MHz (Megaherz) = 1 000 000 cycles per second.
(Frequency in MHz) × (Wavelength in Metres) = 300
i.e., as the frequency increases, the wavelength decreases.

** A possible exception to this statement, the tuned loop, is discussed below, but note that the directional properties of a single loop are, in this context, very poor, and can only be improved by using two or more loops, spaced half a wavelength or more apart.

advanced signal processing developed in the last decade or so may reduce it to about 1000 Hz, but only at the price of a marked deterioration in 'naturalness'. Most engineers would agree that this is an optimistic estimate of the minimum bandwidth required to convey the human voice. As a comparison, if the words are transmitted in written form (as a telegram) at a rate equivalent to normal speaking, the required bandwidth could in principle be reduced to about 20 Hz.

c) *Background Noise.* The electrons surrounding the atoms in all matter are in continuous motion, generating 'thermal noise', a random e.m.r. signal including all frequencies, which is an ultimate limitation on the weakest signal which may be received. Thunderstorms and other atmospheric phenomena, and man-made electrical equipment, generate additional noise which at most radio frequencies is considerably higher than this. It is difficult to conceive of any type of receiving system which can operate on a signal appreciably weaker than the noise *in the same band as that occupied by the signal*. This means that the faster one tries to signal, or the more complex the information, the wider the band and the higher the level of noise which must be overcome.

d) *Interference.* It is particularly difficult for a receiving system to extract information from signals which are mixed up with unwanted signals of a similar type. (An example is the 'Cocktail Party Effect', the difficulty of carrying out a conversation against a background of a high level of other voices.) To avoid this, most man-made radio systems allocate a different band of frequencies to each signal but, as indicated below, this technique has attendant disadvantages. Alternative techniques are available (such as 'spread spectrum') but these add very considerably to the complexity of the signal, and so increase by a large factor the bandwidth that it occupies.

Let me apply these principles to the study of a hypothetical telepathy link, assuming for convenience that the signal passed is roughly comparable to speech. I begin with the very lowest frequencies, following the suggestion, discussed in detail by Taylor, that, 'We would . . . expect the frequencies of electromagnetic radiation used for telepathy to be those generated by bodily processes, say between 1 and 5000 cycles a second.' The objections of aerial size, bandwidth and interference at these frequencies are insuperable, even more so than at the higher frequencies of VLF discussed below. Taylor seems particularly impressed that frequencies within this band may be received, with relatively little loss of strength, on the other side of the world. He ignores the fact that this effect is merely a freak of the geometry of the earth and its surrounding ionosphere, which focuses the signal at the antipodes of the transmitter. As such it does not apply to intermediate ranges, nor to communication through space (as to a space vehicle), a disturbing limitation in such a basic concept.

An even more fundamental objection seems to have been totally overlooked. The 'brain wave', at, say, 10 Hz detected on electrodes on the surface of the skull (and the prime contender for telepathy in this context) *does not exist at any point within the brain*. What the EEG electrodes detect is the sum total of the indirect effects of a myriad of neural impulses, each undetectable as a separate event. Each pulse is a tenth of a volt or so in amplitude and lasts about a thousandth of a second, and they are generated in a three-dimensional pattern within the skull. The low-frequency waveform itself can convey no more than a general idea of the rhythm at which part of the brain is operating. It is difficult to conceive how it can indicate with any accuracy the location or direction of the actual nerves contributing to it, still less how it can contain any information on the nature of the 'thoughts' creating it. The situation can be compared to that of a passer-by outside a concert hall, who can faintly hear the throb and beat of the music, possibly being able to discriminate between a waltz and a march, but who cannot hear the tune, or the notes of any of the instruments.

Dismissing the possibility of the 'biological' frequencies, the next stage is the 'Very Low Frequencies' (VLF) considered by Bentine. This term is usually applied to radio waves between 3 and 30 kHz, but similar comments apply also to the LF band, extending up to 300 kHz. Such waves can travel long distances around the world and still penetrate water (even sea water) to some extent.

As noted above, for an aerial to be reasonably efficient, one of its dimensions should be at least an appreciable fraction of the wavelength at which it is to operate, which, for the VLF band defined above, is 10 000 to 100 000 metres (6 to 60 miles). To meet this objection, Taylor and Bentine have both suggested that the whole of the nervous system of the body may in some way form an extremely long aerial, but this theory is not tenable. If one took a plastic tailor's dummy and crammed it in a haphazard way, or in a regular pattern, with miles of fine insulated wire, it could be no better as an aerial (at very low frequencies) than a solid metal body of the same shape (see below). What happens is that for every length of the wire running North-South (say), farther along the

249

same wire is a similar length running South-North, which picks up a signal an almost exact negative of the first, resulting in a net signal of nearly zero. However, let us take the same principle to absurdity and assume that one could arrange the wire in the dummy to the best advantage, irrespective of the fact that it may not then resemble any organ or structure in the human body. Then the 'best' arrangement of the wire would be a loop (possibly of a large number of turns) following the outline of the body, but this again would still be extremely inefficient because of the small proportions of the loop compared with the huge wavelength involved. An improvement could be made (in principle) by 'tuning' the loop to the frequency of the signal, but this would introduce the 'Bandwidth' problem, as any improvement in sensitivity by this means inevitably reduces drastically the range of frequencies over which the loop will operate.

Atmospheric noise in these bands is very high, most of it generated by thunderstorms up to several thousand miles from the receiver. As a consequence of the severity of the Aerial Size, Bandwidth and Noise problems at VLF, signals below 15 kHz are limited to navigation systems which pass no information, while frequencies below 9 kHz are not used by man at all.

Despite the limitation (because of the Bandwidth problem) to low-speed telegraphy signals, the advantages of long range and water penetration are such that frequencies up to 100 kHz are heavily in demand for 'Maritime Mobile' transmissions to ships and submarines. As such, they are strictly controlled by international agreement, on the basis of 'world-wide allocation', i.e., only one radio transmitter in the world is allowed to operate on any given frequency. This being so, any interference created by a psychically active person passing near to a receiving aerial could scarcely pass unnoticed. In order to achieve the maximum range, the transmitters in the VLF band are among the most powerful in the world, and the aerials the largest. If such waves were used for paranormal communications, any psychic living within several miles of such a transmitter would find the experience mind-blowing in a very literal sense.

The Bandwidth problem is a fundamental restriction in another respect, in that it also governs the number of different signals which can use the band simultaneously without interference. If one accepts the figure derived above of 1000 Hz as the absolute minimum in which a speech signal can be passed, and assumes this as applying to telepathy, then if all radio waves between 10 and 300 kHz were used for this purpose, no more than 290 such signals could exist simultaneously without mutual interference, and this must suffice for all humanity! And bear in mind that the very factor advanced as the advantage of these waves, that they can travel over huge distances, would ensure that a large percentage of the world's population would be within effective range of any one 'receiver' – a magnificent 'Cocktail Party' indeed!

I feel confident in dismissing LF and lower frequencies from further consideration.

Most of the above objections apply also (but less absolutely) to higher frequencies up to several hundred Megaherz. Man's use of radio waves over the whole of this band is so intensive that it is most unlikely that 'peculiar signals' could exist for long without their origin being traced, and I have read no reports of spiritualists or clairvoyants being unable to operate in the vicinity of the Crystal Palace TV transmitters, Fylingdales radar station or the aerials of the Police network.

There seems to be no organ in the human body which remotely resembles any of the many known or imaginable aerial or other radiating systems at any of these frequencies, although Bentine[4] advances the idea that the whole of the human body may act as an aerial. A six-foot vertical 'metal man' would be most effective for frequencies of about 30-50 MHz, *provided its feet are insulated from the ground and the transmitter and receiver are connected between the earth and the soles of the feet,* which is precisely the reverse of Bentine's suggestion. If the bare feet are in contact with the earth, it is difficult to imagine how it can operate effectively as an aerial at any frequency, unless one also postulates one or more 'insulating gaps' at appropriate places in the body. Bentine's other suggestion, that the attitude of the body in certain postures such as praying or meditation alters the characteristics of the aerial to be favourable to a particular frequency is equally untenable. Such changes would only cause minor degeneration of performance.

Telepathy has been demonstrated with one or both parties enclosed in screened rooms ('metal boxes'), and with one of them in a submarine.[84] Most radio waves are easily screened by metal enclosures, and frequencies higher than LF do not penetrate earth or salt water to any appreciable extent.

The objections listed above apply most powerfully to frequencies below about 1000 MHz (wavelengths longer than 30 cm). Frequencies well above this limit may conceivably be transmitted and received by devices comparable in size with some of the organs in the human brain. Unfortunately, such wavelengths are easily stopped by metal barriers, by hills, by water and, not being reflected by the ionospheric layers surrounding the earth, by the curvature of the earth's surface. They would seem to be totally unsuitable for long-range communications such as have been observed in Telepathy experiments.

I repeat, I cannot see any way in which radio waves of any wavelength can be used in the normal manner for paranormal communication, and I am not at all surprised that this is also the conclusion derived from experimental investigations.[31]

However, some objections can be met by attributing to radio waves 'abnormal' characteristics which are not in accord with accepted scientific and engineering concepts. If the existence of a Fourth Dimension is assumed, for instance, then the long ranges achieved cease to be a problem, and the whole radio spectrum may be reviewed with this in mind. Wavelengths longer than about 1 cm are still unlikely (mainly because of the lack of a suitable radiating structure in the brain), while Ultra-Violet rays and shorter wavelengths cause damage to human tissues. The range between these two is the most likely location, with particular emphasis on the 'Far Infra-red' frequencies emitted as thermal radiation by bodies at about blood heat. The rest of the discussion follows as in Chapter 8.

2. The EPR Paradox[63] (page 64)

In 1935, three physicists, Albert Einstein, Boris Podolsky and Nathan Rosen, published a paper on what became known as the EPR paradox – from their initials. The EPR paradox was based on a hypothetical experiment which would, by logical deduction, prove that the behaviour of a photon (the basic particle of energy) could be affected by what was happening to other photons *some distance away*, in complete contradiction to accepted principles. In 1964, Dr J.S. Bell published 'Bell's Theorem', which not only established the EPR paradox on a purely mathematical basis, but showed that it applied equally well to structures of any size, and in 1972 the experiment was carried out and the theory confirmed; 'an operational connection was established between events and structures which should have no connection at all'. Many experiments carried out since then have confirmed this conclusion.

Newton and his contemporaries could not accept that any force could be applied through a vacuum. We know now that there are at least three such forces: electrostatic, magnetic and gravity (*pace* Cosmologists, Nuclear Physicists and research on the 'Unified Field Theory'). However, the presence of any of these can be detected experimentally in the intervening space through which they 'travel', and each follows the 'Inverse Square Law' characteristic of energy travelling in straight lines. In the EPR case no intermediate effects are detectable, and there is no predictable law of variation with distance, so there can be no explanation in orthodox physical terms. The theory suggests that one object can affect another some distance away simply because they both exist in the same universe, which behaves in some ways like a single organism. To some, this 'explanation' borders on the mystical, and the EPR paradox exemplifies the kind of dichotomy which is all too frequent in modern scientific thinking, in which the truth of the immediate inferences (particularly those confirmed experimentally) is accepted, but the more fundamental conclusion – that there is something seriously wrong with the fundamentals of man's concept of reality – is quietly ignored. The comparison of the EPR approach with the hypothesis of a fourth dimension is continued on page 64.

3. Time as a Dimension (page 65)

The discussion of Time as a potential extra dimension also requires some clarification and extension, beginning with the associated subject of 'imaginary quantities' in mathematics. When a mathematician is tackling a physical problem, and comes across quantities which have no physical existence, he refers to them as *imaginary* (in the sense of 'not real', rather than meaning 'existing only in the human imagination'). For instance, suppose I throw a ball into the air and fire a shot at it with a rifle. If the bullet strikes the ball I would call it a 'Hit', and if it does not, a 'Miss'. A mathematician studying the situation may calculate the paths of the ball and the bullet and according to the results declare that they collided at a 'Real' point (a Hit) or an 'Imaginary' point (a Miss). The factor which distinguishes such imaginary quantities is usually represented by the symbol 'i', (or sometimes 'j'), defined as:

$$i \times i = -1 \text{ or } i = \sqrt{(-1)} = (-1)^{1/2}$$

Any real number, whether positive or negative, when multiplied by itself, gives a positive answer, so 'i' cannot be a real number. Despite this, it can be used in calculations using the normal rules of arithmetic and give answers which are real (if 'i' has been eliminated) or imaginary (if 'i' occurs in the answer).

Another factor of great importance is that in many contexts the quantity 'i' operates as a rotation through 90°. To illustrate this, let us draw two axes through an origin, and label the axes in 'Real' and 'Imaginary' units as in Figure 19. Now if we start from point A, with a real value of +3, and multiply it by 'i', we arrive at B, with a value of 3i, having rotated by 90° around the origin. Multiplying by 'i' again gives $3 \times i \times i = 3 \times (-1) = -3$, and again we have rotated through 90°. Two more rotations return us to the start, since:

$$i \times i \times i \times i = (-1) \times (-1) = +1$$

These concepts of 'i' as an imaginary quantity or as a rotation, while at first sight and in these elementary exercises a rather pointless procedure, result in a completely straightforward and consistent mathematics which is in daily use by engineers to solve very practical problems. For instance, it is used freely by electrical engineers in problems relating to the generation and distribution of electricity, and by electronic engineers in the design of radio equipment. In such cases, even though 'i' may be imaginary, quantities involving it represent physically measurable states.

I have discussed these characteristics of 'i' because they are of immense importance in the present context, particularly with reference to some conclusions arising from Einstein's Special Theory of Relativity. I am no expert on the subject, and give only a bald and over-simplified version, but most library books on the subject cover it adequately for present purposes.

In the latter half of the 19th century and the first years of the 20th, a number of experiments were carried out to try to determine the nature of the 'ether', a hypothetical medium presumed to fill all space and to 'carry' electro-magnetic radiation (following the line of thought of Newton and his contemporaries, who believed that 'action at a distance', particularly through an intervening vacuum, is impossible). Some puzzling and apparently contradictory results were obtained and, in attempting to explain these, men like Fitzgerald and Lorentz studied again the fundamental principles underlying measurements of length and velocity. The main effect of Einstein's Theory was to continue and clarify this work, and to extend it considerably. He came to the rather startling conclusion that the length of an object is not a fixed quantity, but changes if it, or the measuring equipment, is moving during the measurement process. While movement is taking place, the object apparently 'shrinks' by an amount which depends (among other things) on the velocity of light!

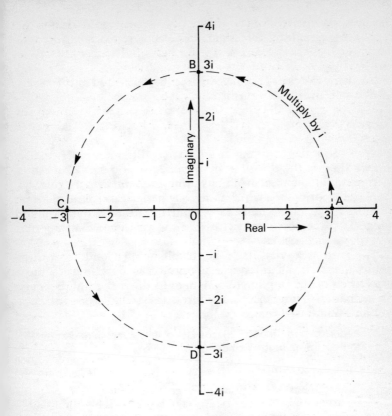

Figure 19.   Illustration of 'i' as a rotation

Similarly, the measurement of time was found to be affected by the movement of the observer. If two events (say a flash of lightning and the impact of a stone hitting the ground) were seen by a stationary observer as happening simultaneously, then a moving observer would detect a time interval between them. Minkowski manipulated these conclusions still further, and ended up with a 'Space-Time Continuum', which can be (over-) simplified as follows. If the distance between the diagonally opposite corners of the rectangular block in Figure 1 (see page 41) is calculated by classical methods (using the Theorem of Pythagoras, so dear to the hearts of generations of mathematics teachers), the result is:

$$S = (L^2 + H^2 + W^2)^{1/2}$$

But if the block is moving during the measurement, then by Minkowski's calculations it is:

$$S' = (L'^2 + H'^2 + W'^2 - c^2T^2)^{1/2}$$
$$\text{or} \qquad S' = (L'^2 + H'^2 + W'^2 + (icT)^2)^{1/2}$$

where L', H' and W' are lengths which may differ from L, H, and W, (depending on the direction of movement), and T is a measurement of time. There seems to be in this equation a 'fourth dimension' in the form (icT), which is *an imaginary measurement of length at right angles to the other three*, and the form of the equation suggests (by comparison with that for a sphere) that '*Space is curved in a time dimension*'.

Although relativity itself is established beyond reasonable doubt, there are still differences of opinion as to its interpretation. One focus of this argument is where to draw the line between mathematical symbols and physical facts. For instance, Minkowski himself remarked that:

. . . henceforward time and space in themselves vanish to shadows, and only a union of the two exists.

– but Herbert Dingle wrote:

The four-dimensional continuum is essentially metaphorical . . . we are leaving prose for poetry. The representation is beautiful, and scientifically permissible if we do not forget it is symbolic . . .

The 'space' which is the metaphorical continuum has first been wrongly identified with ordinary three-dimensional space which is familiar to everyone, and then the 'curvature' of the continuum has been identified with the curvature of a two-dimensional surface [Sic!] such as a sphere, and accordingly we are told that 'space is curved'. Thus a complicated set of misinterpretations of symbols, resulting in something *which is meaningless and quite impossible to imagine*, has been presented as a great discovery of a physical truth . . . All the inconceivable statements which have been made about it [relativity] are the result of confusion of symbols with what is symbolised. [My italics]

The reasoning seems to me to be typical of the illogical attitude of science. The variations in the orbit of the planet Mercury (explained by Einstein) and the deflection of light from stars by the gravitational field of the sun (predicted by Einstein) had been hailed as complete vindication of his theories. No-one suggested that these were mere symbols and not completely physical effects. Why should the effects of gravity be considered physical, while other conclusions based on exactly the same initial assumptions and the same reasoning (such as the 'curved space' concept, which implicitly requires an additional dimension, and the identification of time with an additional dimension) are dismissed as 'symbolic'? The only answer is that implied by my italics in the quotation above, the assumption that anything that cannot be imagined by man is *therefore* meaningless.

It is interesting to note a comparable situation. In 1861 James Clark Maxwell established theoretically that any change in the electric current in a wire would create an electro-magnetic disturbance which would move away from the wire in a way which was mathematically identifiable as a wave movement. Some of his contemporaries insisted that this was merely a beautiful piece of symbolism and should on no account be mistaken for a real wave, which was an unimaginable impossibility. It took the practical demonstrations of Lodge and Hertz some 27 years later to prove that these 'symbolic' waves were very real indeed – and very useful.

Even without this apparent precedent, I cannot accept the 'beautiful-mathematical-symbolism' school of thought. The quantity (cT) is dimensionally (Velocity × Time), which equals Distance, and an additional dimension must be at right angles to all the others – and the imaginary quantity establishes just that. All such clues point to this being a possible answer to our conundrum.

The final step, expanding Minkowski's continuum to include an imaginary fourth spatial dimension identical to the first three, only requires the addition of an extra term, making it:

$$S' = [H'^2 + W'^2 + L'^2 + (iF')^2 + (icT)^2]^{1/2}$$

where F is a linear spatial fourth dimension.

By Minkowski's theory, the quantity S' should be constant for an object moving at any velocity in any direction in four dimensions. Whether such an equation is compatible with experimental observations is a matter for specialists in the field.

4. Multiple Universes

Consider the model of the hypercube in Figure 8(b) and the requirements listed on page 51. If all eight cubes are identical, including the 'outer' one, then all eight must occupy the same volume of three-dimensional space, yet remain 'outside' each other when viewed in four dimensions. It follows that a given point (say the centre) of one cube will coincide in three dimensions with the equivalent points of the other seven cubes, being separated from each of them by a fourth dimension only, just as in the atlas analogy (see page 63), the centres of all the two-dimensional universes are separated only in the third – by the thickness of a page. So one may imagine each cube of the hypercube as comprising the space of one three-dimensional universe. The concept clarifies the ability of two objects to apparently occupy the same volume of three-dimensional space – as the hands of Manning and Webbe (see page 97), and the bodies of Derek Manning and Webbe (see page 148).

The idea of multiple universes is included in some theories in Cosmology. The current view of a Black Hole is that it is an intense concentration of matter, which exerts such a powerful gravitational attraction that it 'sucks in' material, which forthwith disappears, and in the TV programme on the work of Professor Hawking (see page 66), it was said that:

> Some interpretations of Einstein's General Theory of Relativity lead to a solution whereby any person or thing which falls into a Black Hole will emerge into another universe.

Is, then, a Black Hole a fourth-dimension point of contact between two three-dimensional universes: like a hole in a page of our atlas analogy? (This idea is studied in detail by Rucker.[73]) For comparison, think what would happen to our little water-bug if he skated too near to an ornamental fountain, a waterfall or whirlpool.

Any such concept of objects disappearing out of our universe into another must also imply the reverse, suggesting that things may 'appear from nowhere'. This idea receives some support from a surprising direction. Kit Pedler[63] discusses the work of David Bohm, Professor of Physics in Birbeck College at the University of London, on the implications of the EPR paradox:

> He develops the view, for example, that an electron or a shower of electrons are constantly popping up into explicate [physically existent] order from the ground base of the implicate [hidden or non-

existent] order in a kind of permanent cosmic dance between electron-like existence, and non-existence: manifest electrons and non-manifest electrons.

One has only to assume that 'implicate' or 'non-manifest' electrons have simply moved into an extra dimension (not an unreasonable suggestion in this context) to see the idea of sub-atomic movement in many dimensions as a plausible hypothesis, and indeed one which may simplify much of the mystique of theory which seems to surround the study of nuclear particles.

There is a possibility that this concept may tie in with some other aspects of Quantum Theory such as Heisenberg's Principle of Uncertainty. If a particle were subject to a random movement in four dimensions (i.e., a four-dimensional Brownian Movement), then its position observed in three dimensions would appear as a three-dimensional probability density, and its existence as a single-dimension probability with a normal (Gaussian) distribution. This is reminiscent in some respects of the situation proposed by both Heisenberg and Bohm, although an attempt to compare the three concepts mathematically is well beyond my competence.

5. Unsymmetrical Dimensions

The suggestion made on page 65 that the fourth dimension may be unsymmetrical about our universe raises some very interesting possibilities. If we drop a stone into water, the sudden change in density as the stone strikes the surface causes much of the energy of the stone to be transferred to the surface layer of the water and to radiate away from the point of impact in the form of ripples. Now compare this with the 'Big Bang' theory of the origin of the universe, in which it is proposed that the whole of our universe originated in the form of a colossal outburst of energy suddenly appearing at one point in a featureless void, and that energy, (and the matter created from it) has since then been expanding from the point of creation. Now is there, or is there not, a distinct similarity between the 'Big Bang' in three dimensions, and the 'stone-in-the-pond' in two? Could this huge quantity of energy have been generated by a massive object travelling in four dimensions and striking a change in the 'density of space'?

If one is not a supporter of the Big Bang, then consider the analogy of the pond in a shower of rain. The raindrops are distributed evenly but in a random fashion over the pond's surface, and each generates a burst of ripple energy which radiates outward from the point of impact until it is dissipated over the whole surface. Translating this concept to three dimensions on a cosmic scale, results in a scenario not unlike the 'Continuous Creation' theory of the structure of the universe. This analogy also illustrates another possibility. The impinging raindrops disappear into the pond because they consist of the same substance; similarly, in the Big Bang concept, one does not need to consider the impact of a 'solid' body, but simply a piece of the 'dense' medium travelling through the 'less dense' (like emptying a bucket of water into the pond).

The concept of the Big Bang as the arrival in this universe of a large amount of matter or energy (according to Einstein they are interchangeable) from another, ties in neatly with the discussion of poltergeist noises (see page 73). It was suggested that the sudden materialisation of a body in a room would displace air, and create a sharp 'crack' of sound waves. In the same way, a similar materialisation in space could create 'space waves' – or electromagnetic radiation. Chapter 5 discusses a number of mysterious sources of energy discovered or postulated by modern science, and the equally mysterious sources of energy in many reports of paranormal occurrences. In virtually all such cases the energy is identified as (or can best be interpreted in terms of) 'radiation': hardly a surprising observation in view of the above discussion.

However, despite the interesting possibilities inherent in an unsymmetrical fourth dimension, there are no doubt difficult mathematical and philosophical problems arising, so suppose one takes a purist attitude and insists that all spatial dimensions must be identical and therefore symmetrical? Then we are still faced with very severe conceptual problems, even in the case of our two-dimensional bug, who must be surrounded by the same kind of space *on all sides*. It is not enough that he must be unaware of up and down movements, but movement *in any direction* must be inherently possible to him (albeit possibly involuntarily and unknown to him) and any such movement must produce no detectable change in fundamental physical laws. One could picture him as living, not on the surface of a body of water, but on a very thin membrane or web – except that the web or membrane cannot have any physical reality to him. It must be a non-physical plane. Unfortunately, we are so conditioned by life in a world where the force of gravity is a major controlling factor on all things that it is difficult to imagine movement restricted to an undefined surface which has no physical existence. It is even more difficult to imagine that surface being capable of movement at right angles to its own plane, and it becomes well-nigh impossible to transfer these concepts to an additional dimension. Difficult or not, that may be the situation, and as I have continually emphasised, the fact that it is unimaginable does not in itself prove it untrue. It is obvious that I am getting into very deep water indeed – far more appropriate for discussion by Professor Hawking and his students than for me.

COLOURS NAILED TO THE MAST

'Here I stand – I cannot do otherwise'
Martin Luther

As a 'lapsed scientist' myself, where do I stand at the end of my exploration? I emphasise what I said in the first chapter: I have no personal experience to offer, I have introduced no new facts, and I have proved nothing. That does not by any means imply that my own views have not been modified, and the reader may ask how much I believe of my own reasoning. My first answer is to assert that my own beliefs are irrelevant. To justify this opinion, let me suggest that there are two distinct meanings of the word. In the religious context, 'belief' is an instinctive and emotional reaction to something beyond logic. It may be, as Jung and Hardy argue, a vital part of human experience, but it is nonetheless irrational, uncontrollable and often undefinable, and as such forms no part of the kind of logical arguments that I have tried to use. As Jung so succinctly put it: 'A belief proves to me only the phenomenon of belief, not the content of belief.' Whatever my own faith may be (and 'faith' is a far better word for this kind of 'belief with the heart') I have tried to reduce its effects to a minimum.

'Belief with the head', based in theory on a logical process of weighing evidence for and against, is almost as personal a process. As I have pointed out with reference to the attitude of some scientists to the paranormal, a man will only believe a thing when he is prepared to accept the evidence offered, and in that sense no-one will ever believe anything against his will: as long as he can find or invent reasons for disbelieving. So again, my own conclusions are irrelevant. Provided that I have given the evidence on which I base my opinions (and this again is a better word than 'beliefs'), and the reasoning I have applied to that evidence, I can, and should, do no more.

Nonetheless, if the reader should insist, pointing to a specific incident discussed in this book (such as Manning's meeting with Webbe or Tony's possession by the rabbi), and ask 'Do you really believe that to have happened?' I can only answer: 'I don't know, but I am prepared to consider seriously the possibility that the account *may* be true – and to accept the implications if it proves likely to be so!'

A specific question of this nature is a favourite ploy of the sceptic, but its very selectivity makes it unhelpful. A far more productive approach is to consider two diametrically opposed theories:

a) The universe is basically deterministic and materialistic, and present-day knowledge includes most of the 'laws' controlling it. Any report of an event which patently breaches any of those laws may *ipso facto* be rejected as untrue, and study of such events is unsound in principle;

b) Man is an evolving creature with inherent limitations in his sensory organs and the processes of perception, and in his intellect. It is therefore possible that 'real' events may occur which are beyond the borderline of what is acceptable to his conscious mind, and so outside the limits of his normal experience and the knowledge based on that experience. Should such an event be indirectly or partially detected, it may be beyond the capacity of his intellect to interpret the information correctly.

Given the whole panorama of apparently paranormal events, and allowed only a straight choice between those two possibilities to explain them, I have no alternative but to opt for the latter. The sheer quantity and the very diversity of the evidence, and the degree of agreement which I have traced between widely differing approaches and fields of thought cannot possibly be due solely to coincidence, so there must be 'something in it'.

But this decision results in a most strange contradiction. It is usually accepted that belief in the paranormal is illogical; that it is founded in instinctive 'wishful thinking' and cannot stand up to logical analysis. Yet here I am, at the end of a considerable exercise of deliberate thought and 'logical' reasoning, having reached the conclusion that many paranormal events are probably quite real and potentially explainable in physical terms, and indeed, the alternative conclusion – that they are all non-existent – is totally irrational.

What makes the situation worse is that my instinct, gut reaction, or 'heart' if you like, which should (in popular belief) welcome the reality of the paranormal, actually rebels at the idea that I may be closely surrounded by unknown worlds filled with unknown entities who may have immediate contact with my most private thoughts, and may even have control over my actions and emotions without my knowledge.

But, says my logical head, are not these exactly the characteristics one associates with the concept of 'God'? And I, in common with very many of mankind, believe, instinctively and by faith, in God.

And there the matter rests.

BIBLIOGRAPHY

This Bibliography is intended as an index to all works quoted substantively in the text, and as a useful cross-reference between names. Page numbers in square brackets [p169] refer to a specifically relevant passage in the reference work. Where necessary, cross-references to specific books are given by initials in square brackets (as 'Manning [TL]' = The Link).
* I do not claim to agree with, to have understood or even to have read the whole of all of the works listed, but those I have found particularly interesting and informative are marked with an asterisk.

1. Bander, See Manning [TL]
2. Batcheldor, See Watson [L, p301]
*3. Bentine, Michael, *The Door Marked Summer*, Granada Pub, 1981
4. Bentine, Michael, *The Doors of the Mind*, Granada Pub, 1985
5. Blakemore, Colin, *The Mechanics of the Mind*, CUP, 1977
6. Blakemore, Colin, *The Mind Machine*, BBC Publications, 1988
7. Bohm, David, See Pedler [MOM p157]
8. Broad, Prof. C.D., See Ornstein
9. Castaneda, Carlos, *The Teachings of Don Juan*, Penguin, 1970
10. Chomsky, Noam, See Magee [p173]
11. Collins, H.M. & Pinch, T.J., *The Construction of the Paranormal*, See Wallis
12. Dingle, H., *The Special Theory of Relativity*, Methuen, 1940
13. Dolby, R.G.A., *Reflections on Deviant Science*, See Wallis
14. Dunne, J.W., *Experiments with Time*, (5th Ed.), Faber, 1939
*15. Elliott, J. Scott, *Dowsing, One Man's Way*, Neville Spearman, 1977
*15A. Evans-Wentz, W.Y. (Ed), *The Tibetan Book of the Dead*, OUP, 1960
16. Eysenck H.J. & Sargent, C., *Explaining the Unexplained*, Weidenf. & Nicolson, 1982
17. Findlay, Arthur, *On the Edge of the Etheric*, Corgi, 1971
*18. Ford, Arthur, *The Life Beyond Death*, Abacus, 1974
19. Freud, See Wollheim [p169]
20. Fuller, John G., *The Airmen Who Would Not die*, Souvenir, 1979
21. Geller, Uri, *My Story*, Robson, 1975, Corgi, 1977
22. Geller, Uri & Playfair, G.L., *The Geller Effect*, Jonathan Cape, 1986
*23. Gooch, Stan, *Creatures From Inner Space*, Rider & Co. 1984
24. Gooch, Stan, *The Paranormal*, Wildwood House, 1978

25. Gregory, Prof. R., Visual Illusions in Space, *New Scientist*, Aug. 1962

*26. Guirdham, Arthur, *The Cathars and Reincarnation*, Spearman, 1970

27. Guirdham, Arthur, *We are One Another*, Turnstone, 1982

28. Hampe, Johann C., *To Die is To Gain*, Darton, Longman & Todd, 1979

29. Hansel C.E.M., *ESP, A Scientific Evaluation*, Scribner, 1966

30. Hardy, Sir Alister, *The Divine Flame*, Collins, 1966

*31. Hardy, Sir Alister, *The Living Stream*, Collins, 1965

32. Hardy, Sir Alister, *The Spiritual Nature of Man*, OUP, 1979

*33. Hardy, Sir Alister, *The Challenge of Chance*, Hutchinson, 1973, (with Harvie, Robert and Koestler, Arthur)

34. Harrison, M., *Fire From Heaven*, Sidgwick & Jackson, 1976

*35. Heywood, Rosalind, *The Infinite Hive*, Penguin, 1978

*36. Heywood, Rosalind, *The Sixth Sense*, Penguin, 1978

37. Humphreys, Christmas, *Exploring Buddhism*, Geo. Allen & Unwin, 1974

*38. Inglis, Brian, *Natural and Supernatural*, Hodder & Stoughton, 1977

*39. Inglis, Brian, *The Hidden Power*, Jonathan Cape, 1986

40. Inglis, Brian, *The Unknown Guest*, Chatto & Windus, 1987

41. Iremonger, Lucille, *The Ghosts of Versailles*, Faber & Faber, 1957

*42. Iverson, Jeffrey, *More Lives Than One*, Souvenir, 1977

43. Janov, Dr Arthur & Holden, Michael E., *Primal Man, The New Consciousness*, Abacus, 1977

44. Jung, Carl Gustav, *Memories, Dreams, Reflections*, Fount, 1978

*45. Kennedy, Revd David, *A Venture in Immortality*, Colin Smythe, 1973

46. Koestler, Arthur, *The Act of Creation*, Pan, 1975

47. Koestler, Arthur, See Toynbee and Hardy [TCOC]

48. Kolakowski, Leszek, *Bergson*, OUP (Past Masters), 1985

49. Lodge, Sir Oliver, See Ford and Heywood [TSS]

50. Lethbridge, T.C., *A Step in The Dark*, Routledge & Kegan Paul, 1967

51. Magee, Brian, *Men of Ideas*, OUP, 1982

*52. Manning, Matthew, *In The Minds Of Millions*, W.H. Allen, 1977

*53. Manning, Matthew, *The Link*, Colin Smythe, 1974, Corgi, 1975

*54. Manning, Matthew, *The Strangers*, W.H. Allen, 1978

55. Miller, David (Ed), *A Pocket Popper*, Fontana, 1983

*56. Moody, Raymond A., *Life After Life*, Mockingbird, 1975, Bantam, 1986

57. Muldoon, S.J. & Carrington, H., *The Projection of the Astral Body*, Rider & Co, 1929-58

58. Morison & Lamont, *An Adventure*, Macmillan, 1911, 1913 (Pseudonyms for Moberley, C.A.E. & Jourdain, E.F.)

59. Myers, Sir Frederic, See Ford, Heywood [TSS], et al.

*60. Ornstein R. (Ed), *The Nature of Human Consciousness*, (Incl. Papers by Tart, Broad, etc.), Viking Press, W.H. Freeman, 1973

61. Owen, Dr A.R.G., *Can We Explain the Poltergeist?* Helix, 1964
62. Owen, Dr A.R.G., See Manning [TL App. 2]
63. Pedler, Kit, *Mind Over Matter*, Thames Methuen, 1981
64. Penfield, Wilder, See Blakemore
*65. Pike, Bishop J.A., *The Other Side*, W.H. Allen, 1969, Abacus, 1975
66. Playfair, Guy Lion, *The Flying Cow*, Souvenir, 1975
67. Popper, Sir Karl, See Miller
68. Price, Dr G., See Heywood [TSS p187]
69. Price, Prof. H.H., See Toynbee [Koestler p255]
*70. Puharich, A., *Beyond Telepathy*, Souvenir, 1962
71. Pullar, P.,*The Shortest Journey*, Hamish Hamilton, 1981
72. Ralphs, J.D., 'Mapping Neural Activity in the Brain by I.R.' *Speculations in Sc. & Techn.*, 14 No.1 1991, Science and Technology Letters
*73. Rucker, R., *The Fourth Dimension*, Rider, 1985
74. Schoeps, H-J., *An Intelligent Person's Guide to the Religions of Mankind*, Victor Gollancz, 1967
75. Schumann, Hans J., *Buddhism – An Outline of Its Teaching and Schools*, Rider, 1973
76. Swedenborg, Emanuel, See Ford
77. Taylor, Prof. John, *Superminds*, Book Club Assoc. (Macmillan), 1975
*78. Toynbee, A. (Ed), *Life After Death*, Weidenfeld & Nicholson, 1976 (incl. Papers by Koestler, etc.)
79. Vaughan, Alan, *Patterns of Prophecy*, Turnstone, 1973
80. Walker, Kenneth, *The Unconscious Mind*, Arrow, 1961
*81. Wallis, R. (Ed), 'On the Margins of Science', *Sociological Review Monograph No 27*, Univ of Keele, 1979
*82. Watson, Lyall, *The Romeo Error*, Hodder & Stoughton, 1974
83. Watson, Lyall, *Lifetide*, Hodder & Stoughton, 1979
*84. Watson, Lyall, *Supernature*, Hodder & Stoughton, 1973, Coronet, 1974
85. Watson, Lyall, *Beyond Supernature*, Hodder & Stoughton, 1983
*86. Wilkerson, Rev. David, *The Cross & The Switchblade*, Oliphants, 1968
87. Wilson, Colin, *Strange Powers*, Latimer New Dimensions, 1973
88. Wilson, Colin, *The Poltergeist*, New English Library, 1981
89. Wilson, Colin, *Afterlife*, Harrap, 1985
90. Wollheim, Richard, *Freud*, Fontana, 1973
91. Zohar, Danah, *The Quantum Self*, Bloomsbury, 1990
92. Zollner, Johann, See Inglis [NAS p281]
93. Zukav, Gary, *The Dancing Wu Li Masters*, Collins/Fontana, 1979

INDEX